The Armchair Companion to **Chicago** Sports

The Armchair Companion to **Chicago** Sports

RICHARD C. LINDBERG

WITH
BIART WILLIAMS

Cumberland House
Nashville, Tennessee

Published by Cumberland House Publishing, Inc., 431 Harding Industrial Park Drive, Nashville, TN 37211-3160.

Distributed to the trade by Andrews & McMeel, 4520 Main Street, Kansas City, Missouri, 64111.

Cover design by Ernie Couch/Consultx
Cover photograph by Downtown Photo, Nashville, TN

Library of Congress Cataloging-in-Publication Data

Lindberg, Richard, 1953-
The armchair companion to Chicago sports / Rich Lindberg with Biart Williams.
p. cm.
Includes bibliographical references (p.).

1. Sports—Illinois—Chicago—Miscellanea. 2. Sports—Illinois—Chicago—History—Chronology. I. Williams, Biart. II. Title.
GV584.5.C4L55 1997
796'.09773'11—dc21 97-23285
CIP

ISBN: 978-1-68162-023-7

1 2 3 4 5 6 7—02 03 01 00 99 98 97

CONTENTS

ACKNOWLEDGMENTS

A book is much like a journey. It all begins with an idea and an inspiration. This project was no different. The idea was conceived by Cumberland House and Connie Goddard of the Goddard Book Group, who contributed valuable research time and editing to the project while coordinating logistics. Carol Carlson reviewed the content of the manuscript, edited portions of the text, and helped us keep faith with the timetables. Our thanks to Jeff Eason, a talented young filmmaker, for his inputting work; also Robert Pruter, sports historian and author; Tom Blair; David M. Patt of the Chicago Area Runner Association; Tom Krish of the *Chicago Sun-Times;* Bob Rosenberg, scorekeeper for the Chicago Bulls and White Sox; Jim Dressel of *Bowler's Journal;* Billy Johnston Jr., co-owner of Maywood Park, Sportsman's Park, and Balmoral Park; and Leslie Peterson of Cumberland House.

INTRODUCTION:

The Genesis of Chicago Sports

What is sport if not remembrance? We recall with pride and a dash of nostalgia that moment of shared glory we experienced in the heat of competition or the spectacle of the professional athlete achieving something much more than a place in the record book.

This is a book about the evolution of Chicago's professional and amateur sports. But it is more than a closetful of dusty memories. It is a careful examination of the athletes, the games they played, and the love affair between a vibrant city and the attainments of the men and women who set their sights on excellence on the colorful and widely divergent playing fields of Chicago.

Sports is a metaphor for life in the Windy City. It is has been said that sports is a big deal in this town. Maybe it is the only deal.

Chicago is all about sports: a kaleidoscopic blend of backroom politics, brawling, social drinking, and the uniting of divergent ethnic groups and social cultures toward a common purpose—bringing home the next championship to the Windy City. Indeed, sports is often a grim tug-of-war between the ideal and the unattainable, the dreams of childhood and the disillusionment of old age.

It has only been within the last 30 years that the social historians and scholars who ponder the urban experience have attempted to link the role played by sports and recreation in the shaping of American culture. For example, until very recently serious consideration of baseball's evolution was dismissed as popular history unworthy of the historian's attention.

However, as we study the rhythms of urban living in major population centers like Chicago, the sporting life emerges as an important and fascinating crosscurrent.

The sporting life had a rather curious and sordid connotation in the last century. From the Civil War era through the waning years of the Gilded Age, the term referred to a class of profligate gamblers whose avocation was intrinsically linked to the liquor business, horserace wagers, backroom bowling matches, prizefighting, dice and cards, and the red-light trade—a den of ill repute was known for many years as a sporting house.

In Chicago the recreational industry was dominated in the

early years by Irish and German immigrants who dared to defy the strong moral bent of Chicago's original settlers, the New England blue bloods who condemned sports and the sporting world as sins against God's will. Their social conventions, class distinctions, religious convictions, and strong work ethics presented marked contrasts to the downtown saloon culture, which was segregated in squalid wooden buildings concentrated near the dangerous wharf or levee districts of the city.

The red-light attractions of the levee and the latest gossip from the world of pugilism and horseracing were publicized in scandal sheets like the *Street Gazette* and other racy tabloids hawked on the corners by young boys. The penny newspapers were circulated among a transient clientele of out-of-town salesmen (known as drummers), business people, and western cattlemen, all desirous of a little action as they wiled away their idle time in the saloons of downtown hotels.

In the last century Mike McDonald was Chicago's leading purveyor of cards, liquor, and dice. He owned the "Store," the most luxurious gambling den in the city. The three-story building at 79 West Monroe Street was virtually immune from police raids during its shady existence because Mike McDonald was smarter, more intuitive, and less prone to reckless behavior than many of his colleagues up and down "Gambler's Row" on Randolph Street, where much of the so-called action was centered in those days.

McDonald syndicated the supporting fraternity into a viable political coalition that elected city office-holders sympathetic to the all-night saloons and illegal gambling games. The humble origins of the legendary Chicago Irish American political machine took root in the late 19th century when this self-anointed "king maker" and his criminal allies in the sporting world marshalled control of the Cook County Democratic Party.

As McDonald sought respectability in his newly chosen field, societal tastes began to change. Slowly the public turned away from the crooked parlor games like faro, euchre, and hazard that they couldn't win. Horseracing, America's first popular spectator sport, captured the imagination of Chicagoans in the mid-1880s. For the first time economic and class differences were temporarily cast aside as society's swells mingled with the gambling riffraff at

Washington Park on the South Side to witness the running of the fabled American Derby.

Wealthy and powerful gamblers like Mike McDonald, whose income derived from illegal vice activities in the 1870s, plunged into the racing game a decade later. In 1891 McDonald financed the construction of Garfield Park, a racing oval located on the West Side. Garfield Park was closed down by the Chicago City Council by legislative fiat a year later. The aldermen did not impose this drastic measure for altruistic reasons or because they believed that McDonald was an evil force to be circumvented at all cost, but rather because Edward Corrigan, the owner of the rival Hawthorne racetrack, had already courted their favor with hard cash on election day.

There was a great deal of money to be made in the world of sports. The politicians sensed it, and the public hungered for the opportunity to view athletic competition. The gamblers and the Yankee high hats—who in the past had condemned the rakish business of sports as a sinful, godless pastime foisted upon the working classes by disreputable criminals—softened their opposition when they realized they too could profit from the new economic incentives.

The genesis of modern professional sports in Chicago closely relates to this symbolic marriage between society's ne'er-do-wells and the respectable monied classes.

Aaron Montgomery Ward, the Chicago mail-order titan who created a beautiful lakefront park to steer the masses away from the crowded tenements and the tedium of inner-city living, added a sporting-goods line to his catalog. Richard Sears was another opportunist whose retail and catalog empire started in Chicago. The Sears catalog added a line of sporting goods within a few years of Montgomery Ward.

German immigrant Ignaz Schwinn and meat packer Adolph Arnold opened the Schwinn Bicycle Company at Lake and Peoria Streets in 1895. Chicago, the city that spawned the cycling craze in the Gay '90s, employed 6,000 workers in bicycle factories in 1896. There were over 200,000 riders, 600 dealers, and over $500,000 spent on biking paraphernalia that year. On Thursday nights 500 members of the South Side Cycling Club filled Grand Boulevard in a *tour de promenade.* Those who violated proper decorum by racing their bikes at top speeds were called "scorchers" and were relentlessly pursued by the Chicago police.

John Brunswick of Cincinnati manufactured barroom supplies, which he peddled among the tavern proprietors allied to the Mike McDonald syndicate—men he would not have otherwise been associated with in the course of daily living. Brunswick eventually relocated his business to Chicago, where he added a line of bowling equipment because the saloon owners demanded it. In many respects Chicago gave rise to the sporting goods industry.

Faro and poker dealers who earned their living in the Loop gambling dens during the 1870s organized the handbook syndicates and poolrooms into a unified force in the 1890s. A poolroom was often nothing more than a storefront, a warehouse, or the back room of a cigar or barber shop where bets were taken and payouts made. With pencils and notepads in hand, an army of traveling handbook men took to the streets, clocking bets on local and out-of-town races. Improvements in technology allowed the results of the races to be transmitted to Chicago saloons and poolrooms via the telegraph seconds after a winning horse crossed the finish line.

Horseracing existed precariously for about two decades until the Chicago City Council and the Illinois State Legislature, in a combined effort to save Chicago from consortiums of touts and gamblers in league with the criminal syndicates, imposed two sets of bans in 1898 and 1904 barring trackside wagering. The second prohibition lasted until 1922. Sullied by the unsavory reputation of the "Sport of Kings," the public embraced baseball. It was, after all, the "last clean sport in America." Or was it?

Professional baseball debuted in 1870 at Dexter Park, a West Side racing ground named after one of the most famous trotting horses of the day. The idea of paying an admission fee to witness a staged sporting event or offering an athlete a salary to play a game struck many Chicagoans as an absurd, far-fetched notion. However, civic pride demanded that the city organize a baseball team to compete with the powerful Cincinnati Red Stockings, who had attained national recognition by winning all 60 of their games in 1869. Results fell far short of rising expectations, but the popularity of the Chicago White Stockings playing at Dexter Park in the summer of 1870 laid the groundwork for the formation of the National League in 1876. Thus occurred in the year of the American Centennial the rise of the modern professional sports league.

The enterprise was spearheaded by Chicago businessman and White Stockings owner William Hulbert, who believed the downtown money interests could offer professional baseball to the public without the odious sporting fraternity lurking about the grandstand. As the first president of the National League, Hulbert banned alcohol sales and bookmakers from the athletic grounds where his teams played.

William Hulbert's contributions were enduring. He was an ironclad disciplinarian who divorced baseball from the class of men who had corrupted horseracing and pugilism for decades. He was only 50 years old when he passed away in 1882.

Gradually his conservatism was invalidated by the brewery and saloon interests who crept back into the game in the 1890s. These self-important potentates with deep and pervasive connections to the urban political machines of the late 19th and early 20th centuries purchased professional baseball teams as a means of self-aggrandizement and as a viable way to peddle their companies' alcohol or food products to the fans in the stands. Paunchy, middle-aged men with sagging jowls puffing thick brown cigars, they strutted through the grandstands with their walking sticks firmly in hand. Instantly recognizable from the mass of fans who paid their two-bit admission price, the owners were a throwback to the historic link between the recreation industry and the levee bosses of yesteryear.

The owners' hypocrisies and their callous mistreatment of the athletes they employed belied the positive images they wished to convey to the public. These same baseball magnates with questionable connections to the politicians and gamblers liked to refer to themselves as "sportsmen." They mingled with society's elite at the posh Onwentsia Country Club, contributed a portion of their gate receipts to socially acceptable charities, and promulgated the mythic, all-American wholesomeness of baseball at a time when many of the ballparks in America, including Wrigley Field and Comiskey Park, were infested with bookies and oddsmakers.

The commonly held view of baseball as the last clean sport in America lasted until 1920, when the first public disclosures were made that the 1919 Chicago White Sox had conspired to lose the World Series to Cincinnati. Until the "Black Sox" debacle nearly ruined the game and forced the owners to take swift and decisive action, they turned a blind eye. Profits were all that mattered to them. Sadly, it remains much the same today.

Old ideas die hard. Until 1920 baseball was the only professional play-for-pay team sport in America. Golf, tennis, and sailing were regarded as highbrow country club sports enjoyed by the socially elite, far removed from the grind of downtown living. It was no coincidence, therefore, that the early golf greens were designed and laid out for wealthy residents in remote Wheaton, Lake Forest, Kenilworth, and Winnetka. The nation's very first 18-hole golf course, patterned after St. Andrews in Scotland, was opened in Wheaton in 1894 by Charles Blair MacDonald, truly the father of Chicago golf. By 1911 Chicago and its surrounding suburbs had already hosted three U.S. Opens.

Among the ordinary people trapped within the vast inner-city slums, golf and tennis were narrowly viewed as games for fops, presidents, and the rich. Beginning in the 1920s the automobile became a staple of middle-class life, affording city residents the opportunity to partake finally in the misunderstood sport of golf at distant suburban fairways. Thereafter, the ancient Scottish game enjoyed a much broader-based popularity.

Football was a rite of autumn that took place across the college campuses of the nation from September until the Thanksgiving holiday. Amos Alonzo Stagg and a generation of collegiate athletes who played the game with something akin to a religious fervor in the 1880s fiercely resisted the ambitions of private entrepreneurs who would dare compromise the integrity of their sport by creating a class of hired athletes to showcase their talents for money. The prevailing 19th-century attitude as expressed by Stagg was an anachronism that relegated the gridiron game to second-class status for many years to come. The National Football League, cofounded by Chicago Bears owner George Halas in 1920, failed to achieve equal footing with professional baseball and continued to struggle up until the late 1960s.

Baseball became perceived as slow and out of sync by a new generation of sports enthusiasts who demanded fast-paced, nonstop action that mirrored the accelerated pace of life in the space age. Younger journalists assigned to the sports beats of the metropolitan dailies were less interested in the "national pastime" than the older gentry of writers who had entered the profession when baseball was still the meal ticket. Football, hockey, and basketball were little more than November-to-March diversions for snowbound Chicago scribes anxiously counting down the days until baseball's spring training camps opened.

After veteran baseball columnists Warren Brown, Dave Condon, John Carmichael, Gene Kessler, and John Justin Smith finally retired from their respective Chicago newspapers, their treasured memories and collected baseball wisdom were abandoned and forgotten. The younger reporters who replaced them on the sports desks simply did not share the same interests and passions. These reporters came of age when Howard Cosell, with his razor-sharp, Vietnam-era style, gave baseball the last rites. Cosell, a commentator on ABC's Monday Night Football, considered the summer game to be a decaying and dying relic of America's agrarian past reserved "for little boys and very old men."

As a result, baseball suffered a drop-off in the free newspaper publicity that had been vital to its success since the earliest days of the National and American Leagues. Nowadays an assignment to cover the NCAA Final Four basketball tournament is a much more coveted plum for the MTV generation of reporters than one to cover the World Series.

Continuous labor strife, poor marketing, and greed shown by players and owners alike soured many fans on professional baseball in the 1970s and 1980s, despite the continued popularity of beautiful Wrigley Field. Set within a pleasing urban tapestry on the city's North Side, the home of the Cubs has become a yearly destination for thousands of out-of-town tourists, vacationers, and weekend junketeers from Iowa, Wisconsin, Michigan, Indiana, and other nearby states who come, not to watch the Cubs play baseball, but to see and experience Wrigley Field.

Currently professional football in Chicago is something of a religion. In addition, the whole city is a stage for athletic endeavor, and everyone plays some part. If we are not playing softball or hardball, running, exercising, bowling, golfing, swatting a tennis ball, or shooting hoops, we are watching someone else do it. The impact of cable television, the proliferation of instant news, 24-hour sports talk stations, and intensified media scrutiny into every phase of an athlete's life on and off the playing field have bestowed upon our sports heroes instant celebrity status. Escalating ticket prices, the unavailability of seats for most of the important tournaments and professional events, and the unwillingness of the players to sign an autograph without first checking with their agents or receiving compensation for the privilege have all failed to dissuade Chicago fans from lining up at the ticket windows.

So many sports teams have come and gone. So many vanquished dreams that underscore the strength—and frailty—of the sporting enterprise in our town. Alas, where did they go—the Chicago Rockers, Rockets, Cardinals, Studebaker-Flyers, Hornets, Aces, Cougars, Tigers, Gears, Whales, Fyre, Majors, Winds, Packers, Zephyrs, Stags, and Bruins? They all enjoyed brief notoriety, an occasional spectacular flourish, and then vanished into the night because their promoters were daydreamers, greedy charlatans, or simply misinformed about the demographics of the Chicago market.

As sports fans, we recall the triumphs and failures of all of our teams as vividly today as we did in our youth, when they made us smile, laugh, or cry. Our athletic heritage and the memories of games, players, and events from bygone days is our birthright. Moreover, the milieu of professional sports, despite its less than auspicious beginnings, provides us with an important identity, gently reminding us of who we are within the framework of life in Chicago.

This volume has been assembled with great care. The book brings together for the first time a timeline of the significant occurrences in Chicago sports from the earliest days in our emerging frontier city. The book is more than just a survey of the "Big Four": baseball, football, basketball, and hockey. While we have given these major sports their due, we also recognize that library shelves are cluttered with volumes of history dealing with this subject matter. Biographies, team histories, encyclopedias, and fan memoirs abound. However, there exists a bibliographic void when it comes to books dealing with the history of Chicago bowling, horseracing, tennis, sailing, and even golf.

The standard how-to volumes, offering tips and advice for the weekend sportsman, fill a critical need within the genre of participation sports, but the reading public should not lose sight of the history of the colorful athletic endeavors that have gone before in each of these areas. Unfortunately, that is what has happened over the course of time.

We have attempted to address this oversight with the source book of Chicago sports history you now hold before you. It is a potpourri of facts, trivia, data, nostalgia, and historical analysis designed to entertain and enlighten generations of sports enthusiasts for years to come.

The Armchair Companion to **Chicago** Sports

CHAPTER 1

Covering All the Bases: Chicago's First Sport

The Windy City has always been known as a good baseball town. The pennants haven't always been snapping in the breeze above Chicago ballparks, but Chicago fans love talking and arguing baseball even more than they love their beer and hot dogs at the games. That the city's teams have provided so little to brag about has overshadowed other contributions to the game made by Chicagoans, particularly William Hulbert and Charles Comiskey, who played a prominent role in the development of the major leagues.

Hulbert, who began as a player, converted the game from a barnstorming venture run by the players to a profitable business. A stockholder in Chicago's entry in the early Players Association, Hulbert lured four-star eastern players to Chicago—a group that included Boston hurler Al Spalding and Philadelphia slugger Cap Anson. Faced with disciplinary action by the association, the two-fisted Hulbert went ahead and organized his own circuit. He called it the National League, and the Cubs team he helped start remains the oldest continuous franchise in the circuit.

Charles Comiskey, an alderman's son, chose sports over politics and planted the White Sox on his native South Side soil at the turn of the century. The White Sox were one of the first teams in the new American League. A year later Comiskey and the other American League owners defied the established order and declared the league to be a major one. By forcing the National League to sue for peace, Comiskey and his associates established the second of the two circuits we know today.

1870

A gathering of dignitaries, politicians, industrialists, and dashing military figures like General Philip Sheridan, fresh from his Indian campaigns in the West, turned out to preview Chicago's first professional baseball team—the Chicago White Stockings—at their Dexter Park home, an elegant racing oval and partially covered public grandstand located on the city's West Side.

It was a matter of civic pride, this baseball business. The White Stockings were organized by local promoters to challenge the Cincinnati Red Stockings, America's first professional team, whose 1869 nationwide tour awakened the country to baseball's possibilities as recreational entertainment. The Red Stockings won all 60 of their games in 1869, humiliating every team that stood in their path.

Chicago, not to be shown up by the Queen City team in their 1870 engagement, invested heavily in player talent in anticipation of the fateful showdown scheduled for September 7.

The White Stockings defeated the weakened Red Stockings 10-6 on Cincinnati's home grounds, hastening a raucous celebration back home. The White Stockings and the sport of baseball had taken root in the city of Chicago.

"The Chicago club is a $20,000 article, and for that money a dozen of the best ballplayers in the country may be had!"

ANONYMOUS OUT-OF-TOWN REPORTER, JULY 1870

1870

On August 23 history records that the first baseball game played between two African-American teams was held at Ogden Park on the West Side between the Blue Stockings of Chicago and the Pink Stockings of Rockford, Illinois. The Chicago team won easily by a score of 48-14.

Q: Who were the Blue Stockings?
A: The players were employed at various Chicago hotels as waiters, doormen, and porters.

1871

A former dump site at 22nd Street and State Street became home to the White Stockings, an independent team in 1870, that joined the newly formed National Association. With the snaky underhand tosses of George "Charmer" Zetlin the White Stockings entered October in first place. Then a fire engulfed the 22nd Street grounds, along with a good piece of the rest of the city. The White Stockings were forced to play their final seven games on the road; homeless, they lost the title. Though the scores aren't known—the *Chicago Tribune* did not provide baseball results for two weeks after the great fire—the outcome is.

1872-1873

There were no teams in town, a situation modern-day fans could claim has happened in a few more recent years.

1874

Playing their games on a site just one block south of the old field, the White Stockings rejoined each other and the Association.

1876

Led by newcomers Al Spalding, Ross Barnes, and Cap Anson, the Whites (52-14) romped to the first National League title. Using William Hulbert's bonus money, Spalding started a sporting goods business in Chicago. At one point Spalding planned on outfitting the Whites in a different hat for each position—until a *Tribune* sportswriter ridiculed the idea, writing that the players would look like a bed of Dutch tulips.

1877

William Hulbert became president of the league and took his new responsibilities seriously: He expelled New York and

Philadelphia for schedule violations, banished four Louisville players suspected of taking bribes from gamblers, and in 1881 kicked Cincinnati out of the circuit for serving beer on Sunday.

1878

Al Spalding retired and Chicago played only .500 ball. During the season the White Stockings employed a left-handed catcher, Bill Harbidge—which was not so much of an oddity because the catcher stood well back of the plate, and the hurlers still used an underhand motion, though they were allowed to put some snap on their pitches.

Q: When were pitchers allowed to throw the ball shoulder-high?

A: In 1884, to compensate for the longer distance between home plate and the mound (50 feet).

1879

Cap Anson was promoted to playing manager. The Whites were in the race till an August slump sent them tumbling to third.

> *". . . the White Stockings, the Silk Stockings, Anson's Gang, Hulbert's Hired Men, etc., having been bringing disgrace upon this city and execrations upon their own heads by the extraordinary capable manner in which they have allowed themselves to be beaten by clubs which a few weeks ago they would have scorned to acknowledge had any show of defeating them."*
>
> CHICAGO TRIBUNE, REPORTING THE DEMISE OF THE WHITE STOCKINGS

1880

With the services of catcher Michael "King" Kelly, the White Stockings breezed to the National League title. Baseball's first superstar, Kelly performed a daring hook-slide, which was popularized in the sheet music tune "Slide Kelly Slide."

Q: What other sort of performing did Kelly become known for?

A: Capitalizing on his fame, Kelly toured the vaudeville circuit doing a song-and-dance routine. An irreverent Irishman, he also spent considerable time with John Barleycorn, which led him to miss his regular afternoon appointment. This put him at odds with the martinet Cap Anson.

1880

Another free spirit on the White Stockings team was reserve outfielder Billy Sunday. After waking in the gutter one day following a particularly raucous evening, Sunday saw the emptiness of his life. He eventually became a traveling evangelist speaking out against the evils of drinking.

Q: How did Billy Sunday get a rise out of the congregation?
A: The athletic Sunday would bolt from the pulpit and slide across the floor while clutching a Bible.

"The town that Billy Sunday couldn't shut down."
JOHN KANDER, ON CHICAGO

1881

On September 19, despite the nation's official day of mourning after the assassination of President James Garfield, the White Stockings took to the field. This so outraged *Chicago Tribune* owner Joseph Medill that he banned coverage of baseball for the following season. The ban was temporarily lifted when William Hulbert died in April.

1882

After winning their third straight flag, Cap Anson's White Stockings engaged the American Association Cincinnati Reds in the first World Championship games. After the teams had traded shutouts, the games were canceled when Cincinnati was threatened with expulsion by the league president.

1884

In opposition to the reserve clause, St. Louis realtor Henry Lucas organized the Union League. A. H. Henderson, a Baltimore matress manufacturer, organized the Chicago entry. They were nicknamed the Browns, but the fans sarcastically dubbed them the Onions. One Arm Daly, who before his ball career had lost his left hand in a gun accident, did most of the mound work. The mediocre Onions (34-39), who began play on May 22 at Union Ballpark at 39th and Wentworth, were shifted to Pittsburgh in August. Unable to compete with the well-coffered National League and American Association owners, the Union League folded after one season.

Q: What record did White Stocking Ned Williamson make that summer that would stand until Babe Ruth broke it in 1919?

A: He blasted a record 27 home runs. Twenty-five of his swats occurred at Lakefront Park at Randolph and Michigan in what is now Grant Park.

1885

Cap Anson and his champion White Stockings took on Charles Comiskey's American Association St. Louis Browns in the first official World Series. The games were marred by player fights, umpire baiting, and unruly spectators, then ended in a three-game tie.

Q: One of Chicago's wins was forfeited. Why?

A: Comiskey had removed his team from the field to protest an umpire's decision.

1886

Renewing their feud, the White Stockings and Browns clashed in a $15,000, winner-take-all match. St. Louis captured the title by winning the final three games at home. Chicago had lost the championship game when Curt Welch stole home under King Kelly's high tag. That steal was dubbed the "$15,000 slide."

Q: How did White's president Al Spalding respond to this loss?

A: He refused to pay the players' fares home from St. Louis; then over the winter he sold his star players, including Kelly, to Boston for the unheard of sum of $10,000.

1887

Talentless, the White Stockings dropped to third place and would go another 20 years without a flag.

> *"If Chicago is to have cheap players it ought to have cheap admission."*
>
> CHICAGO TRIBUNE

1887

The game of softball—a quintessential Chicago summer pastime—was invented on Thanksgiving Day by George Hancock and fellow members of the Farragut Boat Club, headquartered in the 3000 block of Lake Park Avenue on the South Side.

It seems that Hancock and his friends were bored with the traditional Thanksgiving football games, so they devised a version of baseball that could be played indoors during the cold and snowy season. Hancock took a glove, wrapped it into a ball using heavy tape, and then began swatting the object around the boathouse with a stick. These were the humble beginnings of the game known as Indoor Ball, which after many years evolved into 16-inch softball—a rite of summer at hundreds of city and suburban parks.

The former site of the Farragut Boat Club along the shore of Lake Michigan has been appropriately marked by softball enthusiasts as the location of the first softball game.

Q: When did Indoor Ball actually go outdoors?

A: After World War I the popularity of indoor baseball slowly waned. However, for many years a 12-inch softball was sold and marketed as an indoor ball by the sporting goods companies.

1888

Cap Anson led a group of major league players, mostly Chicagoans, on an around-the-world tour. Similar tours would be taken by the White Sox in 1913 and 1924.

> *1. There is everything to hope for and nothing to fear.*
> *2. Defeats do not disturb one's sleep.*
> *3. An occasional victory is a surprise and a delight.*
> *4. There is no danger of any club passing you.*
> *5. You are not asked fifty times a day, "What was the score?" People take it for granted that you lost.*
>
> ELMER F. BATES (1889), ON THE ADVANTAGES OF FOLLOWING A LOSING TEAM

1890

In response to the new salary classification scheme by the baseball magnates, the players organized the Players League. About 50 of them jumped to the new circuit, including some prominent White Stockings who were happy to escape the grasp of manager Cap Anson.

Charles Comiskey left the Browns to manage the Chicago Pirates, a South Side team that played its games at the future site of Comiskey Park.

Though peace was restored between players and owners, the settlement doomed the financially insecure American Association.

1893

In conjunction with the Columbian Exposition, the White Stockings moved into new grounds at Polk and Lincoln. The ball field featured box seats on the grandstand roof for the lace-and-surrey set. West Side Park would serve as the National League team's home base for 23 seasons.

Q: What's now located where the old Whites once played?
A: The field was near the present site of Cook County Hospital.

1897

In what still stands as baseball's worst drubbing, the White Stockings scored 36 runs against Louisville. After the season Cap Anson was fired by new owner James Hart. With Anson no longer at the helm, the White Stockings were called the Orphans.

Q: Anson had several careers after he left the team. What were some of them?

A: After managing the New York Giants for a few seasons, he wrote his autobiography, then served as Chicago City Clerk from 1905 to 1907. For a while he also performed on vaudeville with his daughters.

1900

Despite James Hart's objections, Charles Comiskey transferred his minor league St. Paul Saints to Chicago, but they had to observe Hart's stipulation that his team not be located north of 35th Street. Comiskey chose an abandoned cricket stadium at 39th and Wentworth for his ballpark and nicknamed his team the "White Stockings."

Q: Why had Comiskey chosen the National's old moniker White Stockings?

A: James Hart had insisted that Comiskey not use the word *Chicago* in his team's name, so Comiskey used the National's former name to identify his club as a Chicago entity. White Stockings was later shortened to White Sox to accommodate the newspaper headlines.

1901

The upstart American League declared itself a major league, precipitating a war with the established National League. Charles Comiskey beefed up the Sox with jump-coat National Leaguers and captured the American League's first official flag. The West Siders' leading hurler, Clark Griffith, was lured to the South Side by a lucrative contract. Accompanying Griffith across town were teammates Nixey Callahan and Sandow Mertes, whom Comiskey met at the train station and whisked over to Sox headquarters past a sleeping James Hart.

1901

Andrew Rube Foster, recognized as the father of black baseball in Chicago, signed a contract to pitch for Frank Leland's Chicago Union Giants, a powerhouse team belonging to the integrated semiprofessional city league whose neighborhood popularity in many respects rivaled that of the Cubs and White Sox in the first decade of the century.

Foster was a brilliant organizer, an early and strident champion of civil rights for the African-American baseball player, and something of a genius when it came to promoting the sport in that racially charged, highly segregated era.

In 1907 Foster took over as manager of the Leland Giants. A brilliant tactician who maximized every opportunity, Foster guided his team to an astounding 110-10 record that season. Rube Foster, more than anyone else in the city at that time, put black baseball on the map.

Q: Where did the Leland Giants play their home games?
A: The team played at the Auburn Park Ball Grounds, located at 79th and Wentworth Avenue on the South Side until 1911 when they moved into Charles Comiskey's vacated wooden grandstand at 39th Street and Wentworth Avenue.

1902

Because of all the defections, the National's skipper Frank Selee brought in youngsters to play, hence the nickname Cubs. Frank Chance manned first base, and Joe Tinker was at shortstop. Late in the season a spunky eastern leaguer named Johnny Evers arrived in town to complete the Cubs' famous trio. On September 15 Tinker, Evers, and Chance completed their first double play.

1903

After the two leagues agreed to a peace treaty, the Cubs and Sox met in a 14-game city series match, which ended in a seven-game tie. Cubs hurler Jack Taylor lost his last three assignments amid rumors that he'd gone down for the bucks. Whoops! During the regular season, Sox shortstop Lee Tannehill committed 76 errors, four of them on May 6 when the Sox were charged with a record 12 boots in an 8-6 win over Detroit.

1904

Mordecai "Three Finger" Brown won 15 of 25 decisions in his first year with the Cubs. As a youngster, Brown had caught his hand in a thresher and lost part of his index finger; he used the stub of the mangled finger to put extra spin on the ball. Hurler Ed Walsh joined the White Sox. Baseball's first strikeout artist, Walsh showered American League hitters with a blazing spitter that Detroit outfielder Sam Crawford swore "disintegrated on the way to the plate."

Q: How did Walsh moisten what became known as his "slippery eel" pitch?
A: He sprayed the ball with saliva concocted from slippery-elm bark tablets and chewing gum.

1905

Cubs skipper Frank Selee, who was suffering from tuberculosis, was replaced at the helm by Frank Chance, but his keystone mates Joe Tinker and Johnny Evers weren't on speaking terms by season's end. Before an exhibition game in Bedford, Indiana, Evers caught a cab, leaving Tinker and several other players behind at the hotel. Then during the game Tinker and Evers exchanged harsh words and fists flew. After that the two rarely spoke to each other, and communicated only when necessary during a game.

1906

Back on top, the Cubs had a 116-36 season and were considered by many the greatest ball club of all time. Then the hitless-wonder White Sox (93-58) upset them in the World Series.

To accommodate all of Chicago's baseball bugs, the games were reproduced at two indoor arenas: the Auditorium Building on Michigan Avenue and the old First Regiment Armory. An operator stationed at the ballpark relayed an account of the action to each site. The batter's name, number of outs, and the runners' positions were indicated on a large baseball diamond erected on each stage.

Q: Which of the following allowed the Sox to whip the Cubs?

1. The Cubs, having breezed to the title, were too cocky.
2. The old baseball adage about good pitching in a short series prevailed. Sox hurlers posted a 1.67 ERA.
3. Improbable Sox heroes—the nondescript Nick Altrock, who outpitched Three Finger Brown in the opener; utility infielder George Rohe, who produced the clutch hits that won games one and three; and journeyman Ed Hahn, who paced the Sox to victory in the series finale.

A: All of the above.

1907

The Cubs romped to another National League title then defeated the Detroit Tigers in the World Series. Each member of the Cubs starting rotation gained a win. Ty Cobb, who boasted he hit .800 against the Cubs' pitching, had just four hits, and it was the Cubs, not Cobb, who ruled the base paths with 18 stolen bases. Seeing Cubs runners flash by in his dreams, Detroit catcher Boss Schmidt sought medical assistance after the season to help quell his nerves.

1908

The Cubs met the Detroit Tigers again in the World Series and again emerged victorious, which made it the third straight year a championship flag flew over the city of Chicago. It almost was an all-Chicago series. The Tigers defeated the second-place Sox on the final day of the season.

Ed Walsh made 66 appearances and saw action in 14 of the Sox's last 17 games. On October 2 he fanned 15 Cleveland hitters in a loss to future fellow Hall of Famer Addie Joss. Coming out of the pen the next day, he fanned the mighty Nap Lajoie to preserve a 3-2 victory.

Q: How could Walsh strike out 15 batters and still lose the game?

A: Addie Joss bettered him by spinning a no-hitter.

1910

Comiskey Park, a steel-and-concrete edifice designed by architect Zachary Taylor Davis, opened on July 1, with the Sox losing 2-0 to St. Louis before 30,000 fans.

Q: Why did the symmetrical Comiskey Park have such large dimensions (362' x 420' x 362')?
A: Ed Walsh, who accompanied Davis on an inspection of other parks, wanted a spacious pitcher's ballpark.

Q: What happened to the Sox's original stadium?
A: It served as home field for the Negro League American Giants until the Stateway Gardens housing project was constructed on the site in the late 1940s.

1910

On August 27, 1910, at Comiskey Park, a crowd of 3,500 witnessed the first night game to be played in a major league stadium. Nineteen arc lights were installed on the overhanging roof between third and first base to illuminate the diamond for two of Chicago's finest semipro teams: the Logan Squares and the Rogers Parkers. Despite some power shortages the experiment was adjudged a success, but a novelty that would have to wait a few more years at least. There would be no more night baseball in Chicago until the White Sox took the initiative in 1939.

Q: Who managed the Logan Squares?
A: Former White Sox manager James J. Callahan.

1911

Rube Foster quit the Leland Giants in order to form a partnership with a white South Side tavern owner named John C. Schorling. Together they organized the Chicago American Giants, a legendary team that dominated the black baseball circuit on the amateur side and the Negro National League for years to come. Playing at the cramped 39th Street Grounds, the Giants won titles in 1913, 1914, and 1917, and tied for the 1915 championship.

1914

The Federal League began play. Chicago's entry was managed by Joe Tinker and nicknamed the Whales.

Q: How did the new team get its name?

A: The name Whales was chosen in a contest sponsored at the conclusion of the 1914 season. Chicagoan D. J. Eichoff, who won a season's pass for himself and his family, wanted the name to symbolize Lake Michigan, and he said the biggest fish in the lake was a whale. Other entries under consideration were Tots, Chix, Bandits, and Imperials.

1914

On March 14, 1914, less than a month before the opening of the Federal League season, 5,000 enthusiastic North Siders turned out for the gala groundbreaking of Weeghman Park, the privately financed baseball stadium named after the ambitious young owner of the new team that was set to begin play in a month's time.

The Federal League was essentially a midwestern baseball circuit before James Gilmore, a thirty-seven-year-old Chicago businessman, took over as its president. Gilmore and his fellow dreamers envisioned the day when they could challenge the National and American League hegemony and build a third professional baseball league. The grand illusion took shape in the fall of 1913 after Gilmore set in motion a plan to lure big money men from across the country to invest in Federal League teams, draw marquee players from the other two leagues, and build new stadiums.

Charles Henry Weeghman, an avid sportsman who owned ten Loop restaurants specializing in fast, over-the-counter lunch service, was the first to be contacted. Weeghman invested a considerable amount of his capital in the risky venture. He loved baseball and the company of fellow sportsmen, but ultimately he lost his entire restaurant fortune backing a doomed baseball league that fell apart after only two seasons.

Q: What happened to Weeghman Park after the Federal League was forced out of business?

A: Lucky Charley, as the press nicknamed Weeghman before he suffered irreversible financial setbacks, was permitted to buy the Cubs from the Charles Taft family of Cincinnati in 1916 as partial settlement of the contentious two-year-old Federal League war. Weeghman Park, which cost the owner $250,000 to build in 1914, was renamed Wrigley Field a few years after Charles Weeghman sold his majority interest in the Cubs to William Wrigley Jr. and a syndicate of nine investors on December 7, 1918. Two years later his restaurant chain was thrown into a receivership.

Q: Who designed Weeghman Park?
A: Zachary Taylor Davis, the young architect from Daniel Burnham's staff, who also drew up the blueprints for Comiskey Park in 1910. Davis modeled his latest commission after the Polo Grounds in New York.

"We are in the game with a load of money and not afraid to spend it if it will get us the ballplayers!"

JAMES GILMORE, TO THE CHICAGO PRESS, MARCH 1914

"Boys! Call us the Blues, because only the blue-bloods get to be Federals!"

CHARLES WEEGHMAN, ADVISING THE PRESS TO CALL HIS 1914 TEAM THE BLUES. A YEAR LATER THE NAME WAS CHANGED TO THE CHICAGO WHALES.

1915

The Chicago Whales, employing former Cubs hurler Mordecai Brown, edged the St. Louis Tip Tops by one percentage point to capture the Federal League title.

Charles Comiskey gave the Sox a championship flavor by securing the services of Eddie Collins, Lefty Williams, and Joe Jackson. The third-place Sox closed out the season with 11 straight wins, then swept the Cubs in the local series.

1916

As part of the peace accord between major league baseball and the Federal League, Chicago Whales owner Charles Weeghman was allowed to purchase the Cubs. Playing at the Feds brand-new park on the North Side, the new team composed of ex-Whales and Cubs finished a flat fifth.

1917

The White Sox acquired first-sacker Chick Gandil and shortstop Swede Risberg, and the team captured the World Series, whipping the New York Giants in six games. Charles Comiskey rewarded his champion players with a case of champagne that sportswriter Ring Lardner said tasted like "stale horse piss."

1918

Over 200 major league players joined the war effort, including Sox players Red Faber, Eddie Collins, and Swede Risberg. Opting for defense work were married men Joe Jackson, Lefty Williams, and Happy Felsch. Comiskey labeled the factory workers slackers and promised they would never play for the Sox again.

Q: Why did these slackers rejoin the team in 1919?
A: The gate-conscious Comiskey reneged on his promise.

1919

In retaliation for Charles Comiskey's niggardly ways, eight Sox players consorted with New York mob kingpin Arnold Rothstein to throw the World Series, but the players were double-crossed by the gamblers and received little of the promised money.

> *"I don't know what's the matter, but I do know something is wrong with my gang. The bunch I had fighting in August for the pennant would have trimmed this Cincinnati bunch without a struggle, the bunch I have now couldn't beat a high school team . . ."*
>
> KID GLEASON, AFTER A REDS VICTORY

Q: What players were expelled the following year when the scandal erupted?
A: The "Black Sox" included Joe Jackson, Happy Felsch, Buck Weaver, Swede Risberg, Ed Cicotte, Lefty Williams, and

Fred McMullen. The eighth conspirator, Chick Gandil, had retired prior to the season.

"I done it for the wife and kiddies."

BLACK SOX HURLER ED CICOTTE

Q: Were the Black Sox players innocent or guilty?

A: It all depends. The eight Black Sox defendants were found innocent in a civil court because an important document had been pilfered, leaving the prosecution with an impossible task of proving fraud on the players' part. Newly appointed baseball commissioner Judge Kenesaw Landis delivered the final verdict, suspending all eight players for life.

1920

In the discordant winter of 1920, a time when the ill-fated White Sox were on everyone's mind, Rube Foster organized the Negro National League, a professional association of African-American players fielding representative teams in the South and Midwest. An East Coast counterpart was founded in 1923, and it lasted until 1929.

The eight-team Negro National League was formally chartered in Kansas City in February 1920. The Chicago Giants remained under Rube Foster's careful control until 1926, when he suffered a severe mental breakdown and had to be rushed to the state insane asylum. Under Foster's firm but guiding hand, the NNL managed to maintain its financial independence from white baseball up until 1931, the year the league was forced to temporarily disband due to the hardships wrought by the Great Depression.

Q: In what years did the Chicago American Giants capture the NNL pennant?

A: The Giants finished on top in 1920, 1921, 1922, 1926 (second half of a split season), 1927 (first-half champions), and 1928 (second-half champions).

Q: How did they do after Gus Greenlee, a notorious Pittsburgh racketeer and owner of the Pittsburgh Crawfords, revived the dormant NNL in 1933 with an infusion of gangster money?

A: The Giants (now referred to as Robert Cole's American Giants) won first-half pennants in 1933 and 1934 and second-half pennants in 1944 and 1949—now playing under their former name, the Chicago American Giants.

Q: Who were some of the great African-American stars who played for the Giants in their heyday?

A: Shortstop Oscar Charleston, in the opinion of many the greatest NNL player of all time, was a member of Foster's 1920 champions. Third baseman and manager Dave Malarcher was a standout infielder for much of the 1920s. Ernest Willie Powell was the pitching ace of the 1926-1927 champions. Sandy Thompson won the batting title in 1927 with a blistering .441 average. First baseman George Mule Suttles; outfielder Norman Turkey Stearnes, who won the 1935 batting title; and shortstop Willie Wells (elected to the Hall of Fame in 1997) were the catalysts of the 1933 success.

"We are the ship, all else the sea!"

MOTTO OF THE NEGRO NATIONAL LEAGUE,
COINED BY RUBE FOSTER

1925

The White Sox got back in the limelight when catcher Ray Schalk gave Chicagoans a thrill by stabbing a baseball dropped from the brand-new Tribune Tower, a distance of 456 feet. Though he missed the first three drops, he snared the fourth one.

Q: Did Schalk establish some sort of record with this feat?

A: No. Washington Senator backstop Gabby Street and Sox catcher Billy Sullivan had each caught a ball thrown from the Washington Monument (550 feet).

1926

New Cubs manager Joe McCarthy led the team back into contention; the astute McCarthy, over a twenty-four-year period on three teams, never once finished in the second division. McCarthy recommended the Cubs sign Giant farmhand Hack Wilson. A barrel-chested leprechaun (5'6" and 190 pounds), he won the first of four home-run titles. Dubbed the poor man's Babe Ruth, Wilson celebrated life like the Babe, drinking and chasing women.

> *"I've never played drunk. Hung over, yes, but never drunk."*
>
> HACK WILSON

Q: What happened to the Cubs' home field this year?
A: It was named Wrigley Field after the chewing-gum magnate who'd bought the team.

1927

Over the winter Charles Comiskey added an outfield upper deck to his already spacious ballpark, increasing the seating capacity to 52,000. Zachary Taylor Davis was again called upon to oversee the renovations. Davis promised Comiskey that, with the addition of elevated runways leading from the right and left field upper deck to the ground floor, a capacity crowd could exit the park in five to six minutes.

> *"Comiskey Park, enlarged and improved beyond the imagination of fans who haven't seen it, will be finished in every detail when the American League opens here on April 20, 1927. The new plant then will be ready to vie with Yankee Stadium in New York as the greatest baseball plant in the world."*
>
> ED BURNS, *CHICAGO TRIBUNE,* MARCH 1927

1929

As Charles Comiskey had done a decade earlier, Cubs owner Bill Wrigley had begun assembling a championship club piece by piece, and this year the team acquired the fellow they needed to win the flag—Rogers Hornsby. But the great Cubs ball club saw its season end in an embarrassing five-game World Series loss to Connie Mack's Philadelphia A's.

Q: Why was it such an embarrassing loss?
A: For one, journeyman hurler Howard Ehmke struck out 13 Cubs in the opener, making a series record; in game four Hack Wilson lost a ball in the sun, which helped the A's mount a 10-run seventh inning for a comeback win.

Q: What role did the White Sox play in the Cubs' defeat?
A: Several White Sox players, who had contested the Cubs in the city series, prepared a thorough scouting report for the A's pitchers.

1930

Joe McCarthy, who was on the hot seat after losing the '29 World Series, was fired with four games left in the season and replaced by Rogers Hornsby. On the South Side, Sox rookie Smead Jolley brought some unintended laughs to drab Comiskey Park. Though he stung the ball well, his glove struck a Statue-of-Liberty pose on fly balls, costing the Sox games. The Sox then tried to make Jolley a catcher, but his habits of missing countless balls and leaving his mask on while chasing fouls ended the experiment.

Q: What was Smead Jolly's best position?
A: He'd have been a great designated hitter, but unfortunately the rule wasn't adopted until four decades later.

1930

Rube Foster passed away on December 9 after spending the last four years of his life confined to a mental institution in Kankakee, Illinois. Thousands of mourners passed by his casket at the funeral home on 47th Street. According to the *Chicago Defender,* the casket was closed at the usual hour a ball game ends. In 1981 Foster received a long-overdue tribute from the sportswriters; many of them were too young to have seen him play. For his lasting contributions to the national game, Foster was elected to baseball's Hall of Fame.

Q: How did Rube Foster acquire his famous nickname?
A: In his younger days Foster had defeated Rube Waddell, one of Connie Mack's great pitching stars, in a barnstorming game pitting the Leland Giants against the Philadelphia A's.

"Now some of the players we would meet would tell us about the hardships they had and so forth and they did—but I never experienced that until after Robert Cole and those people got the American Giants and that is when I quit. With Rube everything was high class. I got my money every first and fifteenth of the month."

DAVE MALARCHER, WHO SUCCEEDED RUBE FOSTER AS GIANTS MANAGER

1931

White Sox manager Donie Bush was given a leave of absence to comb the country for some ballplayers. Gone two weeks, Bush returned empty-handed, but in a better frame of mind to finish the campaign.

"The Sox need a catcher, an entire new infield and an outfield with wallop."

SOX MANAGER DONIE BUSH, 1931

1931

White Sox founder Charles A. Comiskey passed away at his Eagle River, Wisconsin, vacation home on October 26. The Old Roman (his nickname since the 1890s) was a well-respected and venerated figure during his lifetime and a hero to the working-class Irish of Bridgeport who lived a few blocks from the stadium he built with his own money. It was only much later that baseball historians reconsidered Comiskey's callous handling of his players and recast him in the role of villain. However, he remains a true pioneer of the national pastime, and for his accomplishments as one of the founders of the American League the Old Roman was elected to the Hall of Fame in 1939.

Q: Who owned the White Sox after Charles Comiskey died?

A: Ownership of the ball club passed to Comiskey's only son, John Louis. In 1939 J. Lou Comiskey died, and his widow, Grace Reidy Comiskey, operated the White Sox with her daughter Dorothy until Grace suffered a fatal heart attack on December 10, 1956. Chuck Comiskey, grandson of the Old Roman, co-owned the White Sox with Dorothy until 1959, when Bill Veeck acquired the team after a long and bitter stock fight that was eventually resolved in a federal court.

"The South Side rooters are still in a class by themselves in the way of unswerving loyalty to the White Sox and to Comiskey, which is one and the same thing. Comiskey lived, breathed, and died baseball. Very few have ever been so thoroughly wedded to their business. For 55 years baseball was his very being, and 31 of those found the name of Comiskey blended with that of the White Sox, and evidently it will remain that way for generations to come."

CHICAGO HERALD & EXAMINER EDITORIAL, OCT. 26, 1931

1932

Mounting a late surge, the Cubs captured the pennant; a late addition, shortstop Mark Koenig (.353) provided the pennant spark. But the ex-Yankee Koenig was voted only a half share by his teammates, prompting the revenge-seeking Yanks to sweep the Cubs in four games in the series. In game three Babe Ruth, while jawing with the Cubs bench, supposedly called his home-run shot.

"If he had pointed to the bleachers, I would have knocked him down on the next pitch."

CUBS PITCHER CHARLIE ROOT

1933

Baseball's first All-Star Game was played in Comiskey Park on July 6 before a sellout crowd of 43,000 fans and 102 working reporters. The star-studded event was billed "The Game of the Century" by *Chicago Tribune* sports columnist Arch Ward, who conceived the idea of a dream game pitting the greatest stars of the two professional leagues against one another on neutral ground. The fans voted for their favorite players—Al Simmons of the White Sox was the leading vote-getter in 1933.

The White Sox earned the right to host the game after winning a coin toss against the Cubs.

At first the All-Star Game was intended as a one-time event coinciding with the 1933 World's Fair hosted by Chicago. However, the game was sold out 45 minutes after the State Street ticket window opened for business on July 2. The success of the first game convinced the owners to schedule a yearly All-Star Game to be rotated among all of baseball's major league cities.

Q: Who won the first All-Star Game, and what was the score?
A: The American League defeated the Nationals 4-2. Babe Ruth of the New York Yankees clubbed the first home run.

Q: What other years did Chicago play host to baseball's immortals?
A: The All-Star Game returned to Comiskey Park in 1950 and again in 1983. Wrigley Field was the site of the 1947 game, the second 1962 game, and, finally, the 1990 game.

"This is an announcement of the greatest baseball game ever scheduled. It will bring together the strongest team that can be recruited from the National League against the best that can be assembled from the American League."

ARCH WARD, NOTIFYING CHICAGO FANDOM, MAY 19, 1933

1933

The centerpiece of the Negro League baseball season was the yearly East-West All-Star Game, which was inaugurated the same year as the Major League All-Star Game and in the same locale. The teams were selected in a random poll conducted by two widely circulated African-American newspapers—the *Chicago Defender* and the *Pittsburgh Courier.*

Twenty thousand fans turned out to watch the greatest Negro League players from the western team defeat the stars of the east 11-7 at Comiskey Park in 1933. For every year thereafter until 1950, when the final East-West Game was played, attendance rarely dipped below 45,000. In fact, the East-West Game out-drew the Major League All-Star Game in 1938, 1942, 1943, 1944, 1946, and 1947.

They came by train, they came by car. It was the most important sports event of that era for black America, and with the exception of 1946, when the game was shifted to Washington, D.C., Comiskey Park was the home of every East-West Game.

Q: Who was the winning pitcher for the victorious West team in the 1933 All-Star Game?

A: Willie Foster of the Chicago American Giants.

1935

With a 21-game winning streak in September the Cubs vaulted past the Cardinals and Giants to capture their third title in six seasons, then lost the World Series to the Detroit Tigers in six games. The team's hitters failed in the clutch, its fielders committed some inopportune errors, and several players engaged in foolish bouts of bench jockeying and umpire baiting. Manager Charlie Grimm was tossed from one game. After the series, commissioner Landis leveled hefty fines on Grimm and three Cubs players.

1936

Finishing in the first division for the first time in 15 seasons, the Sox sported five .300 hitters and a 20-game winner. Shortstop Luke Appling won the batting title and supplied a club-record, 26-game hitting streak.

1937

Chicago Times columnist Irv Kupcinet foolishly intervened in a dispute between another sportswriter and Cardinals hurler Dizzy Dean in a Tampa, Florida, hotel lobby. While hollering at Dean, Kup was sent sprawling into a flowerpot from a punch thrown by Dean's teammate Ducky Medwick. As peacemakers moved in, Kup righted himself and, ignoring Medwick, lunged after Dean who took cover behind a couch.

Q: Did Kup ever square accounts with Old Diz?
A: The following year they shook hands and later became good friends.

1937

In July workmen began constructing the Wrigley Field bleachers and scoreboard. When the renovation was complete, the home of the Cubs took on the familiar look that has endured to the present day.

Q: Whose idea was it to plant ivy vines on the outfield wall?
A: Bill Veeck, future owner of the White Sox and son of Cubs executive William Veeck Sr. While carpenters hammered away on the bleachers and gardeners planted the ivy, Veeck tried unsuccessfully to plant three Chinese elm trees on each side of the scoreboard. The trees wilted and died in the gale-force winds sweeping off Lake Michigan.

1938

Jackie Robinson, the gifted infielder who was named the Southern California Junior College's Most Valuable Player for 1938, appeared at the White Sox Spring Training headquarters in Brookside Park, Pasadena, California, that spring with a team of semipros. The Pasadena team was scheduled to play a charity exhibition game against the big league ball club.

The date was March 14, 1938. Despite pounding out two hits in five at bats against four Chicago pitchers, Sox manager James Dykes was unimpressed with the young African-American ballplayer. No one dared challenge baseball's exclusionary policy concerning blacks, least of all the curmudgeonly Dykes—who harbored deep resentments against African-Americans throughout his managerial career.

Jackie shattered baseball's seemingly impenetrable color line in his rookie season with the Brooklyn Dodgers in 1947.

Q: Who eventually broke baseball's color barrier in Chicago?
A: Orestes Minnie Minoso of the White Sox, on May 1, 1951. He made history when he stepped up to bat for the first

time in Comiskey Park and drilled a home run off Vic Raschi of the New York Yankees. Ernie Banks broke the Chicago Cubs' color line two years later when he made his debut against Philadelphia on September 17, 1953.

1938

Continuing their three-year pennant string started in '29, the Cubs streaked to the title. The Cubs bumped the Pirates from the top spot on September 28 when player-manager Gabby Hartnett slugged his famous "homer in the gloamin." That shot gave the Cubs a 6-5 victory in a game about to be called on account of darkness. But, as in 1932, the Cubs were swept in the series by the Yankees.

1939

To help rescue itself from a pool of red ink, the White Sox had lights installed during the season; 13-year-old Charles Comiskey pulled the switch to illuminate the park. The first night game was played on August 13, the Sox defeating the Browns 5-2. Two weeks later over 50,000 fans attended a game under the stars against the Yankees.

Q: What Sox player would inspire a movie starring Jimmy Stewart?

A: Promising Sox hurler Monty Stratton lost his right leg in an off-season hunting accident, but he later mounted a comeback in the minor leagues pitching on an artificial leg.

1940

The Sox started the forties with a whimper, not a bang. On opening day, they endured a no-hitter from Cleveland's Bob Feller.

Q: When was the only time the players started and finished a game with the same batting average?

A: April 16, 1940. The Sox hitters started at .000 and finished at .000.

1942

After America's entry in World War II hundreds of players traded their baseball flannels for service fatigues. For the duration of the war baseball teams consisted of military 4-Fs, career minor leaguers, and grizzled veterans. In the last City Series match the White Sox whipped the Cubs. It was the eighth straight victory and 18th title in 25 meetings for the Sox.

1943

Afraid that interest in the game would wane, Cubs owner P. K. Wrigley started a Women's baseball circuit in the Midwest—The All-American Girls Professional Baseball League. The women played in skirts on a condensed field using a smaller ball.

1945

On a ragtag Sox team put together for wartime play, 37-year-old Tony Cuccinello kept things interesting by vying for the batting title against the Yankees' Snuffy Stirnweiss. When the Sox's finale was rained out, Cuccinello lost his bid by one percentage point.

A Cubs squad captured the National League pennant, pitting them against the Detroit Tigers, which did not have one starter under age 30. The series was marked by lackadaisical fielding and terrible base running. The sixth game, a comical Cubs overtime win, was labeled the worst game ever played in America. Detroit managed not to play as poorly as the Cubs did.

"I don't think either of them can win."

Warren Brown, a Chicago sportswriter,
when asked for his series prediction

1948

Chicago: first in industry and commerce and last in the National and American League.

The Sox had their worst season in franchise history (51-101), resulting in the dismissal of general manager Les O'Conner. On the North Side the Cubs, employing kiddy corps from their feeble farm system, finished in the cellar for the first time in 24 years. Trying to save face, new general manager Jim Gallagher called the Cubs the best team ever to finish last. Owner Phillip K. Wrigley didn't concur and drafted an apology to the Chicago fans that was posted in all the Chicago dailies.

Chicago fielded a women's baseball team, the Colleens, which joined the Cubs and Sox in last place that year.

> *"This year's rebuilding job was a flop. If one system does not work we will try another."*
>
> P. K. Wrigley

1949

The Boys Benefit Games, a mid-season charity game between the two Chicago clubs, commenced in 1949. The games ended in 1972. A yearly Cubs-Sox match resumed in 1985. The Sox dominated the later matches (7-0-1) and overall held a 18-to 13-game edge in the annual game.

Q: Have the Cubs ever beaten the White Sox in intercity play?
A: Yes. In preseason meetings the Cubs hold the edge (95-86).

1950

You can't tell the players without a scorecard. The White Sox colorful Go-Go era was about to be ushered in at Comiskey Park under wheeler-dealer general manager Frank Lane. Billy Pierce, Nelson Fox, Chico Carrasquel, Minnie Minoso, and Sherm Lollar would be stolen in lopsided deals by Lane, making the Sox winners.

The seventh-place Cubs, dubbed the Whiff Kids, dropped 17 double-headers. Former Brooklyn Dodger farm director Wid Mathews replaced Jim Gallagher as director of player personnel.

> *"Mr. Mathews' job is to produce a winning team as soon as possible."*
>
> Phillip K. Wrigley, when asked what Mathews's job would entail

1951

Chicago was tingling with excitement over the Go-Go Sox, who won 23 of their first 32 games. After 11 straight wins on the road, the team was greeted by a cheering throng at the LaSalle Station then rushed to City Hall to receive the keys to the city from Mayor Kennelly.

Q: How long did the Sox streak run?
A: After 14 straight wins they moved ahead of the Yankees into first place. The rivalry ignited when the New Yorkers' stalling tactics on one rainy day during a crucial July game canceled a Sox winning ninth-inning rally.

1952

The "mayor" of Addison Avenue, Hank Sauer, paced the Cubs to a fifth-place finish, winning an MVP award on the way.

Q: How did the fanatics in the bleachers pay homage to Hank Sauer?
A: An avid pipe-smoker, Sauer was showered with packets of tobacco.

1953

The Sox posted their best record in 34 seasons but still couldn't catch the super-heated Yankees.

The Cubs first black players, infielders Gene Baker and Ernie Banks, arrived in mid-September. A Korean War vet, Baker was the first black player signed by the organization. Banks, purchased from the Negro League, entered the lineup on September 17 and was hitless in three at bats. Two days later, he drilled a single off the Cardinals' Vinegar Bend Mizell.

Q: What pitcher served up Ernie Banks's first home run?
A: St. Louis's Gerry Staley, who would later serve with the Sox.

1955

Ernie Banks hit five grand slammers, but alone he couldn't move the Cubs out of the throes of the second division.

> *"Without Ernie Banks, the Cubs would finish in Albuquerque."*
>
> JIMMY DYKES

1956

Sox rookie shortstop Luis Aparicio won Rookie of the Year honors after capturing the first of nine straight stolen base titles.

1957

The Sox-Yankee rivalry, which had been brewing for a while, culminated in a bench-clearing brawl in Chicago. Sox outfielder Larry Doby took exception to a tight fastball and both benches emptied. During the melee, Enos Slaughter exchanged blows with the Sox's "Big Walt" Dropo. Slaughter came away with a lumpy face and a uniform torn to shreds. In late August the Yanks returned to town three games in front and proceeded to sweep a three-game series. The *Chicago Tribune* reported the sad news in small-print headlines.

> *"What happened to the go-go?"*
>
> CASEY STENGEL, THE YANKEES' MANAGER

1959

The Sox capped the fifties with their first title in 40 years, and the Sox took care of the hated Yankees, whipping the Bronx Bombers 13 games to nine for their first series win over the New Yorkers in 35 years.

Drawing further attention for the team, new owner Bill Veeck introduced a carnival atmosphere at Comiskey Park: firework displays, flying saucers, raffles. Attracted by his antics, a record 1,400,000 fans passed through the turnstiles.

Q: What controversy followed the Sox's win?
A: Air-raid sirens piercing the eardrums of Chicagoans—a

high jinx that wasn't well received in those Cold War days. An initial clamoring for an official investigation eventually died down. Years later it was revealed Mayor J. Richard Daley, South Sider and Sox fan himself, gave the order to turn on the sirens.

1960

Gambling that with more power the Sox could repeat their 1959 record, Bill Veeck traded the best youngsters of his farm system for sluggers Roy Sievers, Minnie Minoso, and Gene Freese. The mighty Sox led the league in hitting but finished third behind the Yankees with the hard-to-beat duo of Roger Maris and Mickey Mantle and Baltimore.

Q: Who set off the Sox scoreboard for the first time?
A: Sox outfielder Al Smith (May 1).

Q: Did the scoreboard ever go off for an opposing player?
A: Yes. For Ernie Banks after he homered in a Boys Benefit Game.

Q: What did a South Side alderman propose as a way to mark the Cubs' mediocre playing?
A: He proposed that Addison Street be renamed Eighth Place. In response two North Side alderman suggested Ernie Banks Street would be a better name. Mayor Richard J. Daley, a die-hard Sox fan but a politician nonetheless, vetoed both proposals.

1961

In ill health, Bill Veeck sold his majority stock in the White Sox to partner Arthur Allyn, a local businessman.

After 14 straight second-division finishes, the Cubs were ready to try anything. And they did. Owner P. K. Wrigley announced there would be no head coach, instead a group would take turns managing the club.

The team's problems—poor pitching, a flimsy defense, and an unproductive offense—could not be solved by committee. In

1961 the ball club rode losing streaks of seven, eight, and nine games backward to seventh place.

Q: Who was the first head coach?
A: His dedication to the system got Vedie Himsl opening-day coach. With limited managerial experience—in Class D ball—a decade earlier, he posted a 5-6 record before being dispatched to San Antonio. Harry Craft replaced him, then the two switched places amid a Cubs six-game losing streak.

Q: How did the college of the coaches work the following year?
A: In year two the Cubs lost a record 103 games. There was dissension among the coaches. When new man Charley Metro dropped a lineup proposed by Elvin Tappe down the toilet, then publicly aired his doubts about the concept, he was fired. Metro was later hired by the Sox as a scout.

1963

Some stability returned to the Cubs' dugout when the group coaching system was all but abandoned, as the Cubs posted their best record in 18 years (82-80).

Q: What was another cockeyed program the Cubs adopted during the revolving coach period?
A: In what was utterly regarded as a whim, P. K. Wrigley appointed a retired air force colonel named Robert Whitlow to a new post of athletic director. Expected to act as a liaison between the front office and the field manager, the superfluous Whitlow was largely ignored by the ballplayers and coaches and resigned three years later.

1964

Desperate for pitching help, the Chicago Cubs concluded the worst trade in team history—perhaps for all time. Outfielder and future Hall of Famer Lou Brock was sent to the St. Louis Cardinals on June 15 in trade for two washed-up pitchers and a no-name outfielder. Brock garnered over 3,000 hits and 900 stolen bases in his lengthy career. The three players the Cubbies received in return are memorable only for the infamy of the trade.

Q: Who did the Cubs receive for Brock and pitchers Jack Spring and Paul Toth?
A: Pitchers Ernie Broglio and Bobby Shantz and outfielder Doug Clemens.

"Brock for Broglio? P. K. Wrigley is still swallowing his gum over that one!"

EDWARD KIERSH, AUTHOR

1966

Wrigley hired Leo Durocher, the guy from the wrong side of the tracks, to stick a needle in the Cubs' collective backsides. Even under the positive Durocher, the Cubs finished 10th, attracting a meager 635,000 fans. Durocher's talents were far more effective on the South Side when his prodigy, Eddie Stanky, took charge of the White Sox and chiseled a ball club from the same crusty mold as himself—feisty underdogs scrounging for every run, every victory.

1967

Rabid Cub fans were bitten by the pennant bug as the team climbed seven rungs to third place. With 18 of 20 wins by early summer, imploding Cubs fans went crazy giving standing ovations to every player entering and leaving the batter's box. Though by late July the pennant was but a dream; the Cubs ended the season in third place.

The White Sox gave the pennant race a good go, occupying first place from June 14 to August 13 and remaining in contention after that. Only a game and a half separated the four contenders the final week. Of the four, the Sox faced the easiest schedule with two patsies, Kansas City and Washington, on tap for the five remaining games. Their vaunted pitching staff primed and ready for action, the Sox had the bunting in stock, the champagne on order, and the city on hold. But there would be no victory party, no bubbly, no key to city hall, as the Sox lost all five games.

> *"Detroit, Minnesota and Boston now can be relieved because the laughing stock of the American League race is out of it. All year long the elephant has been fearful of the mouse, that's why my boys can go back to their home towns with their heads high."*
>
> EDDIE STANKY, AFTER THE SOX WERE ELIMINATED

1968

After fifteen straight losses over two seasons, Eddie Stanky was canned in July, much to the players' delight, as his fiery ways had flickered out in a cold clubhouse. The fans' affection was wavering, too, as only 800,000 of them—a third of that total represented games in Milwaukee—showed up for games. Riots in the neighborhood surrounding Sox Park produced season-long anxieties. Resurrection seemed at hand when owner Arthur Allyn rejected an offer from Milwaukee and sold his majority stock to brother John Allyn following the 1969 season.

1969

Twenty games over .500 and sporting an 8 1/2-game lead on June 6, the Cubs were rolling toward the title amid a swirling mass of "Cubmania" typified by the boisterous Bleacher Bums. But as the Cubs' balloon rose in the National League East, the pins of destruction lay underneath as a tired, no-depth ball club entered September after dodging points of controversy: manager Leo Durocher's battles with the press, the player's time-consuming endorsements, third baseman Ron Santo's heel-clicking victory act.

On September 4 the Cubs held a five-game lead. Then the pennant flag collapsed on them. The champion Mets started the Cubs' fall with a big two-game sweep in New York.

Q: Why did the Cubs fold?

1. Underachievers. Dr. Harvey Mandell, a Chicago psychologist, theorized the Cubs may have had an unconscious desire to lose. The players were afraid of success and the subsequent responsibility.

2. Daytime baseball and Durocher's refusal to rest his regulars.
3. The Mets. The New Yorkers had a better club, especially in pitching.

A: 2. and 3. for sure, and perhaps 1., too.

1970

Blown out in the season opener, the Sox went on to lose the most games in franchise history (56-106). Attracting only 495,000 fans to Comiskey Park, they were out-drawn by the minor league team from Hawaii.

Q: An attraction called the Big White Machine got attention that dull year. What was it?
A: A 1929 White Ford that catcher Ed Herrmann drove around the ballpark after each Sox home victory—a total of 31 (31-53) times in 1970.

1971

With Leo Durocher calling his players "babies in need of nipples," many of them quit. Father and sons squared off in a clubhouse shouting match in late August. Though P. K. in a published statement that ran in all Chicago dailies supported Durocher, he resigned the next season. Old reliable team player Ernie Banks retired after the season.

After the worst season in Sox history, new housekeepers Rollie Hemond and Chuck Tanner made sweeping changes from new uniforms (glitzy red-and-white pinstripes finished off with red Adidas running shoes) to new bodies (Mike Andrews, Pat Kelly, Jay Johnstone, Tom Bradley). The flamboyant Harry Caray replaced the venerable Bob Elson on the airways, but Caray's foghorn voice was barely audible as the Sox were broadcast on two low-watt suburban stations.

Still, the Sox emerged from the basement in July, then nosed out California for third place.

1972

Newcomer Richie Allen, despite preferring a cigarette break to batting practice, clubbed a league-high and club-record 37 homers, including two inside-the-park jobs in one game.

Q: What was the zenith of Allen's extraordinary year?
A: On June 4 he crushed a three-run, pinch-hit, ninth-inning homer off Sparky Lyle to give the Sox a double-header sweep over the Yankees. Many of the 51,904 delirious fans lingered on in a daze for an hour after the swat.

"Play him, fine him, and play him again."
GENE MAUCH ON RICHIE ALLEN

1974

With P. K. pleading for the fans' patience, the fresh-start Cubs still finished last. Ron Santo went crosstown to the Sox, and late in the season, Dick Allen emotionally announced his retirement, then changed his mind. Suspicious of his intent, the Sox sold his contract to Atlanta.

1975

Spraying baseballs about, Bill Madlock (.354) won the batting title. Madlock's bat still would have been of little use in a Cubs' embarrassing 22-0 loss to the Pirates at Wrigley Field.

Q: 22-0?
A: Yes. But the game was played under unfair conditions. Every time Pittsburgh batted the wind blew out. When the Cubs batted the wind shifted completely around and stopped the balls dead. Pirate Rennie Stennent (7-7) was particularly blessed. Twice he had two hits in one inning.

Announcer Harry Caray lost favor with the Sox players and was axed by John Allyn after the season but was rehired by new owner Bill Veeck, who wisely let Chuck Tanner sign with Oakland.

"Harry Caray is a no-good bleep."

CHUCK TANNER

1976

The nation's bicentennial was the Cubs' centennial, and the team celebrated by having Cap Anson's daughter toss out the first ball. Then the Cubs went on to spend another year in the second division.

"Barnum" Bill Veeck was back at Comiskey Park along with the fireworks and dancing dogs. Veeck dressed the Sox in clam digger uniforms, shorts optional, and hired '50s pitching guru Paul Richards as skipper. Original Go-Go'er, 53-year-old Minnie Minoso, was activated in September and had a single in eight at bats.

1977

New general manager Kennedy with some off-season moves transformed the ugly-duckling Cubs into handsome contenders under kingpin Herman Franks, but when wicked-pitch reliever Bruce Sutter strained his arm, the Cubs collapsed like a deck of cards without their ace in the hole.

Prior to the All-Star Game, an out-of-character Sox ball club dubbed the "Hitmen" (192 home runs) stormed into first place, then pitching and defense problems slowly dropped the Sox out of the race. They set a new single-season attendance record in Comiskey Park. For the moment, the White Sox were back on top among Chicago fans.

1977

On April 12 Philip Knight Wrigley, affectionately known as P. K. to his closest friends and associates, passed away at age 82 at the Elkhorn, Wisconsin, hospital near his summer resort home in Lake Geneva. The soft-spoken, gentlemanly Chicago Cub owner had guided the fortunes of the team since 1932, when his dad, William Wrigley Jr., died. Phil Wrigley preferred to watch his team on television. He rarely attended games in person and preferred to leave the day-to-day operation of the ball club to others. But he always took care of the little guy. In 1945, the last time his Cubbies appeared in the World Series, Wrigley surrendered his own seats so that the average fan would not miss out on seeing the game in person.

Somewhat of a recluse and uncomfortable in the company of the press, P. K. Wrigley shunned the limelight at all costs, but he preserved the integrity of day baseball by refusing to install lights in his ballpark. It was his enduring legacy as an owner.

Q: Who took over ownership of the Cubs following Wrigley's death?

A: Principal interest in the ball club was transferred to P. K.'s disinterested son William, who sold the Cubs to the Tribune Company in 1981. The 1981 sale ended the longest continuous operation of a franchise by the same family in one city.

"It was from Mr. Wrigley that I learned my best lesson—the fan comes first."

CHICAGO WHITE SOX OWNER BILL VEECK, APRIL 1977

1978

The third-place Cubs first free agent, Dave Kingman, was the only player to reach double figures in home runs—28. But overall the towering Kingman (6'6") showed little zest and more penchant for sulking.

With Richie Zisk and Oscar Gamble opting for free agency, the White Sox were just another ball club. The Sox dropped 50 of their remaining 87 games despite starting the season over with a Veeck gimmick, a second-season opener in July.

Proving lightning (Gamble) and thunder (Zisk) don't strike twice, owner Bill Veeck lost on free agent Ron Blomberg and rent-a-player Bobby Bonds. Blomberg batted a mere .231 and was cut the following spring. The well-traveled Bonds had a lackluster start (26 games, .278) and a wiser Veeck terminated Bonds's lease, shipping him to Texas.

"No way I am gonna' wear those God Damn hot pants."

BOBBY BONDS

1979

At Disco Demolition Night on a humid July evening, unruly Sox fans were admitted to Comiskey Park for $0.98 and a disco record, the latter to be destroyed between games of the doubleheader by rock disc jockey Steve Dahl.

While awaiting the big bang, the crowd passed time drinking beer, smoking pot, and launching records Frisbee-style into the field. The eventual explosion set off a chain reaction in the stands and the fans stormed the field. They set fires, dug up home plate, and lifted chunks of turf. The players did a hasty retreat to the dugout, grabbing bats for protection. Riot police had to be called, and 39 people were arrested. The field was left a pockmarked mess, cluttered with broken records and beer cans. The Sox had to forfeit the second game.

> *"These weren't real baseball fans. All I know is we'll make certain we don't try anything like this again. I was amazed. I wish I wasn't."*
>
> Bill Veeck

1980

More playing went on off the field than on with Bill Veeck's White Sox. On a muggy July evening announcer Jimmy Piersall choked sportswriter Rob Gallas, then found himself in a headlock administered by Veeck's son Mike, who was defending his family honor following some past remarks Piersall had directed at Veeck's mother. Manager Tony LaRussa dislocated his shoulder trying to break up a player fight. Another rhubarb featured hurler Ed Farmer and Detroit's Al Cowens, who charged the mound on an infield grounder, rekindling an old feud.

Play wasn't any more professional on the North Side. Cubs cleanup hitter Dave Kingman spent most of the summer brooding and nursing a sore right shoulder on his boat in Lake Michigan. Before his injury he'd missed a game at Wrigley Field, drawing a $1,250 fine and a spanking from the press corps. They were still seething about a spring incident when Kingman dumped a bucket of ice water on a journalist. He was traded in the off-season.

"Bill, Karen and Lee think the Cubs stink."

A BANNER TRAILING A PLANE OVER WRIGLEY FIELD

1981

After losing 20 of their first 22 games, only the players' strike in June saved the Cubs from burrowing out of sight. Not so much fed up but in need of capital, William Wrigley sold the club to the Tribune Corporation during the pause for $20.5 million, ending the Wrigley family's 66-year ownership.

The Sox had changed hands prior to the season. Veeck sold the team to real estate magnate Jerry Reinsdorf and TV tycoon Eddie Einhorn. Their first plays were to sign Boston Red Sox backstop Carlton Fisk and purchase Philadelphia slugger Greg "Bull" Luzinski.

1982

Acerbic Harry Caray replaced the mellifluous Jack Brickhouse at the Wrigley Field mike by season's end and the Cubs improved a notch to fifth.

1983

Something had started working for the White Sox, who won 59 of 85 games and clinched the Western Division title three weeks before season's end!"Winning Ugly" was the Sox battle cry in 1983, and their spirited play nearly landed them in the World Series.

The Eastern Division champion Orioles' torrid season matched that of the Sox, but Baltimore bested the Sox three games to one in the American League play-offs.

1984

Ending a 38-year hibernation, the Cubs bolted out of their second-division lair to capture the National League Eastern Division title. But the cynics, especially Sox fans, shouted "told you so" when the Cubs choked in the play-offs, losing three games in a row after taking the first two contests.

Q: How did the Cubs' fortunes rise so fast?
A: Magic Man Dallas Green. In an active day of trading just before opening day, Green acquired Phillie outfielders Gary Matthews and Bob Dernier and A's reliever Tim Stoddard. Those deals made the Cubs contenders, then Green put them on top with two mid-season blockbusters—securing hurlers Rick Sutcliff (Cy Young winner) and Dennis Eckersly. A previous Green acquisition, Ryne Sandberg, won the MVP award.

1985

Pete Rose, arguably the greatest player not in the Hall of Fame, equaled Ty Cobb's record for most career hits when he lined a fifth-inning single up the middle against the Cubs on September 8, 1985. It was the 4,191st hit of Rose's illustrious career, and it occurred in a tie game at Wrigley Field that had to be suspended because of darkness.

Q: What Cub and former White Sox pitcher surrendered the milestone hit to Rose?
A: Reggie Patterson.

> *"I thought about going over and shaking Rose's hand. There still is time to do that. I was just thinking of the next guy up."*
> REGGIE PATTERSON, ON MAKING HISTORY

1987

First in home runs and last in the National League East. The Cubs out-slugged the division champion St. Louis Cardinals by 105 round-trippers but were outscored by the clutch-hitting and speedy Red Birds, 798-720. Dallas Green took leave in October following a power struggle with Tribune Company executives.

Andre Dawson had been reluctantly signed by Green, who was still smarting over past free-agent busts. Dawson won National League MVP honors.

1988

On a thundering August 8 Wrigley Field sparkled when the lights went on for the first night game. The proceedings were washed out and the first official after-dusk contest was played the next evening. Six more late contests were played in '88, transforming pastoral Cubs Park into an urban nightspot.

Q: What was the score of the first night game?
A: Cubs 6, Mets 4.

Q: Who flipped the light switch, illuminating Wrigley Field?
A: It wasn't Charles Comiskey Jr. or a lot of other likelies, but nonagenarian Harry Grossman, age 91, who could remember back when the Cubs snarled with the Tinker, Evers, and Chance bunch.

The White Sox slogan that year was "Anything Can Happen," but the real issue was where—Chicago or Florida? Owners Reinsdorf and Einhorn pondered the franchise move when plans for a stadium were slow-going, particularly in light of the Cubs' night game agenda passed by the City Council. Repair work on the Dan Ryan Expressway added to the perceived second-club status of the Sox.

An unsympathetic Illinois assembly made the move southward look imminent, but just before the final tick Republican governor and alleged Cubs fan Jim Thompson joined forces with Chicago Democrats to pass a stadium bill at the stroke of midnight on July 1 that kept the Sox in town.

1989

The Cubs' second division title in five seasons—who would have thought? In spring training manager Don Zimmer had been optimistic: "In my heart we're better." But first-place better? Yes, with a hungry ball club and some unexpected players stepping up to do the job—Jerome Walton, Mike Bielecki, Les Lancaster, Mitch Williams.

The play-offs against the San Francisco Giants were slam-bang affairs. Fifty-two runs were scored in the five-game series. The

Cubs out-hit the bay area bombers but didn't produce as many clutch hits and lost the series in five games.

1990

Manager Jeff Torborg's spring plans went pleasantly astray during the regular season. His projected platoon players—Sammy Sosa, Robin Ventura, Lance Johnson—earned full-time berths and a number of not-counted-on arms—Sam McDowell, Alex Fernandez, Scott Radinsky—performed well, propelling the Sox into contention. Rookie first-sacker Frank Thomas, up in August, bolstered the Sox lineup.

1991

A new state-of-the-art ballpark and a first-place finish were perhaps asking too much. But the Sox, with enough good things happening, finished second for the second straight year.

New Comiskey Park had all the amenities of a modern park: escalators, wide concourses, comfortable seats, novelty stores, a Sox Hall of Fame, Diamond Suites, a Stadium Club, and a state-of-the-art scoreboard with a jumbo video screen. On opening day there was some discussion about the steeply built upper deck. This nosebleed section soon became a focal point of discontent, more so when the club was going bad.

Q: What was opening day like?
A: Forget it! New Comiskey Park was inaugurated with a 16-0 drubbing by the Detroit Tigers.

1991

In a remote corner of distant Kane County—a landfill site no less—minor league baseball premiered in Northeast Illinois. The Wausau, Wisconsin, Timbers, a Class-A Midwest League affiliate of the Baltimore Orioles, moved their struggling operation to Geneva, Illinois, located approximately 40 miles west of downtown Chicago.

In the summer of 1991 the Timbers were reborn as the Kane County Cougars, and one man's gamble turned into an overnight financial and artistic success. The Cougars, playing in a $5 million, scaled-down replica of the new Comiskey Park, drew 240,290 fans into the stadium and shattered the Midwest League attendance record originally set by the Peoria Chiefs in 1989.

The Kane County Events Center, renamed Elfstrom Stadium in honor of the man whose vision and fortitude lured the Timbers to Illinois and helped convince a private firm—Waste Management Inc.—to donate $2.15 million to the building fund, quickly became a popular and affordable destination point for suburban baseball fans.

The Cougars supplied the thrills by clinching the Northern Division title in the second half of the split season, but the promotions and marketing wizardry of General Manager Bill Larsen made all the difference in the world. Borrowing a page from the late Bill Veeck, the front office sponsored a series of wacky promotions and giveaways. On All-Faith Night, for example, fans showing up with church bulletins entered the stadium for half price.

Larsen and his associates needed all the faith, hope, and charity they could muster before the season started, but by year's end the Cougars were a big success.

Q: Who is Phil Elfstrom?
A: The former president of the Kane County Forest Preserve, who whipped up support for the Cougars and the new stadium bearing his name.

"It couldn't have been done without the gift from Waste Management. The ballpark will show off their landfill. It will bring renown to Kane County."

PHIL ELFSTROM, JANUARY 1991

1993

Was it ever in doubt? In a rather matter-of-fact pennant run, the Sox occupied first place permanently from June 22 till the end of the season.

Roberto Hernandez, Wilson Alvarez, and Alex Fernandez blossomed into competent hurlers. Jack McDowell (Cy Young) and Frank Thomas (Most Valuable Player) turned it up a notch. Second baseman Joey Cora put in a surprise performance. But the Sox lost the play-offs in six games to a stronger and more experienced Toronto Blue Jays club. Jack McDowell was KO'd in the opener, then knocked from the box again in the pivotal fifth game.

1994

The story without an ending. Baseball fans could only wonder what would have happened. On August 15 the players went on strike and, when the dispute lingered into September, the entire season was canceled. Up until that point, everything was going as planned for the Sox. They had bolstered the lineup with free agents Julio Franco and Darren Lewis. Frank Thomas was enjoying his second MVP year. The staff was the best in baseball. And in baseball's hottest rivalry, the Sox held a game edge in their division over Cleveland, whom they had whipped in the season series 7-5.

> *"Baseball's 1994 summer was filled with shining stars. Only one shiner will be most remembered—the black eye that ended it."*
>
> TONI GINNETTI, *CHICAGO SUN-TIMES,* SEPTEMBER 15, 1994

1996

Chicago: Down for the count but never out. The Cubs, hovering around .500 entering September, couldn't draw the wild card as they lost fourteen of their last sixteen games. As in the Billy Williams-Ernie Banks days, some players stood above the others—Sammy Sosa, Mark Grace.

The Sox also lost their bid to be the fourth-best team. Frank Thomas missed 20 games, which cost him his third MVP award. Still, Thomas made it a record six straight seasons of a .300 average, 20 or more homers, 100 RBIs, 100 walks, and 100 runs.

> *"If Babe Ruth was hitting behind Frank, half the teams would pitch to the Babe."*
>
> TERRY BEVINGTON, SOX MANAGER

1997

Proving their mastery over the Cubs once again, the White Sox captured two of three games in the new Comiskey Park—only this time it counted for something. Interleague play, the dream of many baseball visionaries including the late William Veeck (Bill's father), became a reality in 1997.

Q: What former Cubs player, now with the Sox, singlehandedly destroyed his ex-teammates in the series?
A: Outfielder Dave Martinez. He hit .375 with two home runs and four runs batted in.

"Cubs fans are great fans. That's why I don't want them here. Sox fans are more demanding. They're more knowledgeable about the game. They don't like *to watch bad baseball."*

Sox owner Jerry Reinsdorf, on keeping Cub fans out of Comiskey Park

CHAPTER 2

A Sport for Kings and Paupers: Horse-racing in and around Town

Wagering on horseflesh has been around since the beginning of time, and since Chicago's beginnings racetracks have appeared in the city in one form or another. Many of the early gatherings were quickly dispersed by the police, only to just as quickly reappear somewhere else. Other racetracks were legitimate businesses supported by the Chicago National Jockey Club, organized back in 1844.

The fashionable set viewed the races as social events; wage earners went to the tracks to wager. And since they couldn't all get to the tracks, gambling dens sprang up in the city, offering games of chance and a racing book. A patron could lose more than his shirt at some of the rougher establishments around town. To deter crime a law was passed forbidding bookmaking in the city, but the ban hardly stopped the gamblers, who paid off the police and the politicians for protection. In 1895 the first of two prohibitions against thoroughbred racing was enacted by the state legislature. It lasted just two years.

A loophole in the code allowed a legal bookmaking operation at the track. Gambling syndicates fought over the lucrative racetrack book; murder and arson were often part of the action. Gambling wars raised the ire of Chicago's bluenoses and in 1904 the area tracks were shut down. Still, the gambling went on; the advent of the wire services allowed patrons to bet on out-of-state races. Parlor operations flourished in the back rooms of saloons and on steamer boats on Lake Michigan.

After some experimental non-betting meets, racing returned for good in Illinois in 1924, with a pari-mutuel wagering system stemming the mob's influence in the industry. Syndicates turned to the lucrative business of owning tracks—Al Capone's criminal organization financed and ran Sportsman's Park in Cicero, for example. Later racetracks were taken over by wealthy businessmen and large corporations.

Today, the sport of kings, be it the thoroughbreds or the trotters, is played out all year on Chicago area ovals. The industry is wholeheartedly supported by the state, whose coffers are filled by the tax revenue generated on and off the tracks.

1845

Chicago's first racetrack was carved out in the open prairie at Dexter Park on the Southwest Side. The first event held at that crudely graded oval was a two-mile saddle race; Lady Jane won it in 5:26. The Dexter Park track would eventually be swallowed up by the Union Stock Yards.

1866

Dexter, son of the great harness horse Hambletonian, outstepped George Patchen to win a $5,000 match race at Dexter Park. But the most memorable moment at Dexter Park occurred during a match race in late September between trotters Cooley and General Butler. Cooley won the first two heats; General Butler took the next two. Before the final heat William McKeever, the owner and driver of General Butler, went to a nearby tavern and boasted about his horse. When the race resumed that evening, McKeever propelled General Butler to the lead, then both horses disappeared in the backstretch. Moments later, the fans heard the familiar hoof beats of the horses heading for home. Cooley came first, followed by General Butler, dragging an empty carriage. Men with lanterns ran up and down the track trying to locate McKeever. They found him on the ground near the final turn, dead from a blow to the head. A plank was found nearby. The case was never solved.

Q: What happened to the purse?
A: All bets were off after the discovery of McKeever's body.

1884

Washington Park opened near Garfield Park, just west Midway Airport. At the fashionable Washington Park, socialites hugged the rail along with the hoi polloi. Civil War general Phillip H. Sheridan was the track's first President. The great African-American jockey Isaac Murphy won Chicago's inaugural American Derby aboard Modesty. Murphy would later return to Chicago and capture two more derby titles.

1890

Businessman Edward Corrigan purchased 119 acres of land in Cicero, erected a grandstand, and opened Hawthorne Park on May 20 with a five-race card. Six thousand people attended the opener. A horse from the Corrigan stable, Brookwood, won the feature race.

1891

Republican mayor Hempstead Washburne shut down the notorious Garfield Park racetrack. Unlike Washington Park, Garfield Park attracted some unsavory types, which led to complaints from the people in the surrounding area.

First Ward alderman "Bathhouse" John Coughlin, who represented the racetrack owners' interests, fought the ban in the city council. Ignoring the council's edict, the track owners opened the park anyway, and after the last race, the police moved in and made scores of arrests. Left unmolested by the police, Bathhouse John spent the evening bailing out his friends. In another police raid two days later, a wealthy Texas horseman and a policeman were killed in a shoot-out. After that incident, the Garfield Park race course was shut down for good.

> *"You can't shut up a man's property. You can't do that! It's unfair. It's unfair. It's . . . It's . . . un-American, that's what!"*
> "BATHHOUSE" JOHN COUGHLIN, FIRST WARD ALDERMAN

1895

Because of the Garfield Park incident and the flourishing illegal betting rings, the Illinois General Assembly banned racing. Three years later, following some vigorous campaigning by the horseracing lobby, the ban was lifted.

1902

Mobsters resorted to extortion to gain exclusive bookmaking rights at Hawthorne Park. They set the grandstand on fire, a blaze that also destroyed the paddock. Hawthorne Park was rebuilt in seven weeks with a more durable concrete and steel structure.

1903

Sullied by a decade of internecine warfare between opposing gambling syndicates seeking the right to make book at the tracks, the Sport of Kings came increasingly under fire by the Chicago Civic Association, the clergy, and other reform groups who assailed the character of the men who ran the races and clocked the bets.

Despite these setbacks, the turf sports continued to flourish in popularity. In addition to elegant Washington Park on the South Side, there were five other premier racetracks, all within commuting distance of downtown Chicago. The Windy City had truly become the midwestern hub of thoroughbred and harness racing by the turn of the century.

Q: Can you name the other racetracks operating in Northeast Illinois at this time?

A: (1) Hawthorne, located in Cicero; (2) the Harlem Jockey Club in West Suburban River Forest; (3) the Roby Fair

Association and Racetrack, operated by Chicago gambling boss John Condon in Roby, Indiana, not far from Whiting; (4) Ingalls Park in Joliet; (5) and the Garfield Park Driving Association, a harness racing oval located at Central Avenue and 12th Street in the Austin neighborhood.

"Chicago has become a racing center second to none in the country, and the blue grass breeders can send their thoroughbreds to no course where they will hear a greater cheer of approval as they come under the wire than here in the city by the lake."

CHICAGO INTER-OCEAN, JUNE 21, 1891

1904

The city council banned racing, a ban fostered by Mayor Carter Harrison, who had vowed to end the bookmaking operations in Chicago. Washington Park was torn down in 1906. A new Washington Park was later erected (1926) in Homewood, Illinois.

"It is my intention to witness the sport of kings without the vice of kings."

CARTER HARRISON II, CHICAGO'S MAYOR

1905

Chicago's first gambling cruise ship, the *City of Traverse,* set sail from the Illinois Central Slip at 68th Street on June 29 with a full compliment of sporting men, who crowded into the staterooms of the 36-year-old Lake Michigan steamship. A gambling syndicate headed by Big Jim O'Leary, Harry Perry, and Charles Social Smith took advantage of a loophole in Illinois law that permitted gamblers to place legal bets as long as the vessel was moored 22 miles southeast of Chicago. The politicians and the church reformers were outraged.

Dr. Lee DeForest, who pioneered wireless telegraphy, installed his invention on board the steamer in order to accommodate the crush of gamblers who wagered on out-of-town horseraces.

Q: Did the city of Chicago finally succeed in closing down the objectionable boat?

A: Yes. Captain Herman Schluetter of the Chicago Police Department built a wireless station on the Indiana shoreline to intercept and jam the boat's wireless signal. On July 10, 1907, the license of the gambling boat was revoked. The *City of Traverse* was later sold to the Graham & Morton line.

> *"Schluetter doesn't know the inside story. The* City of Traverse *quit running because the police wanted $1,700 graft!"*
>
> BEN R. HYMAN, ATTORNEY FOR THE GAMBLING SYNDICATE

1909

Ed Corrigan sold Hawthorne Park to businessman Tom Carey, who tried to revive the racing business. On Labor Day 10,000 people jammed Hawthorne Park to watch and bet the thoroughbreds. After the second race deputy sheriffs shut down the main book in the racing secretary's office. Still, a lot of wagering took place as the fans used hand signals to get a gambler's attention, then secretly exchanged pieces of paper.

> *"With yesterday's grand attendance still before me I cannot help but state that it's my belief that the rehabilitation of the game in this state is not far distant."*
>
> TOM CAREY

1916

Under a better political climate a 13-day experimental meet was sponsored by the Illinois Jockey Club at Hawthorne Park. An estimated 20,000 people were on hand for the opener. The feature race, the $10,000 American Derby, was won by Dodge, who was ridden to victory by F. Murphy. On opening day 100 deputies were on duty. Ten people were arrested for gambling, eight of them for bookmaking.

> *"Let me tell the folks in the box I am pinched."*
>
> LEE H. MEYER, A GAMBLER

1921

A Senate judiciary committee heard testimony from Howard C. Barber of the Society for the Prevention of Crime (in New York no less!). "Chicago is the racetrack gambling center of the nation," he warned. "Chicago is once more overrun with handbooks boasting protection from high officials in city hall." Within a year's time Barber's worst fears were realized: Legalized thoroughbred racing returned to Chicago.

> *"On top of one of Chicago's skyscrapers is an office which has a system of trunk lines running all over the country! It is the distributing center of all the racetrack gambling news. Three men operate this. The head man gets 50 percent of the profits and the other 50 percent is divided among the other two. In the building at 431 S. Dearborn Street is the mysterious office of General News Bureau. It has five telephone trunk lines and a local switchboard employing many operators. The bureau is owned and operated by Mont Tennes, long accepted as Chicago's handbook king."*
>
> Howard Barber, May 11, 1921

1922

Racing returned to the Chicago area for good as Hawthorne Park staged a 13-day non-betting meet. As an added attraction on opening day, the great horse Exterminator ran against the clock. Exterminator was trying to eclipse the track record of 2:04 for the quarter-mile. He was timed in 2:10. The poor time was blamed on the new sand-filled track.

1923

The Illinois Derby was inaugurated at Hawthorne. In Memoriam won the inaugural event. The Illinois Derby, which is now based at Sportsman's Park, is run after the Kentucky Derby and attracts some of the best three-year-olds in the country.

1924

Gambling in the form of pari-mutuel betting is allowed at the Chicago area racetracks. Kentucky Derby winner Black Gold captured the seventh running of the Chicago Derby at Hawthorne.

Q: What is pari-mutuel betting?
A: It is a French term meaning "a bet among ourselves." Put simply, the people bet against each other. The state, acting as an agent, holds the money being wagered on a race and pays the winning ticket holders the proper amount based on the number of tickets sold.

Q: Why did the state allow pari-mutuel gambling?
A: It was the lesser of two evils. Pari-mutuel gambling eliminated the gambler's book. Gambling syndicates no longer could determine the odds or take a percentage of the purse.

1926

Matt Winn, a Kentucky horseman who popularized pari-mutuel betting machines at the nation's leading racing grounds, built Lincoln Fields, a thoroughbred track located on the site of a former German settlement in South Suburban Crete, Illinois.

The track was an instant success, which forced the hand of the conservative Illinois legislature to legalize pari-mutuel betting the following year. Winn operated Lincoln Fields until 1947, but no races were run there from 1943 until the owner sold his interest to Edward Fleming, one of the stockholders.

The State Racing Board permitted Winn to locate his racing days at other tracks.

Q: What famous boxer used Lincoln Fields as a training site?
A: In preparation for his match at Soldier Field against Gene Tunney, the great Jack Dempsey trained there in 1927. The next year aviatrix Amelia Earhart visited Lincoln Fields and was honored with a race in her name.

"Churchill Downs is my first love as a race track, but Lincoln Fields is the one in which I take the greatest pride because it was built under my supervision and was the dream come true of a racetrack perfect in all its appointments."

COLONEL MATT J. WINN

1927

Arlington Park opened in Arlington Heights, Illinois. Financial backers included Laurence Armour (Armour and Company), John Hertz (Yellow Cab), and Major Frederic McLaughlin (Chicago Blackhawks). The oval featured an 18,000-seat steel and glass grandstand and two racing strips—an outer strip and an inner grass course.

1929

Arlington Park introduced four stake races: the Arlington Classic, the Arlington Handicap, the Stars and Stripes, and the Arlington Lassie. The Arlington Handicap was won by Misstep, who had also captured the inaugural Hawthorne Cup (1928).

Q: Today how many Grade 1 stake races are run in the Chicago area?

A: Three. And all three races are at Arlington Park: the Arlington Million, the Beverly D, and the Secretariat.

1930

In May the Appellate Court of the State of Illinois finally outlawed dog racing, driving the Hawthorne Kennel Club—an Al Capone operation that earned $2 million in illicit revenue for the mob—out of business. Since 1927 the Capone gangsters, with their battery of high-powered attorneys in place, staved off final action in the courts for the closing of the track. The Cook County sheriff was powerless to lead raids against the track because of court injunctions bought and paid for through Capone's political "clout." Indeed, it paid handsome dividends to have "friends" in high places protecting you—if your name happened to be "Scarface" Al Capone.

Q: Where was the Hawthorne Kennel Club located?
A: At 17th Street and Halsted on the South Side, near the Hawthorne Race Track.

1931

Hawthorne became the first major track in Chicago to use an electric timer. Fraction times were posted on the scoreboard as the horses raced around the oval.

1932

Sportsman's Park opened on the site of the old Hawthorne Kennel Club. The park was backed by Al Capone's organization. To accommodate the thoroughbreds, the oval was increased from a quarter mile to a half mile. Horsemen were lured to Sportsman's because of the healthy purses: $36,000 a week, a guaranteed $1,000 for the feature event. The president of Sportsman's was Edward O'Hare, who basically oversaw the mob's operations.

Q: Is that the same O'Hare for whom the airport is named?
A: Yes and no. O'Hare field is named after Ed O'Hare's son Butch, who won the Congressional Medal of Honor for valor as a fighter pilot during World War II.

Q: Was Edward O'Hare ever immortalized for anything?
A: No. The senior O'Hare, who started out as a bootlegger in St. Louis, wasn't even held in high regard by his mobster friends. O'Hare was gunned down by Frank Nitti's henchmen outside Sportsman's Park on November 8, 1939 in retaliation for snitching on Al Capone during the government's probe of Big Al's finances.

1933

Benjamin Franklin Lindheimer was chairman of the Illinois Commerce Commission under Governor Henry Horner, elected to office in 1932. Lindheimer was also a horseman and very interested in boosting his personal fortune by driving out the last of the crooked gamblers and mobsters—the bane of thoroughbred racing since the 1890s. Lindheimer believed that public confidence in the Sport of Kings would be bolstered, and in all likelihood more people would come out to the tracks to wager if the mobsters were expeditiously removed from the grounds.

He set in motion a plan to clean up the tracks by arranging for the creation of a state board known as the Illinois Racing Commission. Its first task was to identify and bar all persons engaged in illegal business, bookmakers, and other types of undesirables from operating state racetracks. The formation of the IRC was a prelude to a larger scheme Lindheimer had in mind: It was his burning ambition to become the czar of the local racing industry.

1933

The famed runner Equipose won the Hawthorne Gold Cup and the Arlington Handicap. Equipose, who won the Preakness in 1931 and was voted Horse of the Year in 1932 and 1933, left his imprimatur upon Chicago racing with a gritty performance at Arlington Park in the summer of 1932. He set a record in the mile-long Delevan Stakes on June 30. He captured the Stars and Stripes on July 4 and concluded this extraordinay streak with a decisive win in the Arlington Gold Cup on July 9. Four horses bowed out of the Gold Cup rather than face the famed "Chocolate Soldier," leaving a field of just three starters to run the race.

Q: How is Equipose remembered?

A: Arlington Park honored the horse with a stakes race in his name. An offspring of Equipose named Equifox won the first Equipose Mile Handicap in 1941.

"He bounded forward as if wings and not four good legs were carrying him along in his journey."

FRENCH LANE, *CHICAGO TRIBUNE*

1935

In February Ben Lindheimer purchased controlling interest of Washington Park at 175th and Halsted in Homewood. He paid

Jack Lynch three cents each—$1.4 million—for 150,000 shares of stock and jumped into track ownership with the blessing of Mayor Edward Kelly, one of the bosses of the Chicago Democratic Machine. Kelly persuaded Lynch that it was in his best interests to cut a deal with his political ally Lindheimer before he was thrown out of the business.

Q: Who was Jack Lynch?

A: Jack Lynch was a notorious gambler and racketeer whose $10 million fortune sprang from his 40 percent ownership of the General News Bureau. The Bureau was a racing wire founded in 1907 by Mont Tennes, an old-time gambling boss who controlled Chicago's lucrative North Side handbook and poolroom operations for nearly a quarter century. The wire service supplied track conditions and betting odds and was an enormously profitable endeavor. Lynch made headlines in 1931 when he was kidnapped by Al Capone's men and later released after a $50,000 ransom had been paid.

1936

With strong political backing in Springfield (and from the Chicago mob), Ben Lindheimer helped draft a bill to legalize 2,500 previously illegal betting handbooks in Chicago on the premise that the added revenue to the state coffers would help pay the salaries of teachers and police. The legislation glided effortlessly through the General Assembly but was vetoed by Governor Henry Horner—a move that cost him the support of Mayor Kelly and the previously loyal Democratic Machine, which had strongly supported the measure. Horner was narrowly reelected to a second term; however, he died before he could serve out the four years.

Q: What were the consequences for Ben Lindheimer?

A: Ben Lindheimer and Governor Horner were like brothers. After the bookie bill was vetoed, Lindheimer promised Kelly he would help dump Horner from the ticket in return for the mayor agreeing to help him acquire a second racetrack—Arlington Park. The transaction was completed on April 16, 1940, when the sale of Arlington Park to Lindheimer and a syndicate of Chicago investors was announced.

1936

Hawthorne Park introduced the photo-eye camera, which produced a finish-line photo within seconds after a race. That year, the camera was needed to determine a winner in an important race. Myrtlewood, the world record-holder in the six furlongs, nipped Clang, the seven furlong record-holder, by a nose. The race was run over a "Myrtlewood" distance of six furlongs.

Q: What's the largest number of horses to hit the wire together at a Chicago track?
A: Three. At Maywood Park three harness horses finished in a dead heat for second place.

1937

A record turnout at Hawthorne. On September 6 37,792 fans showed up for a day at the races.

1938

The great stakes horse Seabiscuit, the leading money winner in 1938, had no racing luck in Chicago; he lost both the Hawthorne Cup and the Arlington Park Stars and Stripes. After the Hawthorne Cup, Seabiscuit trained at Sportsman's Park for his upcoming match race at Pimlico Racetrack in Maryland with the previous year's triple crown winner, War Admiral. Chicago's railbirds flocked to the oval to catch a glimpse of this undistinguished-looking thoroughbred whose stubby legs and chunky body made him look like a duck waddling down the track.

Q: Who won the match race between Sea Biscuit and War Admiral?
A: The tortoise beat the hare. After going head to head with the powerful War Admiral, Sea Biscuit drew away in the stretch run and won by three lengths. The race was broad-

cast coast-to-coast for the benefit of a captivated nation. President Franklin Delano Roosevelt interrupted a cabinet meeting to listen to the race.

1940

Both Hawthorne Park and Arlington Park introduced the Bahr starting gate, which opened and closed electronically. The great stretch runner Whirlaway debuted at Lincoln Fields (Balmoral Park) on June 3. Whirlaway bored out approaching the final turn then, after being righted, came from behind to win the race by a nose. At Arlington Park, Whirlaway, sweeping wide again, would win only one of five races.

Owner Warren Wright and trainer Jimmy Jones were impressed by Whirlaway's speed but perplexed by his straying habit. At first Jones blocked Whirlaway's retreat with a stationary object, then he tried running a stable horse alongside him. Both methods failed. Whirlaway was stubborn, unmanageable, and had a sour disposition. Just to be saddled, he needed countless practice sessions, and he always required a calming walk before a race.

Q: How did Jones finally rid Whirlaway of his straying habit?
A: Whirlaway, it was determined, was afraid of the inner rail so a special blinker was made to cover his left eye.

Q: How did Whirlaway fare after the equipment adjustment?
A: Ridden by Eddie Arcaro, Whirlaway won horseracing's triple crown: the Kentucky Derby, the Preakness, and the Belmont. He returned to Arlington Park and posted a victory in the American Derby.

Q: What was the name of Wright's famous farm?
A: As owner of the Chicago Baking Powder Company, he borrowed the name of his best-known product—Calumet Baking Powder—and called it Calumet Farms.

"Dumbest horse I ever trained."

JIMMY JONES, WHIRLAWAY'S TRAINER

1942

Jockey Tony Skoronski debuted at Sportsman's Park. In a 27-year career Skoronski got nicknamed "Mr. Sportsman's Park." He won over 800 races and took 12 jockey titles.

1942

The Thoroughbred Racing Association of the United States was founded in Chicago for the purpose of centralizing national authority, imposing a stringent code of standards to a largely unregulated industry, and encouraging a high level of ethics among owners and trainers. The association (now headquartered in Lake Success, New York), eventually became the governing body of 54 tracks in the U.S.

1943

Because of World War II, Arlington shifted its schedule to Washington Park. Other tracks cut down on their schedule.

1946

The Hawthorne Cup commenced after a five-year hiatus, and Arlington Park reopened. Designed exclusively for harness racing, Maywood Park also opened that year.

1946

Newly constructed Maywood Park was the first harness track in the Midwest to offer its patrons pari-mutuel betting and a nighttime race card. Built on the 38-acre west suburban site of the Cook County Fair Grounds, where harness racing was once held, Maywood presented a streamlined version of the country races by doing away with the elimination heats.

While the workmen applied the finishing touches to the grandstand, a pre-opener gala was held on the grounds. Members of society, sportsmen, and the media comingled at the buffet table. Afterward, 110 light standards flicked on, and the world champion trotter Greyhound paraded around the oval to polite applause.

Over 11,000 fans of the sulky races attended the opener.

Despite a rainy spring that caused the cancellation of six cards, the meet was pronounced a success.

Q: What new harness racing innovation was introduced at Maywood during the fall meet?
A: The Phillips motorized starting gate. It was the second of its kind in use at American harness tracks.

1948

Warren Wright and trainer Jimmy Jones saddled another triple crown winner: Citation, named for the military honor bestowed on soldiers. Unlike the willful Whirlaway, Citation was evenly dispositioned, beautifully balanced, and extraordinarily versatile. He could set the pace as a front-runner or come from behind to capture the victory.

As a two-year-old, he won his first five starts, including a record-breaking five-furlong event at Arlington Park and his first stakes victory—the Elementary Stakes at Washington Park. After winning the triple crown Citation won the Arlington Stars and Stripes, equaling a track record despite a wrenched hip. He later captured the American Derby at Washington Park. Citation's racing career ended because of a bad foot. He was formally retired at Arlington Park on July 28, 1951.

"He was a Cadillac."

JOCKEY EDDIE ARCARO ON CITATION

1952

With a purse of $100,000 the Arlington Classic became the world's richest race for three-year-olds.

1953

The great gray colt Native Dancer destroyed the field in the Arlington Classic, winning by nine lengths after a thunderous stretch drive. One of the also-rans was James K., who was owned by Chicago businessman Jim Norris. James K., who had lost by a neck to Native Dancer in both the Preakness and the Belmont, lost sight of Native Dancer in the final turn. Native

Dancer went on to add the American Derby to his credits. In his career Native Dancer won 21 of 22 races.

Q: Where was Native Dancer's only loss?
A: Ironically, Native Dancer's only loss was at the Kentucky Derby, when he was bumped at the first turn, knocking him off stride.

"Words can't explain it—you have to be on his back to feel it."
JOCKEY EDDIE GUERIN ON EXPERIENCING NATIVE DANCER'S SURGE OF POWER

Q: What record did Eddie Arcaro establish that year?
A: He gained his 3,000th win at Arlington Park, becoming the first North American jockey to pass that mark.

1955

Willie Shoemaker posted his first Hawthorne win. But the "Shoe" would find himself on the wrong foot at Washington Park before 35,000 fans in the match race of the century between three-year-olds Nashua and Swaps. Nashua, representing the East Coast, and Swaps, representing the West Coast, were also opposites in demeanor. The elegant, chestnut-colored Swaps was docile and sociable; Nashua, a huge bay colt with a broad back and powerful hindquarters, liked to pick up his stable horse by the tail then drop him on the floor and bellow a good horse laugh. The strong-handed Eddie Arcaro never liked riding Nashua. Swaps and Nashua first squared off at the Kentucky Derby. On a fast track Willie Shoemaker took Swaps immediately to the front where he held off Nashua's late bid. Nashua headed east and won the Preakness and the Belmont. Later he would capture the Arlington Park Classic. Swaps returned to California and won four stake races. The gauntlet had been thrown down and a winner-take-all $100,000 match race was set at Washington Park, midway between the two coasts, for August 31. Swaps had warmed up for the event by capturing the American Derby on August 20 at Washington Park. After that, Shoemaker boasted Swaps would beat Nashua by five lengths.

Q: How accurate was Willie Shoemaker's prediction?
A: He was off about 12 lengths. Knowing Shoemaker's penchant for taking the lead, Eddie Arcaro used his whip to urge Nashua to the front. Arcaro continued to pressure Nashua. Three times Swaps challenged and each time he was rebuked. Pulling away, Nashua won by six lengths.

Q: What was Shoemaker's excuse?
A: Shoemaker said that Swaps didn't care for the slow track.

"Swapsie, what happened?"
THE SISTER OF SWAPS'S OWNER, REX ELLSWORTH

1955

Benjamin Lindheimer added Lincoln Fields to his turf empire for the sum of $3,100,000. The old and no longer prosperous track had fallen on hard times. A fire nearly destroyed the grandstand during a 1952 renovation. The stands were rebuilt, but the newly formed Balmoral Jockey Club would not conduct a meet at the track until 1968.

Q: What was the new name Lindheimer and his associates gave to Lincoln Fields?
A: Balmoral Park. In 1965 the track was sold to William Miller, former chairman of the Illinois Racing Board, who invested $5 million into general repairs and renovations. However, it would remain closed to racing of any kind for another 13 years.

"The environment is delightful. While only minutes away from bustling Chicago, Balmoral Park is situated in the serene countryside. Centered in more than 1,000 acres of rolling, heavily wooded farmland, Balmoral Park is the environment Nature intended for horses and horsemen."
WILLIAM MILLER'S PROMOTIONAL BROCHURE, 1965

1958

Round Table, ridden by jockey Willie Shoemaker, won the Hawthorne Gold Cup in a record gallop. With his share of the $124,850 purse, Round Table established himself as the leading money winner of all time. One of the great grass runners, Round Table campaigned coast-to-coast for four years and won 43 of 66 starts.

1960

Ben Lindheimer, the rich, powerful, and politically connected owner of three Chicago-area racetracks (Washington Park, Arlington Park, and Balmoral), suffered a heart attack on June 5 and passed away. Present at the Lindheimer funeral were all the heavyweights from the worlds of politics and racing, including Mayor Richard J. Daley, future governor Otto Kerner Jr., and banker William S. Miller (chairman of the Illinois Racing Commission), who made a pledge to Lindheimer and Ben's adopted daughter, Marje Lindheimer Everett, that he would help the family keep the racing empire alive. Within a few years the resourceful Marje not only maintained what her daddy had built up but expanded it by introducing harness racing at Washington Park and building a plush hotel next door to Arlington Park.

In the ensuing years Washington Park, a beautiful wooden grandstand and clubhouse complete with a turf course and a dirt track, fell into a state of disrepair. There was no racing at the park from 1964 through 1970. Madison Square Garden Corporation bought the property and experimented with the first winter racing dates in Illinois history in 1977, but the public was not interested.

Q: What other professional sport was Marje Lindheimer Everett involved with?

A: In 1974 the National League turned down Marje Everett's bid to purchase the struggling San Diego Padres from C. Arnholdt Smith. Mrs. Everett had moved to southern California, where she operated the Hollywood Race Track. Her money helped keep the struggling Padre franchise afloat in 1973.

"Racing is a dirty business, and to survive you have to play dirty too."

MARJE LINDHEIMER EVERETT, ALSO KNOWN AS THE QUEEN OF LLINOIS RACING

1961

Racing was never more popular in Illinois. In 1961 all previously existing attendance records were shattered at the thoroughbred tracks when 3,079,130 railbirds passed through the turnstiles to bet on the ponies.

1961

Marje Everett purchased control of Arlington Park and Washington Park Jockey Clubs to form Chicago Thoroughbred Enterprises, which was later merged with Gulf and Western Corporation. Beginning in 1964, Washington Park was used exclusively for harness racing until the park was demolished in 1979.

1962

Bill Shoemaker and Candy Spots won the $357,250 Futurity. Candy Spots, who was making only his third start, was a late entry in the race for two-year-olds. Jockey Willie Shoemaker had talked owner Rex Ellsworth into entering his young colt in the event. Ellsworth paid a $25,000 supplementary fee. It turned out to be an excellent short-term investment. Shoemaker guided Candy Spots from dead last at the outset, past some tiring horses, to fourth place at the head of the stretch. From there Candy Spots collared the leader, Never Bend, at the wire, making Mr. Ellsworth $147,250 richer.

1968

Balmoral Park inaugurated harness racing. The Will County track, standing silent and empty since 1955 while its thoroughbred races were run elsewhere, dusted off the cobwebs and welcomed back the railbirds—to wager on the sulkies.

1969

Phil Georgeff made his announcing debut. Eventually known as the voice of Chicago racing, he worked at all the area tracks, calling both the harness and thoroughbred races. Over a 23-year career he would call 96,131 races.

Q: Where did Georgeff's trademark call "They're spinning around the turn," come from?
A: At the request of television producers he devised it as a segue to another spot.

1971

Marje Everett's Chicago Thoroughbred Enterprise was bought by the Madison Square Garden Corporation.

1973

Triple crown winner Secretariat, fresh from a 31-length triumph at the Belmont Stakes, captured the special Arlington Invitational by nine lengths. With hardly any urging from jockey Ron Turcotte, Secretariat defeated a betting pool of three horses, just missing a track record by 1/5 of a second. The barrel-chested Secretariat then paraded in front of the grandstand with his head held high and his ears pricked to the applause.

> *"Chicago hasn't had an animal so celebrated as Secretariat since Mrs. O'Leary's cow."*
>
> A CHICAGO NEWSPAPER REPORTER

1975

By any other name a messenger service is a bookmaking operation, legal or otherwise. In the summer of 1975, the Pegasus Company hung out their shingle and opened for business. For the convenience of horse players unable to make it out to the track, Pegasus delivered their customer's wager to the betting window for a 10 percent surcharge. Chicago police conducted periodic raids against the messenger services. Howls of protest echoed from the racetracks to the General Assembly, but

150,000 patrons availed themselves of the service in the next two years. According to reliable estimates, the messenger services brought in $10 million of added revenues to the local tracks before they faded into turf history.

Chicago's short-lived messenger services were an early tune-up for a far richer prize looming over the horizon: legalized, state-sanctioned, off-track betting.

1977

In the late evening hours of February 6 an extra-alarm blaze swept through the grandstand and clubhouse of Washington Park in Homewood. There were no sprinkler or fire protection devices installed at the 49-year-old track, and the flames, visible for 10 miles, consumed the entire facility. The total loss was pegged at $5 million.

Washington Park had been put up for sale some weeks earlier, but no one seemed interested in acquiring the outmoded wooden grandstand. The greatest horses and jockeys of the age raced at Washington—Nashua, Swaps, Willie Shoemaker, Eddie Arcaro. The list goes on. Today, a suburban shopping mall occupies the site.

Q: Washington Park's seating capacity was 30,000. What was the all-time single-day attendance record?

A: On September 6, 1946, a crowd of 57,036 poured into the stands.

> *"I'll never forget the first day I walked into that place. It was a filthy, dirty place and we had quite a job turning it into a winner. But during the 1940s and 1950s we did fantastic. It was a track for the blue-collar bettors and always had a higher per capita handle than others, as long as things were going well. But when the economy went bad, the track went bad."*
>
> MARJE EVERETT, RECALLING THE GLORY DAYS AT WASHINGTON PARK

1978

Another racing season and another series of fires with suspicious origins at an area racetrack. On November 19, the grandstand at the Hawthorne Race Course caught fire. Flames engulfed the ancient seating area and nearly threatened the stables at neighboring Sportsman's Park before firefighters from five suburbs were able to extinguish the blaze. It was the third fire of mysterious origin to break out at the track in less than three weeks, and the usual questions concerning criminal arson arose. Unlike Washington Park, the Carey family, who had owned the historic racing ground since 1909, would rebuild from the ashes. The new Hawthorne reopened on February 18, 1980, with a harness race. Thoroughbred racing came back on September 29 of that year.

Q: Hawthorne, built in 1891 and one of the few family-owned tracks left in the U.S., is the fifth-oldest racetrack in the nation. What four racing grounds are older?
A: Saratoga, Pimlico, the New Orleans Fair Grounds, and Churchill Downs.

"To rebuild you just can't tell how much it will cost. But we'll rebuild."

ROBERT CAREY

1978

Messina, the first offspring of triple crown winner Secretariat, competed in the Color Me Blue at Sportsman's Park. Showing how far the acorn can fall from the tree, Messina finished third.

At Hawthorne Park, an early-morning fire on November 19 destroyed the grandstand, but it reopened in time for the thoroughbreds in September 1980.

1979

Thirty-four horses were killed in a tragic stable fire at the Balmoral Racetrack in Crete Township, on July 20. Horse owners rushed to the track in a futile effort to save their animals, but as they descended upon this terrible and chaotic scene of devastation, there was little that could be done. The fire reportedly began in a haystack inside one of the few barns on the complex that did not have a sprinkler system installed.

It was another painful episode in a long and shameful history of suspicious racetrack fires dating back to the turn of the century, when the competing gambling syndicates deliberately torched the wooden grandstands of rival operations as a means of intimidation.

1980

Spectacular Bid, who won two jewels of the triple crown, entered the Washington Park Handicap at Arlington Park, ridden by Willie Shoemaker, who was making his first Chicago appearance in 11 years. Shoemaker nudged Spectacular Bid's bit at the clubhouse turn, and his horse accelerated and outdistanced the five-horse field by 10 lengths. To prevent a minus pool, Arlington's management allowed only win and place bets. Spectacular Bid paid $2.10 for a win and a place bet.

Q: How did one railbird make a buck backing Spectacular Bid?

A: By putting the deed to the house down on the nag. One courageous fan bet $120,000 on Spectacular Bid to place and won $6,000.

1981

The world's richest turf race, The Arlington Million, was inaugurated. The race was the brainstorm of track president Joseph Joyce, who conceived the idea one day looking out the window at his verdant but seldom-used oval. The race attracts the best grass runners in the world. Horses from the United States, France, Canada, Great Britain, Hong Kong, Ireland, and Brazil have competed in the event.

Q: Who won the first Million?

A: The first Million was won in stunning fashion by the Kentucky-bred John Henry, with Willie Shoemaker in the irons. John Henry was far back of the pack in the early going. He veered wide at the clubhouse turn and then roared down the stretch to nip The Bart, a 40-1, longshot at the wire. John Henry's come-from-behind victory gave

"The Million" instant credibility. The exciting two-horse finish is depicted in a bronze overlooking the Arlington Park paddock.

"There isn't any doubt in my mind that this will evolve into one of the greatest races in the world. This isn't a one-shot deal."
JOSEPH JOYCE, ARLINGTON PARK TRACK PRESIDENT

1982

Legendary track announcer Phil Georgeff was fired by Madison Square Garden executive John Mooney, who didn't like Georgeff's enthusiastic call. Mooney in turn would be booed by the Arlington Park railbirds. Georgeff was hired by Balmoral Racetrack but resumed his announcing chores at Arlington Park the following year when Richard L. Duchossois took over the operation. Georgeff returned in grand fashion, arriving in the infield on a helicopter before a cheering throng.

"I try to call every race like I bet on the winner."
PHIL GEORGEFF

1983

Chicago's own Rambling Willie retired. A favorite of the harness fans, Rambling Willie greeted the judges over 100 times and amassed over $2 million in his career. He was owned and trained by Bob Farrington, who purchased the gelding for $15,000.

John Henry, after missing the 1983 Million because of an injury, lost the race by a neck to Tolomeo, who became the first European (Great Britain) horse to win the event.

Q: How many other European horses have won the Arlington Million?

A: Four. In 1988, the French horse Mill Native lit up the tote board, paying $83.20 to win. The French horse Dear Doctor won in 1992. Teleprompter and Tolomeo, both British horses, won in 1985 and 1983 respectively.

1983

On July 26, it was announced that Arlington Park, a subsidiary of Madison Square Garden (which is owned by Gulf & Western), was sold to a local investment syndicate headed by Joseph Joyce, the former president of the track, and Richard Duchossois, a wealthy horse breeder. The track had been a money loser for several years, and there was a desperate need for additional capital funds to improve the facilities.

Q: Who were some of the great jockeys to ride their horses to victory at Arlington down through the years?

A: Billy Hartack, Eric Guerin, Johnny Longden, Bill Shoemaker, Eddie Arcaro, Dave Erb, and Steve Cauthen. Shoemaker, Longden, and Arcaro were one, two, and three in lifetime victories.

"We wanted to buy the track for a number of reasons. We want to preserve the class of thoroughbred racing in Chicago. In the years I ran Arlington Park, it never lost money."

JOSEPH JOYCE

1984

John Henry, at the age of nine years, captured his second Million as odds-on favorite. Urged on by jockey Chris McCarreon, John Henry stayed abreast of the leaders, then coasted home to a 1 3/4-length win over the filly Royal Heroine. It was the first victory by a nine-year-old in a major-stakes race in 67 years.

"We've been accused of giving him hormones or steroids. It's not true. Sometimes we give him vitamins in his feed. Only the Almighty knows why he can do what he does."

RON MCANALLY, JOHN HENRY'S TRAINER

1985

Arlington Park was destroyed by fire on July 31. Tents and other temporary facilities were erected amid the rubbish, and three weeks later the Arlington Million was held as planned. Thirty-five thousand fans watched the "Miracle Million." For that achievement Arlington Park received the National Racing Board's Eclipse Award, the first time the award was given to a racetrack.

1987

Bomb Rickles, a 191-1 long shot, won Chicago's premier harness race, the Windy City Pace. Drawing a distant eight post, the horse had won only one of six starts for the year. Driver Neal Shapiro brought him to third place as the horses entered the stretch. As the horses fanned out on the backstretch, Shapiro steered Bomb Rickles to an opening on the rail and urged him to the wire past the pacesetter Set the Trap, who was another long shot.

The $100,000 victory raised Bomb Rickles's bankroll for the year to $110,000. To the lucky bettors, Bomb Rickles returned $385.20 for a win ticket. Bomb Rickles also keyed a whopping $30,000 trifecta.

> *"I just happened to be in the right place at the right time."*
>
> NEAL SHAPIRO

> *"You can beat a race but you can't beat the races."*
>
> OLD RACETRACK SAYING

1987

The Illinois Racing Board on February 5 approved the sale of historic Balmoral Park to a syndicate of local and out-of-town investors headed by relatives of New York Yankees owner George M. Steinbrenner. An alliance of track operators from Sportsman's Park, Hawthorne, and Maywood purchased 50 percent of the stock in order to reduce the glut of racing in Northeast Illinois. Too many racing dates and not enough quality horses spelled mediocrity—and diminishing returns for the cash-strapped racetrack owners.

Q: Who were the previous owners of Balmoral?
A: The Edward DeBartolo family of Youngstown, Ohio. The DeBartolos purchased the struggling harness track in 1973.

Edward DeBartolo Sr., who failed to add the Chicago White Sox to his sizable sports empire in 1980, eventually brought thoroughbred racing back to Balmoral.

"One of the biggest problems in Illinois in recent years is too much racing. Then we were competing with Balmoral. Now we're doing what's best for everyone."

BILLY JOHNSTON, MAYWOOD OWNER

1987

Off-track betting was introduced in Illinois. For nearly two decades, a number of proposals floated around the Illinois State House, but each time the measure was shot down by conservative-thinking legislators who believed that a further expansion of gambling was an open invitation to disaster—and the omniscient Chicago mob who would certainly be involved at some level.

The bill passed through the General Assembly in December 1986, partly because of lobbying pressure from disgusted track owners who had balked at the generous tax incentives given to Richard Duchossois to rebuild his fire-ravaged Arlington Park.

An off-track betting parlor opened in Peoria on September 7 in a converted restaurant and sporting goods store. The first two Chicago OTBs opened in 1988.

Q: What state was the first to legalize off-track betting?
A: New York, in 1971.

Q: Who owned the off-track parlors in Illinois?
A: Unlike similar operations in Nevada, Connecticut, and New York, the OTB parlors in Illinois were controlled by the racetrack owners themselves. The Peoria OTB was a joint venture between Maywood, Balmoral Park, Sportsmens, and Hawthorne.

Q: What impact, if any, did off-track betting parlors have on Illinois?
A: Within five years there were 21 off-track betting parlors open for business in Illinois. The influx of wagering did little for the state, however. Track owners received a tax break

the first year, but the amount of revenue returned to the state actually dropped. In 1980 Illinois collected $70 million from total racing revenues of $1 billion. In 1993 the state received just $47.6 million from $1.3 billion in wagering.

"Bringing more people to betting will increase the purses and increase the quality of the horses. One thing makes the other thing better."

BILLY JOHNSTON, CO-OWNER OF MAYWOOD PARK

1988

Maywood Park answered the age-old question: Who is the fastest—a buffalo or a horse? A one-ton buffalo, appropriately named Harvey Wallbanger, raced against two thoroughbreds. Harvey came thundering down the stretch to finish first and was rewarded with a Ho-Ho.

Arlington Park was closed for construction and The Million was transferred to Toronto's Woodbine Race Course.

1989

Arlington Park reopened and was renamed the Arlington International Race Course. On September 13 Arlington jockey Pat Day had an extraordinary day, winning eight of the nine races. In only two of the races did Day's horse go off as the favorite. Day's only loss was a second-place finish in the third race.

Q: How good was a railbird's hunch about Day that day?
A: Fans who backed Day at the $100 win window took home $3,885, not counting a $163 Daily Double. Day himself won over $10,000 in commissions.

"I'm not a handicapper, but my mounts looked pretty good when I checked the entries."

PAT DAY

Later that year in The Million, Day finished third aboard Yankee Affair. It was Day's sixth loss in the prestigious race. After nine attempts Day finally won The Million in 1994.

1994

Five years after Illinois taxpayers financed the rebuilding of Arlington International Race Course, owner Richard L. Duchossois threatened to close the facility, raze a portion of the backstretch, and plant crops on the site unless the state of Illinois passed legislation allowing him to open a riverboat casino adjacent to the track.

Pari-mutuel wagering and casinos had never coexisted in the same locale, and the politicians were not about to change the stakes to suit the owner of Arlington Park, whose anguished cries of poverty struck deaf ears.

Despite threats to the contrary, Arlington opened on time in 1995 and every season thereafter.

"The backstretch will be down and planted in time for next spring unless I have a positive answer. I'm going to need assurances I can survive in 1995. I lost my ass in Quad Cities Downs.[Editor's Note: Duchossois closed his East Moline, Illinois, track in 1993 after a 37 percent decline in business attributed to the arrival of the nearby riverboat.] I won't do that again."

RICHARD L. DUCHOSSOIS, OCTOBER 1994

1996

At Arlington Park, Cigar, the 1995 Horse of the Year, equaled Citation's record of 16 straight wins with a victory in the million-dollar Citation Challenge. Cigar, the 1-20 favorite, was almost snuffed out. Losing ground, Cigar was forced to the extreme outside by some drifting horses. But he smoked the opposition with a late charge in the stretch to win by a neck. A month later, Cigar was upset at Del Mar Racetrack in California, ending his streak and preserving Citation's name in the record books.

"Citation would kick him [Cigar] in his behind and send him home."

JIMMY JONES, CITATION'S TRAINER

1996

Tony Morgan won his second straight North American harness driving title, garnering a record 853 winners in 3,782 races for the year. The cunning Morgan, a sixth-generation member of a harness-racing family from Kentucky, usually finds a way to finish in the money whether he has the fastest entry or not. Morgan is at his best on Maywood Park's challenging half-mile course.

"When in doubt take Morgan."
TOM KRISH, HANDICAPPER FOR THE *CHICAGO SUN-TIMES*

CHAPTER 3

Ten-Pin Tales: Bowling in Chicago

In the early days of Chicago bowling, not long after Mrs. O'Leary's cow kicked over the lantern that started the great fire, the sport was viewed as an unsavory pastime reserved for saloon idlers, touts, corner hustlers, ne'er-do-wells, and gamblers of the worst kind.

The game was played in dimly lit basements of notorious downtown saloons, and the rules of play and sense of sportsmanship were quite different from those of today. In those early days a patron received from the barkeep two checks upon entering the premises—one for a beer, the other entitling the drinker to bowl a game on the house.

In 1875 Rohan's, the city's first commercial establishment to offer bowling, opened on Lake Street just west of Damen. Bowling alleys back then were half the size of what they are today and six inches narrower. There was no foul line, and the bowler started from the end of the alley and moved as far as he liked toward the pins. The lanes were built with paving blocks supported by a stilt framework with a mattress hung at the end to stop the wooden balls. The narrow alleys forced the pinsetter to place the pins so close together that 300 games were a common occurrence.

As there was no trick to knocking down 12 pins the popularity of saloon bowling quickly dwindled. That was until a

Clark Street barkeep named Peter Maher lengthened the alleys to 60 feet from the foul line to the head pin in 1898. He also set the pins farther apart and widened the lane to 42 inches. In 1900 the weight of the ball was fixed at 16 pounds and the circumference fixed at 27 inches.

With further refinements the popularity of the game steadily increased, particularly among the German immigrants living on the North Side of the city. The barroom atmosphere and air of danger and intrigue that had been associated with the sport of 10 pins disappeared. By the turn of the century there were a number of well-ventilated bowling halls that welcomed family participation. The criminal riffraff lost interest in the game—horseracing was more to their liking.

The year 1895 was an eventful one for the game. The first bowling league was organized in North Chicago, and the American Bowling Congress (ABC) was founded by Moses Bensinger, a business associate of John Brunswick, and other local proprietors with a vested interest in the growing recreational industry. The ABC established rules that, with few modifications, have been observed ever since. The governing body supervised the activities of thousands of leagues and organizations and staged championship tournaments where titles were awarded to teams and individuals.

Company teams, fraternal lodges, and young men and women from all ethnic backgrounds participated in league play. Within a few short years Chicago bowlers were the toast of the nation. Dom DeVito was a star of the 1920s who bowled for the Duffy Florals, one of several semipro teams in different sports sponsored by the Chicago florists. The Florals won a string of titles and were something of a local legend. In the 1940s a tournament was named after DeVito.

Little Jimmy Blouin, a Frenchman from Blue Island, was the American Bowling Congress champion in 1911 and an all-events champion in 1909. He had few peers and was one of the great match bowlers of all time. Jimmy Smith, his rival from those early days, would probably disagree. Smith, an Italian whose birth name was Melillo, was active in the 1890s and continued to dominate the sport through the 1920s. Smith rolled 16

300 games and for a time held the world's record for the highest average spanning three games—a cumulative 771. Smith and Blouin were the very best bowlers in the country during the World War I era, and they kindled early interest in the professional side of the game.

Chicago bowlers continued to dominate the national scene after World War II. Professionals who earned their living from bowling were often sponsored by commercial firms and breweries headquartered in cities with a strong working-class identification. It was no coincidence that team bowling was immensely popular as a spectator and participatory sport in Chicago, Detroit, and St. Louis—cities that produced the greatest names in the game after the war ended.

Through the medium of television and the long-running Championship Bowling program, aired locally on Sunday afternoons, two of Chicago's very best, Joe Wilman and Carmen Salvino, achieved national acclaim.

Named to the Bowling Hall of Fame in 1951, Berwyn-native Wilman was known to his peers as "Black Jack" because he chewed the licorice-flavored gum during matches. Carmen Salvino was a protégé of Wilman and a lifelong resident of Chicago's Northwest Side. Salvino, like many of the famous high rollers, got his start in the game working as a pin boy while in high school. He is a member of the Professional Bowling Association (PBA) Hall of Fame and the Italian-American Hall of Fame headquartered in Chicago. His personal charisma and pride in performance earned him a legion of followers for nearly four decades beginning in 1950.

The sport received wide attention from the Chicago media throughout the 1950s and early 1960s. For many years nationally known touring pros like Don Carter from St. Louis and Marian Ladewig of Grand Rapids published syndicated advice columns offering insider tips to the readers of the *Chicago American.* Ladewig was voted the greatest woman bowler of all time by the Bowling Writers Association of America in 1973. The newspapers promoted the sport, and they employed full-time bowling writers, like Angelo Biondi of the *Daily News,* to report on the big money tournaments and the flourishing amateur game in the city. Sam Weinstein, host of the "Ten-pin Tattler," covered the game for WGN Radio for six decades.

Changing public tastes, the rising popularity of professional and amateur basketball, and jogging, racquetball, and other physical fitness sports in the 1970s adversely impacted the professional side of bowling. The lavish tournaments and the Sunday afternoon bowling shows disappeared from TV in the 1970s. The sport declined in popularity and was unfairly and inaccurately maligned by health-club faddists as a pastime reserved for wheezing, out-of-shape rednecks who smoked fat cigars and sucked down highballs between sets. Today the game receives only scant agate-type coverage in the pages of the daily newspapers.

Still, Chicago was home to a legion of world-class bowlers who left behind an enduring legacy, among them: Buddy Bomar, Hank Marino, Joseph Norris, Ned Day, Junie McMahon, and Carmen Salvino. In many ways the Windy City remains the hub of bowling nationwide. It is a sport ideally suited to the strong blue-collar identity of the ethnic working-class neighborhoods dotting the greater Northwest and Southwest Sides of the city. Team bowling and Chicago grew up together.

1873

The Brunswick Company of Cincinnati, founded by Swiss immigrant John Brunswick in 1845, opened an office in Chicago selling billiards tables and bar fixtures. Brunswick launched his bowling equipment line in 1870.

Q: Why would a company that manufactured billiards tables add saloon fixtures to their line?
A: Billiards tables were originally located in saloons.

1884

The Brunswick Company absorbed two other billiards firms from Cincinnati and New York and renamed itself the Brunswick-Balke-Callendar Company. The corporate headquarters was relocated to Chicago where it built a large warehouse and office facility in an area of the city now known as River North.

Q: The Brunswick Building was converted to other uses a century later. In 1989 the building burned to the ground drawing considerable media comment. Why?

A: The Brunswick Building had become a center for Chicago's burgeoning art gallery district. A dozen galleries were lost or severely damaged in the fire. The second Brunswick Building, constructed in 1913, still stands. It is now home to Columbia College on south Wabash Avenue.

1896

German immigrants belonging to the various fraternal and ethnic lodges who shared a common interest in the sport of 10 pins founded a confederation of clubs known as the Chicago Metropolitan Bowling Association. The CMBA received its formal charter from the American Bowling Congress (ABC) in 1903 for the purpose of sanctioning league play and providing unification through a locally autonomous governing body. It is the oldest continuing bowling organization of its kind in Northeast Illinois. Today the CMBA is headquartered in Oak Park and remains a local chapter of the ABC, representing 35,000 bowlers from the city and suburbs.

1901

Chicago hosted the very first American Bowling Congress Tournament at the Welsbach Building, 68-70 Wabash Avenue, on January 8-11. The second-floor location featured six alleys, a reception room, dressing rooms, and space for 800 spectators. Forty-one five-member teams and 72 two-man teams signed up. The Standard Club of Chicago emerged as the team champion, and their members walked away with a $200 first prize.

Q: Can you guess the total prize money awarded to individuals and teams in the first tournament?

A: $1,592. By comparison, the 1953 "Golden Jubilee" tournament in Chicago lured 43,000 bowlers vying for a total purse valued at $573,860.

"The noise made by the spectators would put a bleacher delegation at a baseball game to shame. There was almost a continual roar of applause from the beginning of play at 3:30 P.M. until the close of the day's sport at midnight."

NEWS ACCOUNT OF THE OPENING SESSIONS OF THE ABC TOURNAMENT, JANUARY 8, 1901

1902

Chicagoan Frank Pasdeloup defeated Charles Ebbets of New York for the presidency of the American Bowling Congress, precipitating a bitter regional "war" that dragged on for many years between East Coast bowlers and the Midwest faction of the ABC.

Q: The easterners were particularly upset over a piece of equipment favored by the Chicagoans. What was it that helped spur a walkout of 100 New York delegates from the 1902 ABC Congress in Buffalo?

A: Chicago bowlers insisted upon using a 24-pound "dodo ball" in their tournaments. The irksome ball was finally outlawed in 1913 after many years of contentious debate.

1906

The Brunswick Company introduced the "Mineralite," a revolutionary bowling ball invented by Michael J. Whalen. It retailed for $20. A year earlier, the American Hard Rubber Company premiered the first hard rubber ball to the sport. It was known as the "Evertrue."

1911

Jimmy Smith won the ABC Tournament with a score of 1,913 total points. That same year, one of Chicago's longest-running and most famous bowling leagues got its start.

Q: What was the name of this league, and who were some of the star bowlers who participated?

A: The Randolph League, featuring ABC Hall of Famer Pete Howley; Hank Marino, named the "Bowler of the Half

Century" by the Bowling Writer's Association of American in 1951; and Dave Luby, founder and publisher of *Bowler's Journal.*

1913

David Luby, a former shoe salesman and avid Chicago ten-pins man, founded *Bowler's Journal,* the oldest continuously published sporting magazine in the United States. The first issue rolled off the presses on November 13, and thereafter it was published every Saturday. (Editor's Note: *The Sporting News,* founded in 1886, is a weekly newspaper periodical, not a magazine.) Mr. Luby published the magazine from 1913-1925. David's son, Mort Luby, took over editorial duties in 1925 and ran the publication during the formative years of Chicago Bowling. In 1956 Mort Jr. assumed command.

The "First Family" of Chicago bowling finally relinquished control of the magazine and sold it to Keith Hamilton and Mike Panozzo in 1994. The new owners continue the publishing mission, but nowadays it is to an exclusive mail-order clientele of manufacturers, proprietors, elite bowlers, and those devoted to the sport.

Q: Three generations of Lubys are enshrined in the Bowling Hall of Fame. Who is the only other American family with three members belonging to a Hall of Fame?

A: Henry Ford, his son, and grandson are in the Automotive Hall of Fame.

"To boost the bowling game, collect news and present it to the world."

THE MOTTO OF *BOWLER'S JOURNAL* SET FORTH BY DAVID LUBY

1921

Louis "Pete" Petersen converted a saloon and frowsy second-floor dance hall at Archer Avenue and 35th Street, smack in the middle of Bridgeport, into one of Chicago's legendary neighborhood bowling emporiums. In 1921 Pete inaugurated

Chicago's first big money tournament, offering a $1,000 prize to the season's top bowler, Harry Steers as it turned out.

Old man Petersen doctored the lanes in order to give the local amateurs a sporting chance and competitive edge against the big-time bowlers who dropped in to hustle some action from the regulars. Pete was a neighborhood guy, and he always took care of his Bridgeport customers.

Q: What was the name of this famous tournament that lasted for decades?

A: The Petersen Classic. By 1993, the last year the gin-soaked old relic on 35th Street was open for bowling, the Classic lured 13,000 bowlers and offered a top prize of $45,000.

> *". . . a locale stark enough in its antiquity to frighten any Madison Avenue image maker right out of his Brooks Brothers suit, the bowlers face a test as grueling as any basic training obstacle course...It is the most discussed and cussed bowling establishment in the world."*
>
> BOWLER'S JOURNAL

1922

Jimmy Blouin won the first and only World's Open in Chicago.

1934

South Sider Joe Norris won the first of two ABC team titles. For 28 tournaments Norris compiled an ABC average of 198. He was named to eight consecutive All-American teams from 1940-1947 and was elected to the Hall of Fame in 1954. Joe Norris was also a notorious practical joker who never shied away from trickery to gain a competitive advantage.

Q: How did Norris aide and abet his cause?

A: He would stuff cotton in the holes of the ball so it wouldn't fit his opponent's hand and would often hide his rival's shoes.

1935

Sam Weinstein, the "Bob Elson of the bowling broadcasters," launched his "Ten-Pin Tattler," radio's first bowling-only program.

Q: Where did Weinstein get his start?
A: He was an editor for Dave Luby's *Bowler's Journal.*

1940

Mort Luby, the editor of *Bowler's Journal,* a trade publication headquartered in Chicago, began his annual selection of pro bowling's All-American team. It was no coincidence that Ned Day, Joe Wilman, Adolph Carlson, Joe Norris, Paul Krumske, and Buddy Bomar—Chicagoans all—were perennial selections year in and year out until *Bowling* magazine, the official publication of the American Bowling Congress, took over the selection process in 1956.

Q: What down-and-out bowler came out of retirement in 1959 to win $10,000 on the television program "Championship Bowling," only to squander his earnings on frivolous pursuits?
A: Ned Day, bowling's first "glamour" boy, who appeared in 15 short subject films in Hollywood during his glory years on the circuit. He died virtually penniless in 1972.

> *"I'll guarantee you, that money was either in the stock market or on the nose of a horse the next day."*
>
> FRED WOLF, HOST OF "CHAMPIONSHIP BOWLING," ON NED DAY'S WINNINGS

1941

Eleven professional bowlers were elected to the new American Bowling Congress Hall of Fame. Selections were made by the Bowling Writers of America who established the criteria for inclusion. To be eligible for consideration a bowler had to first compete in 15 meets.

Q: Two of the 11 charter members were Chicagoans. Can you name them?

A: Harry Steers and Adolph Carlson. Steers was a 21-year-old pin boy when he won the ABC doubles in 1902. He was the first man to bowl in 50 ABC tournaments. Carlson, a husky Swede from Chicago, averaged 197 in 32 tournaments, but never won an ABC title.

1941

Louie Petersen, originator of the Petersen Classic and the Petersen Point System, conceived and promoted the first All-Star Tournament in Chicago for individual bowlers. The event opened at the Chicago Coliseum on time. But it was December 7, 1941—which coincided with the Japanese sneak attack on Pearl Harbor. Nevertheless, Petersen and his fellow bowlers proclaimed that despite the war, the show would go on. And it did—for many years to come. The All-Star attracted more media coverage over the years than any bowling event before or since.

Q: Where was the All-Star tournament played?

A: Various sites, including the Chicago Coliseum and Louis Sullivan's majestic Auditorium Theater, opened in 1888 on Michigan Avenue.

> *"All the while you were bowling, you knew that somebody up there in the stands was betting thousands of dollars on you. Once in a while, one of these high rollers would come down and stuff a five spot in your pocket as sort of a tip."*
>
> DON CARTER, CHAMPION BOWLER, RECALLING THE CHICAGO ALL-STAR TOURNEY

1942

Without warning, Chicago Police Commissioner James P. Allman, on January 12, enforced an ancient city ordinance dating back to 1910 requiring all bowling alleys to close at one A.M. There were 2,500 bowling alleys operating in Chicago at the time, and an estimated half million city bowlers were not pleased by the commissioner's high-handed actions. Their howls of protest reverberated from City Hall to Washington, D.C., where Mayor Ed Kelly happened to be conducting business. After much ado, the matter was peacefully resolved after Alderman P. J. Cullerton of the 38th Ward introduced a measure in the city council to reclassify bowling alleys as "recreation establishments."

Q: What new closing time did the aldermen finally agree upon?

A: Five A.M., provided that the owners of bowling lanes in residential areas soundproofed their walls.

"I think what we want to do is increase the license revenue."
JAMES B. BOWLER, 25TH WARD ALDERMAN—
WHO WAS NOT A BOWLER

1945

Buddy Bomar, a talk-it-up, eternally sunny promoter who was one of the movers and shakers of the Chicago Classic League, won 1945 Bowler of the Year honors.

Q: Why was Buddy Bomar nicknamed "Buffy"?

A: Bomar bowled at Samuelson's Lanes on the North Side. In those days the lanes were coated with shellac and when the temperature dropped, the wood hardened and became very slick. The night before a big tournament Bomar would open all the windows and then buff the lanes to make them even faster.

1949

Chicagoan Peter Howley, elected to the Hall of Fame in 1941 as a "Distinguished Service Member," bowled in his last ABC tournament.

Q: What unique longevity record does Howley hold?

A: Howley played in the first ABC tournament in 1901 and every one thereafter until 1949. He averaged 178 for 46 tournaments.

1950

Illinois's State Attorney John Boyle filed a discrimination suit against the American Bowling Congress on April 22, in an effort to break the historic and continuing pattern of segregation within the ranks of professional bowling. Judge John Sbarbaro, himself an avid sportsman, assessed the ABC a $2,500 fine—which was never paid. However, the organization dropped the segregationist clause at their next convention.

1952

"Championship Bowling," the brainchild of Chicago ad man Walter Schwimmer, debuted on WMAQ-TV. Schwimmer put up $10,000 in prize money to any bowler who rolled a 300 game on his program. It was a large sum of money in those days, and the big names of the sport eagerly signed on. Schwimmer's promotional genius, and the quirky nature of the program, paid handsome dividends. His late-night show was later picked up by a number of stations including WGN, where it remained a staple of their Sunday afternoon programming lineup until 1965.

Q: Who announced "Championship Bowling"?
A: "Whispering" Joe Wilson. Because he did not wish to upset the bowler's concentration, Wilson whispered his play-by-play commentary into his microphone.

1952

The introduction of the automatic pinspotter in 1952 revolutionized the game and threw hundreds of Chicago pin boys into the unemployment ranks. The American Machine and Foundry Company (AMF), utilizing electromagnetic principles, developed the automatic unit for setting the 10 pins and returning the ball to the player.

Q: What Chicago-based company expanded the automatic pinspotter outside U.S. borders?
A: Brunswick-Balke-Callendar installed the Brunswick Automatic Pinsetter in several lanes in England in 1959.

1953

Myrtle Piper established an all-time game high of 269 in the Chicago American Women's Bowling Classic at the Cascade Center. The annual Women's Classic, sponsored by the afternoon Hearst newspaper, was inaugurated in 1927 and continued through the mid-1960s. It was the largest and richest team handicap sweepstakes in women's bowling in the nation at that time. In its heyday 500 teams signed up to play in the Women's Classic.

Q: When did professional women's bowling get going?
A: The Women's International Bowling Congress was organized in 1916, sponsoring prize tournaments drawn along the same lines as the men's events.

1953

Rudy Habetler was the American Bowling Congress's Master's champion for 1953.

Q: Who is Rudy Habetler?
A: He was the original owner of Habetler's Bowling Alley, one of the city's most famous 10-pin centers. It is still open for business at Northwest Highway and Foster Avenue on the far Northwest Side.

1954

"Bowling with the Stars" aired on WBKB-TV on Sunday afternoons at 4:30 P.M. This made-for-TV bowling show offered top prize money to contestants, and it helped turn local bowlers like Carmen Salvino into instant celebrities.

1957

After the Bowling Proprietor's Association of America abruptly moved the All-Star Tournament out of Chicago, the local chapter of BPAA created a new and better tournament for Windy City patrons.

The first World's Invitational Match Game Tournament, an invitational tournament staged every November through the late

1960s, began on November 13. The greatest bowlers of the age—Don Carter, Dick Weber, Billy Hardwick, Ray Bluth, Bob Strampe, Billy Welu, Dick Hoover, and Harry Smith—all top money winners on the pro circuit, participated in this tournament at one time or another. The tournament was broadcast on ABC-TV. Jim Kearns described the action to the viewing audience.

Q: Where was this premier event held?
A: It was held at McCormick Place, where Don Carter of St. Louis won three of the first five tournaments. Later it relocated to the musty Chicago Coliseum on South Wabash Avenue.

Q: Where were some of Chicago's other big money tournaments held?
A: They rotated among some of Chicago's finest recreational centers, like Schuenneman & Flynn's on the West Side, the South Side Chatham Bowl, and the Argo Bowl at 5900 S. Harlem Avenue in suburban Argo.

1958

Before the Professional Bowlers Association (PBA) was founded in May 1958, just about anyone owning a bowling ball and a pair of shoes could stake a claim as a "pro." There were no selection criteria or qualifications established until Akron, Ohio, attorney Eddie Elias, Carmen Salvino of Chicago, and 32 of the game's true immortals organized the PBA. They paid a $50 initiation fee.

Q: How did one become a member of the PBA?
A: Initially, a professional was defined as someone who earned 50 percent of their income from bowling tournaments. This broad designation was later narrowed to bowlers who averaged 190 or better two consecutive years in ABC league-sanctioned play.

1961

In October Leonard Homel of Los Angeles founded the National Bowling League, featuring 80 of the nation's top professional bowlers representing 10 cities in competition for a 10-

pin championship. Promoters sunk $14 million into the venture, constructing bowling alleys inside theaters to maximize gate receipts. Chicago did not field an NBL team and it was probably just as well. The league collapsed before the year was out.

Q: What Chicago bowler signed the league's biggest contract?
A: Carmen Salvino was paid $20,000 by Lamar Hunt, owner of the Dallas Broncos.

"The year in Dallas has helped me. I'm not throwing as fast, as if I had to push the ball through a brick wall. I have a shorter back swing, controlled speed, a smaller curve, and definitely more accuracy. These were all things that veteran Joe Wilman, the 'Berwyn Bomber' tried to tell me about years ago, but I was just a kid then and who wants to listen to an older fellow? Now I know better."

CARMEN SALVINO, AFTER MOVING BACK TO CHICAGO, NOVEMBER 1962

1961

Shirley Garms, a housewife from Des Plaines, was named Bowler of the Year, an honor voted on by the Bowling Writers of America. In 1961 Garms won the City Match Game Championship for the sixth time in 13 years and bowled in the World's Tournament finals three times in four tries.

Q: What was the City Match Game Championship?
A: To become a champion of this annual round-robin tournament, it was necessary to count the total pins knocked down as well as defeat one's opponent.

"Ever since I started bowling in competition, everybody has said I don't have the killer instinct. But when I'm looking at all those pins, I'm not smiling."

SHIRLEY GARMS, 1961

1967

Chicago had 4,648 certified bowling lanes. As the number of "Ma-and-Pa" operations dwindled over the next decade (to be replaced by spacious, modern, suburban emporiums), the number of lanes open to the public dropped to 4,084 in 1977.

1973

The Illinois High School Association (IHSA), the governing body of prep sports, added bowling to the athletic curriculum.

1977

The Chicago Bowling Proprietors Association of America reported that 67 neighborhood bowling centers went out of business between 1967 and 1977. However, an American Bowling Congress survey showed that 115,000 members were rolling in at least one league in 1977. The media may not have been paying attention to the game in the late 1970s, but bowling still outranked baseball, hunting, football, golf, skiing, and the racquet sports in participation.

Q: Only three participatory sports exceeded the popularity of bowling. What were they?
A: Fishing, swimming, and boating.

1979

Working with the scientists at the Amoco Research Center in suburban Naperville, Carmen Salvino designed a revolutionary bowling ball utilizing a weight-block design he had tinkered with for years while traveling the PBA circuit. The new ball, manufactured and marketed by the Ebonite Corporation, was appropriately named the "Thunderbolt."

1980

At the PBA National Championship in Sterling Heights, Michigan, Carmen Salvino scored a record 4,015 for a 16-game set. Salvino, a demonstrative, heel-clicking bowler, averaged 251 for the tournament. That same year he was elected into the Chicago Sports Hall of Fame—one of five halls of fame that Chicago's favorite son of the 10 pins belongs to. Indeed, an opera starring Carmen.

Q: How many PBA titles has Salvino won over the course of a 40-year career?
A: Twenty.

1983

The first issue of *Bowling Digest,* a monthly periodical of Century Publishing in Evanston, rolled off the presses in March.

1984

Southport Lanes (formerly Leo's Lanes) at 3325 N. Southport Avenue was the last hand-set, public bowling alley in Chicago certified for competition by the American Bowling Congress. Owner Leo Beitz, who bought the building from his parents in 1960, clung to old traditions because he could not afford to pay $12,000 per lane—the cost of the new equipment, electrical wiring, and remodeling.

Q: What did Beitz pay his pinspotters in 1984?
A: Forty-five cents a game. On a typical night the last Chicago pinspotters could make $10.80 for three hours of work.

> *"You go through 20 to 30 pin boys a year. Some don't want to sweat. They want to get paid $5.00 an hour and just sit there. They work one day and never come back again. But we never had to take one to the doctor yet in 24 years."*
>
> LEO BEITZ

1985

Most professional bowlers are on the road 30 weeks a year, following the trail of PBA tournaments and the elusive prize money that is minuscule compared to other sports. In 1985 the richest tournament in the land was the Brunswick Memorial World Open, hosted by Brunswick Northern Bowl in west suburban Glendale Heights. The pro bowlers travel the land in motor homes, very often sharing space at all-night truck stops with over-the-road semidrivers. The life of the bowler was never a glamorous or rewarding one. The 50th-ranked bowler on the tour earned $30,000 a year—offsetting $30,000 in living expenses.

Q: What are the three events comprising the "Triple Crown" of professional bowling?
A: The U.S. Open, the PBA National Championship, and the cash-rich Brunswick Memorial World Open in the Chicago suburbs every November.

"Big companies that want to get a customer to impress him might take him to a plush country club or tennis court. Not to a bowling alley. Most people don't even know there is such a thing as a professional bowler's tour. It hurts."
SAM ZURICH, A FLORIDA BOWLER IN GLENDALE HEIGHTS, 1985

1988

The National Bowling Hall of Fame and Museum in St. Louis, Missouri, added a new exhibit to their permanent collection—the shirts worn in league play by an amateur team sponsored by *Chicago Tribune* columnist Bob Greene. Bob's team of lady bowlers got together at the Mont Clair Lanes on Thursday nights—Ladies' Night at the far Northwest Side lanes. It cost Greene just $25 to sponsor the team, whom he introduced to millions of readers in his syndicated column.

Q: What was the name of Bob Greene's team?
A: The "Greenettes."

"We're the same size as the Pro Football Hall of Fame. If this surprises some people it shouldn't. Only a relative handful of men play pro football, but there are an estimated 8.5 million Americans who bowl in sanctioned leagues and another 60 to 70 million who bowl at least occasionally for recreation. The bowling shirt display is the highlight of our museum."
BRUCE PLUCKHAHN, HALL OF FAME CURATOR

1993

The uneven alleys and heavy pins at Petersen's made it one of the toughest lanes in the city in which to crack 200. Despite the hardships imposed upon them, bowlers of all ages loved and reviled this vintage 1904 building with the tin roof and 65-foot-long bar. And when it closed in October 1993, there was not a dry eye in the house.

> *"People, bowlers from overseas, would come to Chicago and what did they ask for? They did not want to go visit a modern American bowling alley in the suburbs. They wanted to go to Archer and 35th Street. They wanted to go to Petersen's. What a fantastic, weird, and wonderful place."*
>
> MORT LUBY JR., PUBLISHER OF *BOWLER'S JOURNAL*

1994

Two legendary stops on the annual PBA Tour underwent significant changes in 1994. The Brunswick Open and the Tournament of Champions (held annually in Akron, Ohio) merged into one tournament and changed its name to the Brunswick World Tournament of Champions. The star-studded event featuring the top bowlers from around the nation was held the first week of November at the Deer Park Lanes in Northwest Suburban Lake Zurich, a luxurious, state-of-the-art facility that opened to the public in 1991. At the 1994 Brunswick Open, Kelly Coffman rolled his seventh 300 game for the year, tying a PBA record, but he did not cart home the top prize.

Q: Who won the 1994 World Tournament?

A: Eric Folker beat David Ozio in the title game to take home $45,000 of the $300,000 purse. It was a very modest sum of money, given the escalating salaries and prize money available to athletes in the 1990s.

> *"People do not think we're athletes. They say we're not athletic enough. Well, we don't make the millions of dollars like golfers, tennis players, or baseball players, but if anyone thinks this is a real easy life, come out and join us!"*
>
> PARKER BOHN III, PBA BOWLER

CHAPTER 4

High-Wheelers to Triathlons: Cycling, Running, and Jumping Chicagoans

The first reported reference to cycling in Chicago was 1879, when city officials attempted to ban high-wheelers from Lincoln Park. These rather precarious machines had made their first appearance on this side of the Atlantic Ocean only three years before at the Centennial Exposition in Philadelphia. By the time of Chicago's Columbian Exposition in 1893, enforcing such a ban would have been as formidable a project as banning roller blades and skateboards from city streets and parks today.

A century ago Americans were ready to indulge in the nation's first recreational sports fad, and it was one for which Chicago was ideally suited. The city's terrain was flat, and it was encircled by a system of wide boulevards. By 1890 the Illinois Cycling Club had 1,000 members and a four-story clubhouse on the West Side—and this was before the introduction of the first "safety" bicycle, the form with which we are familiar today: two wheels of equal size propelled by a chain drive. As soon as the safety bicycle was introduced in Chicago and elsewhere around the nation, lawyers and their office clerks, genteel homemakers and their servants, machine-shop workers and salesgirls—anyone who could save up the necessary $75 to $100—could make themselves mobile.

Further enhancing the city's ability to take up cycling was its rapidly developing industrial strength. Chicago abounded with carriage makers and wheelwrights who, along with talented tinkerers, could not only manufacture but improve upon the new machine. Some say that before the last century's turn, Chicago had become the bicycling capital of the country with its dozen or so bicycle manufacturers and a hundred cycling clubs. Ministers took to their pulpits to complain that cycling was competing with church services on Sunday, but these young cycling enthusiasts in their gaily colored uniforms could not be dissuaded from their new passion.

After the boom came the inevitable bust, but some Chicago bike manufacturers like Ignaz Schwinn and Adolph Arnold were ready for it; another prominent firm known as Gormully & Jeffrey eventually went into automobile manufacture. They produced the car that came to be known as the Rambler a half century later. The passion for cycling even attracted Chicago baseball pioneer A. G. Spalding, who made an unsuccessful attempt to set up a bicycle trust.

In this century's early decades other amateur sports attracted the talents of two incredibly handsome and immensely talented young Chicagoans—William Hale Thompson and Avery Brundage. Though their backgrounds and chosen careers could not have been more different—the privleged Thompson went into politics and the self-made Brundage virtually took over the Olympic movement in this country—both made decisions later in life that compromised their early promise.

In modern amateur marathon and triathlon endeavors Chicago was late in developing. Though both types of races are now popular events, attracting world-class purses and competitors, there's little written record of their history.

1887

The Gormully & Jeffrey Manufacturing Company of Chicago introduced the "American Safety," a high-wheeler priced at a reasonable $76. Propelled by a highly efficient treadle device, it might have become more successful were high-wheelers not soon to become obsolete.

Q: What replaced the high-wheelers?
A: By the late 1880s several bicycle manufacturers in both the U.S. and Great Britain were experimenting with true safety bicycles—those with two wheels of the same size powered by pedals and a chain drive.

1893

Twenty-five-year-old William Hale Thompson returned to Chicago after nearly a decade in the West and within a year was the Chicago Athletic Club's reigning star, competing against Ivy League grads. Cycling, no doubt, seemed too tame a sport for someone who'd learned to break horses; his first coup was to lead the club's water polo team into the national finals.

Q: At what other sports did young Thompson excel?
A: He was extraordinarily talented at a wide variety of games and competed in baseball, handball, swimming, and diving—even performing on the aerial trapeze—but it was in football that he won his greatest fame.

1894

Accompanied by President William Rainey Harper, John D. Rockefeller made a bicycle tour of the new University of Chicago campus, for which the oil tycoon was chief benefactor.

Q: Three years later a Chicago mayorial candidate bolstered his campaign by demonstrating what an avid cyclist he was. His father had campaigned for the same office atop a white horse. Who was the son?
A: The Harrisons became Chicago's first father-son mayoral duo when Carter Henry Harrison II was elected in 1897.

Q: What other role did cyclists play in politics during the great bicycle boom?

A: The hordes of young male cyclists quickly organized themselves into clubs, adopted club colors and uniforms, and spent some of their noncycling hours campaigning for favored candidates.

1895

Honorary judges for the July 4 Bicycle Derby sponsored by the South Side Cycling Club and held at the Washington Park racetrack included a Swift, a Medill, a Spalding, and a Farwell. Advertisers in the official program included a half dozen local bike manufacturers. Other prominently displayed products included the G-D bicycle waist—a sort of Victorian-era athletic bra. "Lady cyclists will only have thorough comfort by wearing [it]," the copy proclaimed.

1896

Young Bill Thompson decided that a football team from the Chicago Athletic Club should go after a national championship, so he assembled a squad of college stars, called it the Cheery Circle, and served as its coach, strategist, and manager, as well as its strongest player. The team won victory after victory against teams from other cities, and on Thanksgiving Day it was scheduled to play the Boston Athletic Club's team for the national championship. Then disaster befell the team. It had been discovered that some members had been treated to free meals by other members—a violation of Amateur Athletic Union rules. But it was only a near-disaster; even without the expelled players, Thompson led the Chicago team to victory.

> *"Fellows, there's only one thing to do. We want the championship, but we've got to expell those men."*
>
> "Big Bill" Thompson, to his other teammates after this decision

"Thompson says the Chicago Athletic Club has taken a stand before the world for clean football."

CHICAGO TRIBUNE, COMMENDING THOMPSON'S DECISION

Q: At this time Thompson was living in the Metropole Hotel on 23rd Street. What was this hotel later known as, and how would it figure into Thompson's future?

A: The Metropole later became the Lexington, known as the headquarters for gangster Al Capone, one of the athlete-turned-politician's least-commendable associates.

Q: Thompson excelled at billiards as well, once winning a championship from someone still famed in Chicago as a hotelier. Who was he?

A: John Drake, then owner of the Grand Pacific Hotel, who would later build the establishment at the head of Michigan Avenue that still bears his name.

1897

A dance was held in Jackson Park for appropriately attired bicyclists, and it attracted 400 men and women, the latter dressed predominantly in bloomers. A reporter covering the event claimed it attracted some 4,000 spectators as well, who were there to observe an event regarded by many as risqué.

"Bloomers beat dresses all to pieces. They don't interfere with the fun, and you can't step on them nor tear them, and you don't have to get a carriage to take the girl home. Bloomers are all right."

CHICAGO RECORD, QUOTING A MALE BICYCLIST

1897

The city banned all but bicycle traffic from Jackson Boulevard into the downtown area.

1897

The First Regiment National Guard Armory at 16th Street and Michigan Avenue provided the dual setting for Chicago's first indoor track-and-field meet on February 26. The one-day competition spotlighted the talents of various collegiate athletes and from the private downtown sports clubs including the Chicago Athletic Association.

1898

On Decoration Day, May 30, the Associated Cycling Clubs of Chicago held a road race from Wheeling to Garfield Park on Chicago's West Side. The course led all the way into the city along Milwaukee Avenue, then south from Logan Square along the boulevards. The route's surface began as gravel, changed to light clay (on which, a map noted, it was "hard to push"), to cedar block (with and without a streetcar line down the middle), and finally to macadam.

Q: Two years earlier, an overly enthusiastic cyclist was arrested for "hooting" at a female cyclist in Lincoln Park. What was the outcome of the case?

A: Speaking in his own defense, the offending cyclist, whose name was Engstrom, claimed he hadn't actually hooted but "chortled," which he said was involuntary—a female cyclist being an odd sight on the streets of the city and therefore beyond his reasonable control. Nevertheless, the judge assessed him a modest fine.

Q: A woman more noted for temperance than for athleticism was so enthusiastic about mastering the cycle that she wrote a book about it. Who was she?

A: In 1895 *How I Learned to Ride a Bicycle, with Some Reflections Along the Way* was published. Its author was Frances Willard, more widely known as president of the Women's Christian Temperance Union.

1899

The great bicycling boom was about to bust, but German-born Chicagoan Ignaz Schwinn and his partner Adolph Arnold, who had established their bicycle business four years earlier, had seen the drop in demand coming and were ready for it.

Q: How had Schwinn and Arnold prepared for the great bicycle bust?

A: They had decided to concentrate on building frames, leaving the riskier assembly and retailing aspects to others. They also experimented with horseless carriages, which would soon become the nation's next craze.

Q: Just how severe would this turn-of-the-century bicycle bust be?

A: According to one report, one milllion bicycles were sold in the year 1900; by 1904 total sales were only a quarter of that.

1900

The American Bicycle Company, more widely known as the bicycle trust, crashed just two years after its founding, much to the dismay of its chief proponent, former Chicagoan A. G. Spalding. The group included two Chicago firms—the distinguished Gormully & Jeffrey and the mammoth Western Wheel Works—and three firms on the East Coast, to which Spalding had recently relocated in search of a way to cash in on the bicycle craze.

Q: What caused the American Bicycle Company's rapid demise?

A: Not only the precipitous drop in demand, but also independent-minded parts suppliers and retailers who refused to cave in to monopolists.

Q: Known earlier to Chicagoans as a player for and later owner of the Chicago Cubs, Spalding eventually got into other sports-related lines of work. What were they?

A: Publishing, with the American Sports Publishing Company now located in St. Louis, and the manufacture of other sporting goods, such as baseballs and catcher's mitts.

Q: Chicago had Booksellers Row on South Wabash and Printer's Row on South Dearborn, and later it would have Automobile Row on South Michigan. But at the turn of the century it had which sporting-related row and where?

A: Bicycle Row, which was located on Lake Street east of the Chicago River.

1902

The first National Scholastic Track-and-Field Meet sponsored by the University of Chicago was inaugurated in Hyde Park. The annual tournament was open to America's top prep athletes and was a headlining event for nearly three decades until the meet was dropped from the university's athletic program in 1933.

1903

The Chicago Women's Athletic Club was established with 700 genteel members whose interest in participatory sports carried over from school years to adulthood.

1912

Avery Brundage—bespectacled product of a broken home, Horatio Alger-like graduate of Crane Manual Training School, and star athlete at the University of Illinois—journeyed to Stockholm on borrowed money to compete in the fifth Olympic Games. He participated in the decathlon and pentathlon against Native American legend Jim Thorpe among others and returned home smitten by the Olympic ideal.

1913

After automobiles busted the bicycling balloon, several bike manufacturers went into the motorcycle business. Schwinn was among them, and as a promotional activity it developed a racing program. In this year a member of Schwinn's Excelsior racing team became the first to break the 100-mile barrier on a motocycle.

Q: A dozen years later, Schwinn would abruptly exit the motorcycle racing business. Why?

A: Motorcycles had become too fast to be safely raced—a record of 125 miles per hour was set in 1923. When a favored young engineer was killed in a race, Ignaz Schwinn disbanded the company's team.

1915

Having given up his job as an engineer with the firm of Holabird and Roche to participate in the Olympic Games, Avery Brundage began a construction firm, which built numerous apartment complexes for Chicago's growing middle class. The firm also built the shrewd Brundage a tidy fortune, which he reportedly managed to make while avoiding bribery and maintaining his integrity. In a city soon to be run by another star athlete, the corrupt mayor "Big Bill" Thompson, Brundage's righteousness won him the nickname "Honest Ave."

1915

Chicago s first six-day bicycle race was judged to be a rousing success. The event returned a tidy $5,000-$6,000 profit to the promoters who leased the Chicago Coliseum on Wabash Avenue in late November to accommodate the crush of fans and a dozen teams of riders who rode a grueling distance of 2,582 miles before a winner was declared. Lawrence Henley tore across the finish line as Chicago's champion of this peculiar new sport—the rage of Paris, France, during the World War I era.

Henley collected a $1,000 cash prize. Second-place finisher Ryan Thomas was awarded $750 amid the cheering of 10,000 fans who filled the Coliseum to witness the conclusion of the punishing 144-hour marathon sanctioned by the National Cycling Association. At one point, city officials threatened to clear the building because of safety concerns.

Q: What famous local sports entrepreneur, who later built the Chicago Stadium, brought the six-day races to Chicago?
A: Paddy Harmon.

1928

Brundage became president of the Amateur Athletic Union, one of several organizations—including the NCAA—that had been competing to supervise U.S. participation in the Olympic Games. Later that year, he took over the American Olympic Association as well, succeeding future general Douglas MacArthur.

Q: Though not himself a Chicagoan, MacArthur had several cousins whose nonathletic careers were associated with the Windy City. Name some of them.
A: Writer Charles MacArthur *(The Front Page)* and John MacArthur, the insurance man whose fortune endowed the Foundation of the same name. Both established their careers in Chicago.

1928

The Armour Tech Relay Games, an annual track-and-field event that attracted upward of 400 competing athletes from 33 midwestern campuses during its heyday in the 1930s, got going in the spring of 1928. Team trophies were awarded in the college division to the athletes scoring the greatest number of points. The best high school relay teams in Chicago also competed for top prizes.

Q: Where were the Armour Relays staged?
A: The University of Chicago Field House.

Q: By what name is Armour Tech known today?
A: The Illinois Institute of Technology.

1929

The brand-new Chicago Stadium first made a name for itself not as a basketball court or hockey rink but as an arena for the phenomenon of the time—the six-day bicycle race.

Q: How did these races operate, and what was their appeal?
A: Six-day races had begun in Paris during the bicycling mania of the 1890s when single riders pedaled continuously around an indoor track to the cheers and frequent betting of raucous crowds. These brutal endurance tests were soon outlawed and replaced in 1915 by team races, in which two or more cyclists competed with other teams in races that began on Mondays and ended Saturdays. Participants were allowed to slow down on the steeply

banked tracks only at nighttime when the revenue-generating crowds had gone home.

Q: A Belgium-born custom bicycle maker on Chicago's West Side was essential to the success of these marathon bike racers. Who was he and why?

A: Emil Wastyn, who became known as one of the nation's greatest bike mechanics, built racers for national six-day stars like Jimmy Walthour and Al Crossely.

1929

Carl Stockholm of suburban River Forest, Illinois, was the most famous six-day bicycle rider of the 1920s. Shot through the kneecap in World War I by an off-duty soldier who was clowning with a loaded gun, Stockholm fought his way back to athletic excellence by riding a stationary bike at the local YMCA. He competed in the 1920 Olympics before returning to civilian life. He was intent upon becoming an architect—or so he thought.

Carl was studying architecture at Armour Institute when he was paid $900 to compete in a six-day bicycle race—a sports fad that in its heyday filled the Chicago Stadium and other arenas across the U.S. to capacity. "Oh hell, I won't be a good architect anyhow," he reasoned.

Within a few years the writers dubbed him the Babe Ruth of bicycling. Women sent him mash notes. Sometimes they even threw their silk underwear at him as he exited the arena. The price he paid for fame was two broken hands, a smashed collarbone, and numerous fractures—the results of 17 falls.

The popularity of the six-day race faded during the Depression. "They tried to revive it after the war but the followers had gone," Stockholm recalled.

Q: Why was the Chicago Stadium ideally suited for six-day bicycle racing?

A: It is a little-known fact that the elongated curve of the building was especially designed for the six-day bike racers. New York's Madison Square Garden was also built with the racers in mind—not the hockey team or the fledgling basketball leagues just coming to the fore.

Q: What happened to Stockholm when his racing days ended?
A: He served as a naval commander during World War II, then owned a chain of dry-cleaning stores around Chicago.

"I was earning more than the president of a lot of small banks. I know because I've been on the board of a lot of banks. After one race I asked for my winnings in cash. Then I went over to 12th and Michigan—that was automobile row back then—and bought a Stutz Bearcat for $1,600."

CARL STOCKHOLM, 1980

1930

The U.S.-British Empire track-and-field competition was held in Chicago. Businessman Avery Brundage played the part of organizer rather than competitor—a role he would reprise for the rest of his life.

1932

Babe Didrikson, who would later win international fame as a leading golfer, participated in the Amateur Athletic Union's national championships held in Chicago. She entered as a one-woman team sponsored by the Chicago-based Employee's Casualty Company—and brought herself instant national fame. She entered eight of the meet's 10 events and established several records, among them the U.S. record shot put throw (39', 6.25"), a world's record baseball throw (272', 2"), and the meet's record broad jump (17', 6"). And she did it all in a single afternoon.

"Ah'm gonna lick you single handed."

"THE BABE" DIDRIKSON,
ON ENTERING THE AFTERNOON'S CONTESTS

1933

The final National Scholastic Track-and-Field Meet hosted by the University of Chicago on June 17 showcased the talents of

Jesse Owens—an up-and-coming prep track star from Cleveland East Technical High School.

Owens set three inter-scholastic records for the 100- and 220-yard dashes and the long jump. The high school senior, whose days of Olympic glory were yet to come, ran the 100-yard dash in 9.4 seconds, leading his Cleveland team to the national championship.

1934

The Schwinn company's turn-of-the-century concentration on bicycle frames proved a sound business decision when streamlined design reinvogorated the bicycle trade. That year, the company introduced the Aerocycle Streamliner, a bike that projected a kinship with aeroplanes and motorcycles—both of which had great appeal to boys too young to pilot either.

Q: Sears, Roebuck & Company, the ubiquitous mail-order merchant, had not only a quarter of the youth bicycle market but in pursuit of that had introduced what habit to a generation of American consumers?

A: Sears bicycles, which cost around $40 each, could be purchased on an installment plan of $5 down and $5 per month—reasonable earnings from a newspaper route.

1935

The Mead Cycle Company, another Chicago firm, rode in with its Mead Ranger done in earth tones of brown and sandy beige. The color scheme was intended to further associate the bike with its cowboy name.

Q: Bicycle manufacturers were not the only companies trying to sell one product through its association with another. What Schwinn product was the ultimate mock motorcycle?

A: Though its battery pack powered only its lights and the primitive coaster brake was enough to slow it down, Schwinn's Motorbike could help any 10-year-old boy stop traffic.

1936

Despite a major international controversy about the appropriateness of holding the Olympics in Nazi Germany, the great proponent of amateur athletics Avery Brundage prevailed in his belief that the games should be above politics. His either naive or self-deceptive belief in Nazi assurances that Jews were not excluded from German teams left him open to charges of anti-semitism for the rest of his life.

Q: Ironically, it was a non-Aryan and Chicagoan who was the most celebrated star of the 1936 Olympics. Who was he?
A: Jesse Owens, the great African-American track star who set a world record of 103 seconds for the 100-meter race and an Olympic record of 20.7 seconds for the 200-meter race. Then he jumped a then astonishingly high 8.06 meters in the high jump, but didn't win a medal.

Q: After his 1936 Olympic performance Owens, dubbed "the world's fastest human," pulled a famous publicity stunt. What was it?
A: Owens boasted he could beat a good racehorse and he proceeded to do so in 100-yard sprints. Owens admitted later that the races were a sham and that the animals were given no chance of winning. High-strung thoroughbreds, as opposed to run-of-the-mill plugs, were always chosen. Starters would always hold the pistol close to the horse's head, so when the gun was fired, the horse would rear up in terror, giving Owens a head start so large no horse could never catch up.

Q: A fellow Chicagoan participated with Owens in the record-setting 400-meter relay team and later became a Chicago politician. Who was this man?
A: Ralph Metcalfe, who shared a gold medal with Owens for the 400-meter relay, was elected a Chicago alderman in 1955, the same year Richard J. Daley became mayor. Later Metcalfe served in Congress, but without Daley's support.

"First you must dream. It all began with the dream."
JESSE OWENS

1938

Frank Schwinn, who had inherited the company his father had started, decided to develop an adult bicycle market, and to do that he teamed with custom bike mechanic Emil Wastyn.

Q: What was the first model their collaboration produced?
A: The Paramount, a sleek, lightweight model resembling the European models that would soon enter the American market.

"It was probably the most important American bicycle that did not turn a cent in profit."
JAY PRIDMORE, IN *THE AMERICAN BICYCLE,* 1995

1941

On May 17 a specially designed version of Schwinn and Wastyn's Paramount set an astonishing speed record—108.92 miles per hour. To achieve this record, set on a long, straight stretch of pavement in California, the two had hired a daring six-day star named Alfred Letourner and a midget-car racer named Ronney Householder, who drove in front of the bike to break the wind resistence.

1943

Schwinn, like other bicycle manufacturers, went into war production, making mainly airplane frames. One project, later abandoned, was a folding bicycle, which its promoters believed could be strapped to parachutes to provide instant transportation upon landing.

1946

With the war over, Schwinn's dream of adults taking up bicycling was realized in part though the popularity of bicycle touring clubs—groups of young men and women who would load their bikes onto cycle trains and head out into the country for a day of touring.

Q: Two developments hampered this dream. What were they?
A: One was the automobile, which was competing with bikes not only for room on the roads but for popularity with riders; the other was the three-speed Enligh import, which adults chose to ride rather than Schwinn's versions.

1947

The Wilson Sporting Goods Company signed Babe Didrikson Zaharias to a lifetime promotional contract worth $8,000 yearly.

1953

Riding the range continued to be a best-selling theme for Chicago bike makers. When the Mead Cycle Company introduced the Juvenile Ranger, it joined the Gene Autry Westerner from Monarch Silver King, also in Chicago. Even girls' bicycles from Schwinn came with fringed handle grips.

1956

Chicago became one of the nation's first major cities to establish a network of bicycle paths.

1959

As the White Sox edged closer to their first American League pennant in 40 years, Mayor Richard J. Daley welcomed the third Pan-American Games to his fair city in the first week of September.

The Olympic-styled competition, held every four years between the nations of the Western hemisphere, was conceived by the Pan-American Sports Organization at a meeting of the Pan-American Congress in Buenos Aires in 1940, and the event competition was scheduled to begin in 1942. However, it wasn't until 1951 in Buenos Aires that the first Pan-Am Games were played. The onset of World War II delayed the start of the good-will games intended to unite the divergent cultures of the Americas in the arena of athletic competition.

In 1959 the United States captured team titles in men's volleyball, water polo, basketball, and men's and women's tennis. Althea Gibson won the women's singles in tennis. Other scheduled events that year included boxing, gymnastics, yachting, shooting, weightlifting, fencing, swimming, baseball, track and field, and equestrian riding.

Q: Where were the events held?

A: Soccer matches were played at Hansen Park; men's basketball at the DePaul Gym; water polo at the Portage Park Fieldhouse; volleyball at Proviso High School; equestrian events at the Oak Park Polo Club; and rowing—believe it or not!—in the murky Cal-Sag Channel.

Q: What future baseball Hall of Fame member who began his major league career in Chicago hit a home run for the United States team in a Pan-American Game played against Cuba at Comiskey Park?

A: Lou Brock, traded by the Cubs to St. Louis in 1964 for Ernie Broglio.

1965

Space travel rather than range riding became the styling trend for bicycles, and Sears Roebuck introduced the SpaceLiner, which at least looked supersonic.

1972

The Winnetka Distance Run became the first official marathon staged in the Chicago area.

1977

Five thousand runners paid a $5 entry fee to compete in the first Chicago Marathon, a scenic but grueling 26.2 kilometer run on Lake Shore Drive. Mayor Michael Bilandic, a runner himself, and his wife, Heather, made a symbolic run past the judge's stand before the first runners crossed the finish line.

"What kind of shoes should I buy?"

BONNIE SWEARINGEN, SOCIALITE AND POTENTIAL PARTICIPANT IN THE FIRST CHICAGO MARATHON

1980

An ultramarathon was held on Chicago's lakefront. The distances were 50 miles and 100 kilometers (62 miles). Twenty-one men and six women completed the longer run, many of them listening to tiny radios to alleviate boredom. The winning men's time was seven and a half hours. The first woman finisher completed the course in just over nine hours.

"Something different bothered me every five miles —my right knee, my left sole, my stomach. . . . I don't need this @#$.

KATHY BLOOM, WOMAN ULTRAMARATHONER

1982

The Chicago Marathon's first-place prizes for men and women were made equal. A benefactor donated $2,000 to the women's purse to even things up.

Q: Who was the benefactor?
A: Jane Byrne, mayor of Chicago at the time.

1983

The first Chicago Triathlon was held. Over 700 competitors dived into the choppy waters of Lake Michigan for the swimming portion of the event; they dried off while pedaling 25 miles along Lake Shore Drive, then ran nine and a half miles back to the starting point. One participant suffered a flat tire approaching the end of the bicycle course and ended up carrying his vehicle across the finish line.

1984

Runner's World magazine picked the Chicago Marathon as its race of the year. Through the years the race has drawn such luminaries as Frank Shorter, Jenny Spangler, and Joan Benoit

Samuelson. Celebrity runners have included Oprah Winfrey, Marty Obermann, Michael Bilandic, Carol Marin, Helmut Jahn, and Steve Baskerville.

1985

Chicago Marathon winner Steve Jones set a course record (2:07:13) but missed the world record by a split second, which cost him a $50,000 bonus. The 29-year-old Welshman had so outdistanced the rest of the pack that he slowed down at the end. After glancing at the clock, he picked up the pace but didn't have enough kick left to smash the mark.

Q: Does Jones's Chicago record still stand?
A: Yes, and in the same race, Joan Benoit Samuelson set a woman's record (2:21:21), which also hasn't been eclipsed.

"I'm not disappointed. I came to win the race and I did."
STEVE JONES

1986

A disqualification allowed "The Terminator" Scott Molina to win his third straight Chicago Triathlon. During the bicycle portion of the race, overall leader Mark Allen was warned about "drafting" and later disqualified. Allen revenged the loss with a triumph in the 1990 Sun-Times Triathlon.

Q: What is drafting?
A: Being so close to another rider that one is sucked along in that person's wake. It is the same as positioning a subcompact car behind a large truck on the highway—the truck pulls along the car.

"If I knew I was disqualified, I wouldn't have pushed so hard. I would have saved myself for another race."
MARK ALLEN

1991

The village of Downer's Grove hosted the U.S. Professional Criterion Championship Race. Eighty of the top racers in the country competed in the 64-lap event on an enclosed one-mile course through the streets of the village. The race became an annual affair attracting crowds of over 20,000 people.

1992

Australian Brad Beven, who trained in a lake full of crocodiles, barely sidestepped a city creature, an automobile on Lake Shore Drive, to capture the 19th annual Chicago Triathlon. The driver, who ignored a barrier and entered a racing lane, almost hit Beven who, after swearing at the motorist, picked up the pace again.

Q: How did Beven respond to this assault?
A: He returned to Chicago in August and captured the Sun-Times Triathlon.

> *"The water I swim in has about five crocodiles in it, and they've been known to get after people. The only good thing about that is I guess it helps make me a pretty good swimmer."*
> Brad Beven

1993

The Chicago Marathon was run on an extremely frigid day. Temperatures in the 30s and a howling gale produced a wind-chill factor of minus 12 degrees. Over 200 runners were treated for hypothermia and other cold-related prolems. The first and third women finishers were accused of pacing and being shielded from the elements by other runners. The charges couldn't be substaniated and the results stood.

1996

Corporate sponsor La Salle Bank raised the Chicago Marathon purse to $275,000, making it the second-largest purse in the country. The 1996 winner, Paul Evans, won a total of $60,000 in first-place money and bonus money. The women's top finisher, Marian Sutton, won $35,000. Michelle Jones and Californian Mike Pigg took home the $5,000 first-place prize in the 14th annual Chicago Triathlon. For Jones it was her third straight triumph and fifth triathlon trophy overall.

Q: One couple received no prize money but countless adulations from the spectators and their fellow runners. Who were they and why?

A: Jamie Parks pushed his wife, Lynn, who had suffered a broken neck in an automobile accident, through the entire course in her wheelchair.

"God gives you one person, and once I knew she was the one, there was no way I was going to let her go. I know I sound like a Hallmark card or something, but I cherish every moment with her."

JAMIE PARKS

1996

Bicycle racing changed its course in the '90s, with a switch to BMX single-gear bikes raced on dirt courses with plenty of banked corners, bumps, and hills. At "The Hill" in Elgin, bikers bolt from an electronic starter's gate to challenge the roller-coaster course.

"For me, BMX racing is like a disease I can't get out of my system. I just love the thrill it gives you."

SCOTT CRAMER, 26-YEAR-OLD RACER

CHAPTER 5

Green Fairways and Blue Waters: Golf, Tennis, and Sailing on the Shores of Lake Michigan

During the Gay '90s—the decade just after Chicago's young swains and office clerks had taken up cycling with a passion and the city's fashionables were dressing up for their apperances at the Washington Park racetrack—attention shifted to a new diversion, one for which the Chicago area's broad open spaces, gentle hills, narrow creeks, and shallow ponds were well suited. Golf came to town, and by the century's turn, the city could boast of a dozen 18-hole courses, far exceeding that of any other city in the nation.

Young men with fortunes made in the meat-packing business, railroad executives whose private cars could wisk them away for an afternoon on the greens, and debutantes with adventuresome natures all took up the game. In rapid succession clubs such as Chicago, Onwentsia, Edgewater, Exmoor,

Evanston, Glen View, and Midlothian were established. And such a profusion of clubs led to a number of champion golfers as well—C. B. Macdonald, Chandler Egan, Bob Gardner, and Chick Evans among them. Soon the commuter rail lines were promoting the idea of suburban developments built around golf courses—hence Indian Hill in Winnetka, others in Flossmoor and Hinsdale, and by the time of the First World War, suburban Olympia Fields in the south.

This early vigor soon dissipated, and Chicago clubs, which had hosted several national championships in golf's first three decades, receded from the national spotlight. They continued to produce champion players and host tournaments, but did so only sporadically. Yet the Western Golf Association still has its headquarters in north suburban Golf, Illinois. Dubsdread, at Cog Hill in far southwest suburban Lemont, is regarded as one of the nation's most challenging courses; the metropolitan area wins kudos nationwide for the superiority of its courses open to the public; big financial deals are still made at the super-elite (and males only) Bob-o-Link on the North Shore.

Though for decades golf's enthusiasts have hardly been restricted to an elite in Chicago or elsewhere, the superlatives that Chicago courses and players can justly claim haven't hit the public's radar screen. Chicago is far more closely associated with the Bulls and the Bears than with the Western Open. And it's hardly at all associated with, either at home or abroad, another sporting superlative—the world's longest, continuously run freshwater sailing contest: the annual Mackinac Race from chicago to Mackinac Island near the Straits of Mackinaw. And though past champion Billie Jean King has been a part-time resident of the Windy City for a decade, world-class tennis can't lay claim to any greater portion of the city's self-image than golf and sailing.

Also not part of the city's self-image is the number of sporting goods and recreational equipment manufacturers located in Chicago. The city may not have produced any champion tennis stars, but Wilson Sporting Goods introduced the first steel racket in its suburban River Grove plant; Wilson and the Brunswick Company produced golf equipment, and two Chicago companies—Outboard Marine in Waukegan and a branch of Brunswick now in Lake Forest—still corner the market on recreational marine equipment.

1872

Young Charles Blair Macdonald, the arrogantly handsome offspring of a wealthy Chicago couple, was sent to St. Andrew's University in Scotland to finish his schooling. He concentrated instead on mastering the game of golf, which was introduced to him by his Scottish grandfather.

Q: How many years did he have to wait until a golf course was built in his native land?

A: Thirteen years; the course at Yonkers, New York, wasn't built until 1888.

1879

The new game of lawn tennis came to Chicago only a few years after a Welshman devised and patented it. It made its first appearance in Chicago at the opening of the New Union Club, where fully suited and bowler-hatted gentlemen could be seen lobbing balls over a five-foot-high fence.

1887

The popularity of lawn tennis, a genteel and patrician sport favored by the wealthy consorts of Chicago's distant suburban country clubs, soared during the elegant 1880s. On August 10 the Western Lawn Tennis Association sponsored a men's singles and men's doubles tournament on the grounds of the Kenwood Lawn Tennis Club. E. W. McClellan, representing the host club, and C. A. Chase won the singles tournament. McClellan and W. Waller of the North End Tennis Club claimed the doubles championship.

> *"For the past four years the game has become extremely popular at our fashionable summer resorts and there is scarcely a private residence with a lawn large enough to accommodate the game where the white tennis net is not stretched out, fastened*

at either end with the familiar poles and guy ropes. It's the proper thing; it is the only game that can be indulged in without the possibility of injury and is a favorite one with those who cannot excel in any game requiring physical strength."

THE GRAPHIC NEWS, JUNE 4, 1887.

1892

Macdonald's enthusiasm for golf finally found fellow adherents in Chicago, and C. B. persuaded his friend Hobart Chatfield-Taylor to persuade his father-in-law, Senator John B. Farwell (whose family had established Lake Forest), to devise a course there. Farwell went along with the notion in order to please British delegates attending the upcoming Columbian Exposition. Not to be outdone, some West Siders also heeded Macdonald's pleas and built their own short course in an area called Belmont, now part of Downer's Grove.

Q: The distaff side of the Farwell family figured prominently in the early annals of golf. How so?

A: In August 1896 Anna Farwell DeKoven wrote an article for *Cosmopolitan* magazine (to which her brother-in-law Chatfield-Taylor frequently contributed) titled "Golf and the New Woman." It was in part a story of the exploits of her sister, Rose Farwell Chatfield-Taylor, whose fondness for the game was likely instrumental in encouraging their father to let part of their estate be used as a golf course.

"What the bicycle has left undone toward the transformation of the life of American women, the game of golf bids fair to complete."

A. F. DEK

1893

The St. George Cricket Club, located at Belden Avenue and Lincoln Park, hosted the U.S. National Lawn Tennis Association doubles tournament on July 25. Through the efforts of several movers and shakers of Chicago's mercantile class, and civic leaders including Cyrus Hall McCormick and John A. Ryerson, the event turned out to be a major success, proving that the sport of tennis was not exclusive limited to eastern high society. Chicago high society, eternally self-conscious about its raw frontier image promulgated among East Coast social elites by the arbiters of Victorian fashion and good taste, appreciated a smashing good game of lawn tennis as much as the next country club sportsman.

1893

The Chicago Athletic Club built its first tennis court.

1894

Members of the Chicago Golf Club, established the year before at the behest of C. B. Macdonald, anted up a total of $28,000 to purchase 200 acres of farmland in Wheaton. There they built a course intended to compete with Great Britain's best; they succeeded, and the club opened the nation's first 18-hole course.

Q: Chicago is thought to have been home to the Midwest's finest public course, too. Where is it and when was it established?

A: It was the Jackson Park course, completed in 1899.

Q: Macdonald was also indirectly responsible for the founding of the Amateur Golf Association, the sport's first governing body. The AGA was later renamed the United States Golf Association. The circumstances were not particularly honorable and involved a widely heralded if somewhat lascivious New York architect. How so?

A: Macdonald, who regarded himself as the true national champion golfer, did not lose gracefully; one ungracious defeat at the Newport Golf Club in Rhode Island led to the staging of an invitational meet at St. Andrew's. The architect Stanford White had suggested champagne to cure Macdonald's hangover, and the thus-impeded Macdonald sliced a ball into a plowed field. His consternation led the five leading U.S. clubs (St. Andrew's, Newport, Chicago, Shinnecock Hills on Long Island, and Brookline in Boston) to establish the USGA.

1894

Golf's first governing body, the Amateur Golf Association of the United States, was founded with five charter members. The Chicago Golf Club in Wheaton, Illinois was the only one among the five founding members not located on the East Coast.

Q: Within a year the Amateur Golf Association was given a new name. What was it?

A: The United States Golf Association (USGA). Today the USGA oversees the rules of the game, and is responsible for developing the official handicap system, and for the testing of new equipment. The organization is headquartered in Far Hills, NJ.

1895

Macdonald won the first official U.S. Amateur Championship, held in October at the Newport Golf Club.

Q: That same year, Macdonald's friend Chatfield-Taylor, who had established a small course in Lake Forest, gathered several friends with names like McCormick, Palmer, Swift, Armour, and Cudahy to build a larger course nearby. What did this club become?

A: After much debate the founders settled on the name Onwentsia, an Iroquois word that reportedly describes a place where sporting young braves would meet with their wives for play.

1897

How to Play Golf, the first book of instruction on the increasingly popular new game to be published in the United States, was written by H. J. Wingham, a reporter for the *Chicago Tribune.* It is reported to have included the first picture ever published of a player in action.

1897

The Chicago Golf Club in Wheaton hosted its first U.S. Open. Joe Lloyd shot a 162, defeating future PGA Hall of Famer Willie Anderson. The 19-year-old Englishman led the tournament all the way through until the final hole when Lloyd snatched victory from the jaws of defeat. His 465-yard drive and eight-foot putt spelled Anderson's doom. It marked the first time that this prestigious tournament was played in the West.

Q: Can you name the years and locations of the U.S. Opens played in the Chicagoland area?
A: 1900—Chicago Golf Club, Wheaton; 1904—Glenview Club House; 1906—Onwentsia, Lake Forest; 1911-Chicago Golf Club; , 1914—Midlothian Golf Club; 1922—Skokie Country Club; 1928—Olympia Fields Country Club; 1933—North Shore Golf Club; 1949—Medinah Country Club; 1975—Medinah Country Club; 1990—Medinah Country Club.

Q: Who were the winners in each of the tournament years?
A: 1900—Harry Vardon; 1904—Willie Anderson; 1906—Alex Smith; 1911—John McDermott; 1914—Walter Hagen; 1922—Gene Sarazen; 1928—Johnny Farrell & Bobby Jones; 1933—Johnny Goodman & Ralph Guldahl; 1949—Cary Middlecoff; 1975—Lou Graham & John Mahaffey; 1990—Hale Irwin.

1898

The Edgewater Golf Club, which would nurture the talent and aspirations of champion Charles "Chick" Evans first as a caddie, and then as the nation's leading amateur golfer, was established in an open field in the Rogers Park area.

Q: What was Evans paid for the first game he caddied?
A: According to his autobiography, it was 35 cents; he related that he carried the golf bag of a Miss Amy Jones, whose father was one of the club's founders.

Q: The Edgewater Golf Course has become blocks of apartment buildings, but Chicago still sports a club connected to Edgewater's most famous player. What is it?
A: The Evanston Golf Club on Dempster Street in Skokie for many years carried the nickname the "Chick Evans's course."

1899

The Western Golf Association, whose membership included most midwestern clubs, was established in Chicago.

Q: For many years it was headquartered in the north suburban town of Golf. How did that community get its name?
A: Albert J. Earling, president of the Chicago & North Western Railroad, and other railroad executives were members of the Glen View Golf Club, which had been established in 1897. A community soon grew up along the railroad siding where Earling and his golfing pals would be dropped off when they wanted to play. Eventually the railroad built a station there, and in 1926 the town of Golf was incorporated at that point. The surrounding community took the name of Glenview.

1900

C. B. Macdonald moved to New York, where he shortly established himself as the nation's leading golf course architect.

1901

Chicago publisher H. S. Stone & Company published the *Golfer's Rubaiyat* by Walcott Boynton, which was written in verse and illustrated with elaborate borders.

1901

Harry Vardon, the famous British golfer who popularized the overlapping grip, was the victor of the 1900 U.S. Open held in Chicago—three years before he turned professional. He shot a 313 in four rounds.

Q: How many tournaments did this golfing superstar win during the course of his career?

A: Sixty-two, including six British Open titles between 1896 and 1914.

> *"His coming over here in 1900 really boosted golf in this country a great deal. When people saw how great he played, they became very excited about the sport."*
>
> HERBERT WARREN WIND, GOLF HISTORIAN, COMMENTING ON HARRY VARDON.

1902

Mrs. Johnnie Carpenter Hall became the first champion of the Western Women's Golf Association. Before marrying she'd played in eight women's open tourneys and won them all. Chick Evans was her caddie each time.

1902

It was one of the most stunning tournament upsets ever recorded in professional and amateur golf. A 19-year-old from the West Side of Chicago named Louis N. James won the U.S. Amateur Championship at the Glenview Clubhouse on July 19. James was a virtual unknown who came from nowhere to defeat Eben M. Byers and 60 of the best amateurs in the country in match play. A graduate of the Northwest Academy, James was the youngest player to win the Amateur Championship. Today, the U.S. Amateur is one of the richest stops on the PGA tour.

Q: The U.S. Amateur Championship is one of the crown jewels on the golfing circuit. In what other years was this tournament held in Chicago, and at what course?

A: 1897—Chicago Golf Club, Wheaton; 1899—Onwentsia, Lake Forest; 1905—Chicago Golf Club; 1909—Chicago Golf Club; 1912—Chicago Golf Club; 1923—Flossmoor Golf Club; 1931—Beverly Country Club; 1939—North Shore Country Club; 1956—Knollwood Country Club, Lake Forest; 1983—North Shore Country Club, Glenview; 1997—Cog Hill.

Q: Who were the winners in each of the tournament years?
A: 1897—H.J.Whigham; 1899—H.M. Harriman; 1905—H. Chandler Egan; 1909—Robert A. Gardner; 1912—Jerome D.Travers; 1923—Max D. Marston; 1931—Francis Ouiment; 1939—Marvin H.Ward: 1956—E. Harvie Ward; 1983—Jay Sigel.

1904

The starting gun for the first annual sailing race from Chicago to Mackinac Island was fired on August 3, sending the 10 contenders off from a point called the Van Buren Street Gap. Any yacht that abandoned the race was required to telegraph the race committee at once.

Q: The race had first been run in 1898.What was the occasion?
A: Five members of the Chicago Yacht Club decided to turn their annual excursions up to summer homes on Georgian Bay near Mackinac Island into a race.The winning boat was the *Vanenna,* which finished in 51 hours.

Q: Who was the winner in 1904?
A: The *Vanenna* placed second (by five minutes) to the *Vencedor,* which made the race in 37 hours and 46 minutes.

Q: Beginning that year, the "Mac" had a distinction that it still maintains today.What is it?
A: Then, as now, it was the longest freshwater cruising race in the world. It also continues to be one of the safest; no lives and only one boat have ever been lost in the race in its near-100-year history.

1904

Willie Anderson captured his third U.S. Open title at the Glenview Golf Club, finishing five strokes ahead of runner-up Gilbert Nicholls.The following year at the Hunt Club in South Hamilton, Massachusetts, he became the first golfer to win four U.S. Opens.

1905

H. Chandler Egan, Chicago's most famous turn-of-the-century golfer, took his second national amateur championship at his home course, the Chicago Golf Club in Wheaton.

Q: Four years later Egan would lose his title to another Chicagoan. Who was he?

A: Robert A. Gardner, a Yale student whose home club was Onwentsia. At 19 he was the nation's youngest amateur champion.

"Golf and outdoor life in the automobile have made me many years younger than I might otherwise have been."

JOHN D. ROCKEFELLER, OIL TYCOON, ON A VISIT TO THE CHICAGO GOLF CLUB

This was also a big year for golf on Chicago's public courses, and the *Chicago Evening Post* sponsored the first city championship matches in Jackson Park. It was 15-year-old Chick Evans's first formal competition and, he recalled later, "marked the beginning of greater things."

1906

Golf's power to sell suburbia—and commuter tickets thereto—was amply demonstrated with a profusely illustrated volume published by the Illinois Central Railroad. Clubs and residents along the line were pictured in elegant attire.

1908

William Hale Thompson, a dashing young Chicago sportsman and heir to his family's fortune, had already made a name for himself as captain of the Chicago Athletic Association's national amateur champion football team when he took up sailing. From 1908 to 1910 he captained his schooner *Valmore* to three consecutive Mackinac victories.

Q: Thompson is more widely known for his political, not athletic, victories. What were they?

A: Running as a Republican, he was elected mayor of Chicago three times—in 1915, 1919, and 1927. Known as "Big Bill," he is more commonly recalled as one of the most easily corrupted mayors in the city's history.

"It makes a better man of you in every way, more able to contest the other trials of skill and resourcefulness of your life, . . . strength, self-reliance, courage, cool-headedness, preparedness and skill are the real trophies after all, and these are worth striving for and worth attaining."

CHARLES H. BURRAS, *VALMORE* CREW MEMBER, ON HIS REASONS FOR RACING IN THE MAC

1909

Ole Evinrude, a Norwegian immigrant, developed the outboard engine in Waukegan. He incorporated as the Outboard Marine Company, manufacturer not only of the Evinrude engine loved by fishermen and skiers alike, but of the Johnson Sea Horse as well. With Wilson Sporting Goods and the Brunswick Corporation, the company helped establish Chicago as the nation's leading manufacturer of recreational sports equipment.

Q: The year 1909 was also a big year for golf in Chicago. *New Yorker* sportswriter Herbert Warren Wind described it as the "high-water mark of Chicago golf," contending that during the first decade of the 19th century, the area produced the best players in the country. Who were they?

A: According to Wind, of eight quarter finalists in the 1909 U.S. Open, seven were Chicagoans. They were: Chandler Egan, Chick Evans, Bob Gardner, Paul Hunter, Mason Phelps, Ned Sawyer, and Albert Seckel.

Q: That year, Chandler Egan lost the U.S. Amateur Championship to Bob Gardner. What happened in the Western Open that year?

A: The Homewood Country Club in Flossmoor sponsored the tournament, and 19-year-old Chick Evans won it.

1909

Walter T. Hayes, gainfully employed by day as an assistant general traffic manager for Sears, Roebuck and Company, began a nearly invincible 14-year run as Chicago's premier amateur tennis player. Hayes, all but forgotten today, was an inconspicuous-appearing man with a thin face and wire-rimmed spectacles who captured 14 Chicago City Championships in singles and doubles play. He won the Illinois State Championship in singles and doubles 15 times, in addition to National Clay Court singles titles in 1911 and again in 1921. Hayes belonged to several fashionable private tennis clubs, including Kenwood, Homewood, and the South Side Club, where he played against the top amateurs of the day.

> *"Mr. Hayes plays tennis just like he handles his business. There is method in every shot and move he makes. Very few players have exhibited any greater skill in the mechanics and psychology of the game and none that we know of have remained so good for so many years as this hardy son of the Middle West."*
>
> *Chicago Golfer and Country Club Review*, May 1930

1910

Vida Llewellyn, a member of the LaGrange Country Club, won the Women's Western Golf Association Tournament for the second straight year, defeating Mrs. Thurston Harris 125-118, at the Homewood Country Club.

Q: Did Ms. Llewellyn ever win the U.S. Women's Amateur Championship?
A: No.

> *"These two are fairly entitled to golfing honors of the year, and, all things considered, are the strongest players in the West, at the present time regardless of the fact that in computing the totals for the record prize, regular attendance may give a player more points than those obtained by a player of superior skill whose appearance in tournaments is infrequent."*
>
> Joseph G. Davis, *Chicago Tribune* golf writer, October 30, 1910

1911

The 100-foot schooner *Amorita* sailed the 333-mile course up to Mackinac Island in 31 hours and 14 minutes, a record that wasn't broken until 1987.

Q: Despite establishing this record, the *Amorita* only placed second in the race. How could this be?

A: It won in elapsed time, but because of a complicated handicapping system, another boat was technically the winner.

Q: Another record, fortunately still unbroken, was established in that year's race. What was it?

A: The swift winds that whisked the *Amorita* up the lake also shoved *Vencedor* onto Fisherman's Reef near Charlevoix, Michigan. Though the boat was broken up by the storm, no lives were lost. *Vencedor* is the only boat to have ever been lost in the Mac.

1911

John McDermott of Atlantic City became the first American golfer to win the U.S. Open after defeating Michael J. Brady and George Simpson in a playoff. The teenager's stellar performance at the Chicago Golf Club in 1911 was a prelude of things to come. He defended his title a year later in Buffalo.

1914

Stricken with a case of food poisoning, Walter Hagen shot a course-record 68 at the Midlothian Country Club to defeat Chick Evans by one stroke (290) and win the U.S. Open.

Q: At first Hagen did not want to play in this tournament. What circumstances nearly held him back?

A: He did not want to travel to the Chicagoland area from Rochester, New York. He finally agreed to participate in the Open, but only after Ernest Willard, the sports editor of the Rochester *Democrat* agreed to underwrite his travel expenses.

1914

Chicago hosted a first-round match of the Davis Cup pitting Australia against Canada. The Australian team included Norman Brookes and Anthony Wilding, who had won two prior cups in 1908-1909. The robust, gregarious Wilding loved gadding about the countryside on a motorbike with a silk scarf draped around his neck. He was the sport's first heartthrob. Brookes was nicknamed the "Wizard" because of his canny play and unassuming manner. Together they defeated the Canadians in both singles and doubles at the Onwentsia Country Club in Lake Forest. War in Europe broke out a few days later, but the Australians continued east to New York, where they edged the Americans in the challenge round.

Q: The story ends in tragedy. What happened next?
A: Ten months later Captain Anthony Wilding was killed by a mortar shell at the battle of Neuve Chapelle.

"I want to tell you that I consider the Onwentsia courts simply splendid; fully as good as any I have ever played on. Chicago, too, judged by what I have seen of it, is one of the finest cities in the world—but I do hope it cools off a bit for the first matches."

ANTHONY WILDING

1915

Beautiful Olympia Fields Country Club, spread across 700 rolling acres and featuring a 72-hole golf course, was founded. Olympia's par 70, 6,490-yard North tournament course was designed in 1922 by Willie Park Jr., winner of the 1887 and 1889 British Open. In its heyday the spacious grounds accommodated a membership roster that swelled to 1,064. The 200,000-square foot Tudor-style clubhouse—the largest in the nation up to that time—was built in 1923 at a cost of $1.3 million dollars. In the 1940s, however, the size of the country club was cut in half. The vacated land was turned over to real estate developers.

Q: What famous college football coach served as the first president of the country club?
A: Amos Alonzo Stagg of the University of Chicago.

Q: What major tournaments were hosted by Olympia Fields over the years?
A: Beginning in 1920 and continuing through 1971, the club hosted five Western Opens, two PGA Championships, and the 1928 U.S. Open. In addition, the Women's Western Open and various amateur and national collegiate championships were held there. Because many of the dues-paying members objected to the presence of spectators trampling over their green fairways and lush lawns, club management discouraged the major associations from bringing the pro tournaments to Olympia Fields.

"Modern ideas meeting physical needs in a pleasurable way."
AMOS ALONZO STAGG, DESCRIBING THE BEAUTY OF OLYMPIA FIELDS

1916

Chick Evans won both the U.S. Open and Amateur championships, establishing himself as the preeminent young American golfer.

1917

Under the leadership of President C. F. Thompson, the Western Golf Association began sponsoring a series of Red Cross matches to aid the war effort. During its first year subscriptions reached $20,000, a record for Red Cross tournaments across the country.

1920

The Flossmoor Country Club hosted the Professional Golfers Association (PGA) Tour, marking the first time this important event was staged in the Midwest. Jack Hutchison, an American golfer who was born in Scotland, defeated J. Douglas Edgar to claim his third PGA title.

Q: Did the PGA Tour ever return to Chicago?

A: Two more times. In 1925 Walter Hagen, the first American golfer to win the British Open, defeated William Mehlhorn 6 and 5 at Olympia Fields in the final. It was Hagen's third of five PGA titles and the second in a run of four straight. Then at Olympia Fields in 1961 Jerry Barber sunk a 20-foot putt for birdie on 16, a 40-footer for par on 17, and a 60-footer on the treacherous 18th hole for a birdie on 18 to force a playoff with Don January. The following day he defeated January to become the tournament's oldest champion.

1921

Japan and India, two surprise entrants in the 1921 Davis Cup, met in a third-round match at the Onwentsia Club in Lake Forest. Led by its two star players, Zenzo Shimizu and Ichiya Kumagae, Japan, a burgeoning tennis power, advanced to Chicago by two defaults. The games drew near-capacity crowds. Many of Chicago's shining lights of high society returned to the sweltering city from their vacation homes to witness the event. The crowd was generally nonpartisan and politely applauded the efforts of both teams. Japan emerged the victor but eventually dropped the challenge round to the Americans.

> *"Of course the main attraction at the tennis matches at Onwentsia was the playing of Mr. Kumagae, Mr. Shimizu, Mr. Sleem, and Mr. Fyzee, but running a close second was the smart attire of the feminine portion of the gallery."*
>
> CHICAGO TRIBUNE, AUGUST 19, 1921

1922

The U.S. Open shifted to the Skokie Country Club where Walter Hagen, the winner of two previous U.S. Opens, was upset by a 20-year-old unknown named Gene Sarazen.

1923

Australia avenged its stunning 1921 loss to Japan with a decisive 4-1 win in the final round of the American Zone match at the

Chicago South Side Tennis Club. Bill Tilden, the "Babe Ruth" of tennis and a member of the American Davis Cup team, lost an exhibition match to Zenzo Shimizu of Japan on the final day of play. The crowd sensed Tilden wasn't giving it his best, which was often the case when he was bored.

Q: How bored was he?

A: Bill Tilden regained his composure and helped his mates sink the Aussies in the challenge round. In 1928 Tilden returned to the Windy City, where his team again defeated Japan at the Chicago Town and Tennis Club during the finals of the American Zone clashes.

1926

Chicago Tribune golf writer Joseph Davis joined with his desk-mate Irving Vaughn (who covered big league baseball), and Herb and Joe Graffis who reported the nine-hole game for a rival newspaper, to launch a new publication—*Chicago Golfer.*

1926

Though Chicago clubs and players appeared early in the annals of American golfing, the same was not true of tennis's early years. The city's name simply doesn't appear in standard histories of tennis—that is, until Charles C. (or "Cash and Carry") Pyle, flush from turning Red Grange into the nation's richest football player, discovered tennis. Pyle offered top player Suzanne Lengle $50,000 to go on tour. She did, and it was an immense success. Professional tennis was born.

1928

The golfing public had come out to watch the great Bobby Jones perform his magic at the 1928 U.S. Open at Olympia Fields. But it was a little-known club pro named Johnny Farrell who stole the show. After a grueling 72 holes Jones and Farrell were tied at 294. Farrell went on to claim the first playoff round and 36-hole playoff to best Bobby by one shot.

1928

The Chicago Golf Club played host to the Walker Cup match, an annual event between the United States and Britain's leading golfers. The U.S. team, lead by Bobby Jones, "smothered their friends from across the ocean," according to a writer for a Chicago society rag. The U.S. won 11 matches and Great Britain only one.

1929

Nat Rasasco established the Northwestern Golf Company, which shortly built itself into the world's largest exclusive manufacturer of golf clubs.

1929

The first Stop and Sock public driving range and practice ground opened for Chicago golfers.

1929-1930

As the horrors of the Great Depression unfolded in America, the first of 40 miniature golf courses were opened in Chicago over the winter by Metropolitan Golf Courses.

Len Waldron, a former assistant to Walter Hagen, was hired to provide golf instruction to the public at various public courses across Chicago, including locations at Belmont and Sheridan Road, Wilson and Clarendon, 66th and Stony Island Avenue on the South Side, Lake Shore Drive and Sheridan Road, and Howard and Malvern near the Evanston-Chicago city limits.

In the 1920s the exploits of Bobby Jones, Francis Ouimet, and other touring pros excited the nation and temporarily established the sport of golf in the public eye. The onset of the depression set back the timetables, but miniature golf, originally intended to sharpen the putting skills of the serious country club player, became a universal pastime to be enjoyed by people of all ages. The sites originally conceived and developed by Metropolitan are long gone—many of them were replaced by high-rise apartments and gas stations or were simply plowed under or landscaped by the Chicago Park District.

Q: What was the original name of the 40 original miniature golf courses in Chicago?
A: The Tom Thumb Golf Course.

Q: Was the putting surface natural or artificial grass?
A: Neither. The Tom Thumb courses were landscaped with cottonseed hulls.

1930

Two students enrolled at Northwestern University as the first Evans Scholars through a program for caddies established by Chick Evans—who had attended Northwestern—and his mother.

Q: For Mrs. Evans, this scholarship recognized the chief interests of both her son, who had discovered his talents as a golfer through his early experiences as a caddie, and her husband. What was his line of work?
A: Charles Evans Sr. was librarian at the Newberry Library.

1931

Though white tennis players in Chicago were not attracting much national attention, the city managed to attract the country's leading black woman player, Ora Washington. She won eight American Tennis Association crowns between 1929 and 1937.

> *"Washington . . . again holds her position as National Champion, having gone through the season without a defeat. . . . Her superiority is so evident that her competitors are frequently beaten before the first ball crosses the net."*
>
> CHICAGO DEFENDER, MARCH 14, 1931

Q: At the turn of the century a black woman began teaching tennis in Chicago. Who was she?
A: According to Arthur Ashe's history of blacks in American sports, a woman named Mrs. C. O. "Mother" Seames had already established legendary status teaching on a single court located on Chicago's South Side.

1932

The Medinah Country Club, located west of the city and somewhat north of the Chicago club in Wheaton, opened its third course, which had originally been intended for women. Once its exceptional possibilities were noted, however, it became the club's championship course, which hosted the Western Open in 1939 and the U.S. Open in 1949.

Q: The Shriners, who had established the Medinah club, were also responsible for a swimming pool that played host to a champion. Who was he?

A: The Medinah Athletic Club, which was built in 1929 is now the Hotel Inter-Continental on Michigan Avenue, includes a large and lovely Moorish-inspired pool in which Olympic champion (and later the Tarzan of the movies) Johnny Weissmuller worked out.

1933

After nearly four decades as one of the nation's leading courses, the Chicago Golf Club had its first major overhaul.

1933

While MacDonald Smith glided effortlessly to the Western Open championship at Olympia Fields, Chicago police were busy arresting a scratch golfer named Vincent Gebhardi—alias "Machine Gun Jack McGurn"—Al Capone's feared trigger man and mastermind of the 1929 St. Valentine's Day Massacre.

Q: What golfer has won the most Western Opens?

A: Walter Hagen at five (1916, 1921, 1926, 1927, 1932). Ralph Guldahl, Willie Anderson, and Billy Casper won four apiece.

1941

The A. G. Spalding Company, established by Chicago baseball pioneer Albert Goodwill Spalding, published *Rules of the Game of Golf* in conjunction with the USGA.

1946

The Island Goats Sailing Society was established to honor those men who had raced in 25 or more Mackinacs.

> *"Some of the contestants were accused of looking and smelling like goats after three or four days at sea, and someone pointed out that goats often lived on islands."*
>
> AN ISLAND GOAT ON THE REASONS FOR THE SOCIETY'S NAME

1948

Illinois was considered to rank second in the number of golf courses nationwide; 181 of the state's courses were located in the Chicago metropolitan area.

Q: What national open tournaments were held annually in Chicago at the time?

A: The Chicago Victory National Open, which raised money to build and maintain courses at veterans' hospitals, and the Tam O'Shanter Open. Together they attracted 125,000 visitors to the city each year.

1949

The USGA's 49th annual open championship was held at the Medinah Country Club from June 9 to 11.

1952

The Women's Western Golf Association's 23rd open championship was held at the Skokie Country Club from June 16 to 21.

1954

Chicago-based *Popular Mechanics* magazine published a guide to 1,870 North American golf courses, written by Harold M. Pond.

1955

On July 28 a dinner was held at Northwestern University to celebrate the silver anniversary of the Evans Scholars Foundation, which had grown since its establishment by Chick Evans to become the world's largest scholarship program supported by private contributions.

Q: In 1950 when the program began, it gave two caddies scholarships to Northwestern. By 1940 that number had grown to 20. How many students did it sponsor in 1955?

A: By its 25th anniversary it was awarding scholarships to over 200 students annually; 20 years later, it was recognized as having helped over 3,800 former caddies through college, over half of them through Northwestern.

1955

The Chicago Saddle and Cycle Club hosted a Davis Cup match between the dominant Australian team led by Lew Hoad and Ken Rosewall, who won their opening-round match against Mexico. Mayor Richard J. Daley personally greeted team members at City Hall.

The night before the matches, the Saddle and Cycle Club hosted a lavish black-tie affair. After feasting on a scrumptious platter of Lobster Newburg, team members and guests were entertained by a male chorus who spiced up the old standards with snappy tennis lyrics.

"T is for the time we spend in practice. . . . Put them all together they spell tennis."

PARODY OF THE OLD STANDARD "MOTHER,"
PERFORMED BY THE DAVIS CUP MERRYMAKERS

1957

The H. D. Wilson Company moved its headquarters from 2037 North Campbell to suburban River Grove and became the Wilson Sporting Goods Company.

1963

Charismatic Arnold Palmer, a golfer since the age of three who made his professional debut in 1954, won his only title in Chicago nine years later, capturing the Western Open at the

Beverly County Club. Palmer became the first golfer to win the fabled Master's championship at Augusta, Georgia, on four occasions. Arnie was the most colorful and famous player in the golfing world during the postwar period, and in recognition of his talent and universal popularity he was named Athlete of the Decade in the 1960s by the Associated Press. Oddly enough, he didn't have much luck playing Chicago's fairways and greens.

Q: What happened to Palmer when he returned to Chicago for the 1968 Western Open at Olympia Fields?
A: He finished in a tie for fortieth place. Jack Nicklaus won the 1968 tourney.

Q: Who were the "Big Three" of golf who put the sport back on the map in the 1950s and 1960s?
A: Arnold Palmer, Gary Player, and Jack Nicklaus.

Q: Who do the experts rate as the greatest golfer of all time?
A: Jack Nicklaus. During his peak years (1962-1978) he won one of every five events he entered. Over his career Nicklaus captured six Masters Tournaments, four U.S. Opens, five PGA Championships, and three British Opens. Ironically it was Bobby Jones, the greatest golfer of the first half century, who founded the Master's Tournament in which Nicklaus excelled for so many years.

"He plays a game [with] which I'm not familiar."
BOBBY JONES ON JACK NICKLAUS

1967

The Wilson Company introduced the first steel racket to the United States. It had been developed by a Frenchman named Rene Lacoste, who is more widely remembered for having given his name to a particular kind of shirt. Wilson rackets were priced at $50 to $60, more than twice that of good wooden rackets.

Q: What other Illinois company was an early manufacturer of steel rackets?

A: The Skilley Automotive Manufacturing Company of Elk Grove Village was also an early maker of metal rackets. The Spalding Sports Goods Company, founded by Chicago baseball's A. G. Spalding but not located in Chicago, produced an early aluminum racket.

1971

Olympia Fields hosted the Western Open—Chicago's crown jewel of golfing since 1899—for the final time. The event was shifted to Butler National, a newer facility located in west suburban Oakbrook, Illinois. Beginning in 1991 the Motorola Western Open was played at Cog Hill Golf and Country Club in southwest suburban Lemont.

Q: Who sponsors the Western Open?

A: The Western Golf Association.

Q: Who captured the 1971 Western Open?

A: Australian Bruce Crampton, who won a two-stroke victory—and $30,000 in prize money—over Jack Nicklaus on the 18th green.

Q: Would Olympia Fields ever again host a major tournament?

A: Another 26 years would pass. But in June of 1997 the U.S. Senior Open was held at Olympia Fields despite a backlash of protest from stodgy club members who fervently desired that the grounds be declared off-limits to the public for purely selfish reasons.

"When people ask me—Bruce, what's you favorite course? I always say, anyone where I can win."

BRUCE CRAMPTON

1971

Virginia Slims, a cigarette manufactured by Philip Morris, Inc., for women, agreed to underwrite the first major U.S. women's pro tennis tournament after Billie Jean King led a rebellion against the discriminatory practices of the sport's governing body. In those days it was nearly impossible for a female tennis pro to earn a living traveling the circuit. The women earned about one-tenth of what the men received in prize money. With the support of Gladys Heldman of *World Tennis* magazine and Joseph Cullman III of Phillip Morris, the Virginia Slims Tournament, with a stopover in Chicago, was launched.

Q: Who won the first Virginia Slims?
A: Rosemary Casals. She received $1,500 in prize money. A decade later the tour was worth almost $1,000,000. No event was scaled at less than $75,000, including the Chicago Slims event.

Q: Where were the Chicago Slims held, and who were some of the winners in the early years?
A: In 1973 Margaret Court defeated Billie Jean King at the Lakeshore Racquet Club. In later years the event was held in the musty International Amphitheater on Chicago's South Side. Martina Navratilova dominated the Slims, winning six consecutive titles from 1978-1983. She downed Evonne Goolagong, Tracy Austin, Chris Evert Lloyd, Hana Mandlikova, and Andrea Jaeger in short order. The 1983 Slims was the final sports event scheduled for the Amphitheater.

1974

World Team Tennis was established, and the Chicago Aces, owned by Jordan and Walter Kaiser, played at the Lake Shore Racquet Club.

1975

Chicago played host to the U.S. Open for the first time in 26 years. The championship games were held, as they had been in 1949, at the Medinah Country Club west of the city. In tennis, Evanston resident Marty Riessen's tennis star flamed brightly when he won the U.S. indoor match in Philadelphia.

Q: Ten years later, at the age of 40, Reissen was still playing on the grand tour. For that he acquired a nickname. What was it?

A: His youthful longevity led many to call him Peter Pan, a character with similar traits.

1977

Chicago made another of its periodic contributions to professional tennis: Photographer Jeanne Moutoussamy, the daughter of a Chicago architect, married tennis great Arthur Ashe.

1979

The first Nanny Goat—or woman—was inducted into the Island Goats Sailing Socety.

Q: When had women first participated in the Mackinac race?

A: In 1905, the race's second official run, a small sloop called the Lady Eileen, which had a two-woman crew, participated.

1983

Billie Jean King, the holder of a record 20 Wimbledon titles and 13 U.S. Open titles, established a residence in Chicago, the headquarters of the World Team Tennis, which she revived with her husband, Larry, in 1981.

The local entry in the reorganized WTT was nicknamed the Chicago Aces, then later the Chicago Fyre. With Ms. King leading the way, the team won the 1983 league championship, playing the shortest season of any professional sports league: just 25 days.

Q: Who originated the concept of team tennis?

A: In 1962 Billie Jean King (then known as Billie Jean Moffitt) and her future husband, Larry King, came up with the idea for a professional league while they were attending classes at Los Angeles State College. But it wasn't until 1974 that World Team Tennis was introduced to the public.

The Chicago Aces, originally owned by Jordan Kaiser, began play in April but the sport failed to stir fan interest or suitable media attention. There was another problem: Ticket prices ranged from $6 to $10—way too high for the average sports fan's budget in 1974. The league collapsed in 1978, two years after Billie Jean King's husband stepped down as president.

Q: Where did the 1983 Fyre play their matches?
A: The Mid-Town Tennis Club on the North Side. Box seat tickets cost $15. Court-side seats were sold for $8.

Q: Who is in charge of World Team Tennis today?
A: Ms. King serves as director of the eight-team league.

"Well, they don't seem to be paying much attention to us. They obviously are more interested in the refreshments."
DAVIS CUP STAR GRAHAM STILLWELL, OBSERVING THE CROWD ON THE OPENING NIGHT OF WORLD TEAM TENNIS AT THE LAKE SHORE RACQUET CLUB, MAY 7, 1974

"I would say I've had as much excitement out of playing Team Tennis as I've had from winning Wimbledon. If we can get enough people to see it, there's no way it will ever die."
BILLIE JEAN KING, JULY 1983

1985

Chicago sailing enthusiasts raised $12.5 million to launch Heart of America, an entry into the America's Cup competition. The effort, skippered by boat maker Buddy Melges of Zenda, Wisconsin, was several million short of what was needed for a successful entry.

1988

The Mid-Town Tennis Club inaugurated an annual sportsmanship award and named it after Billie Jean King. This was only one of King's connections to Chicago; she'd recently dubbed Mid-Town "the best facility in the country," and its manager Pat Freebody resigned that year to join the U.S. Team Tennis, for which King was a commissioner.

Also at Mid-Town, Chicagoan Katrina Adams—unseeded

but "having an impact," according to press reports—pushed Chris Evert to three sets in fourth-round singles at Wimbledon.

Q: Adams, teamed with Zina Garrisson, made a bid for two doubles finals at Wimbledom that year. This would have been a first. Why?

A: The pair would have been the first black doubles team to make it to the finals at Wimbledon. They lost in the semi-finals to a pair from the Soviet Union.

1988

The Medinah Country Club welcomed the U.S. Senior Open, the United States Golf Association's prestigious national championship for men age 50 and over, to Chicago. Gary Player, the well-traveled South African, shot a four-under-par 68 to defeat Bob Charles on August 8.

Q: Player is one of only four golfers to have won all four of the big-money, high-prestige tournaments: the Masters, the U.S. Open, the British Open, and the PGA Championship. Name the other three.

A: Jack Nicklaus, Gene Sarazen, and Ben Hogan.

> *"The average athlete in sports—in all sports—is 32. We've all been brainwashed to think that you're old when your 60. I'm 61 and I'm still winning."*
>
> GARY PLAYER, 1997

1988

Ameritech, a communications conglomerate, and the Western Golf Association announced the inception of the $500,000 Ameritech Senior Open, to be held in Chicago each year beginning in 1989.

1988

Joseph Jemsek, the ex-caddie who built a Chicago golfing empire catering to the man on the street, was honored by *Golf* magazine as one of the "100 Heroes of Golf" at a black-tie

Waldorf Astoria dinner on June 20. In the 1930s Jemsek caddied for the Cog Hill family owner of the South Suburban golf course bearing the family name. After the family refused him a raise in 1939 he secured loans, pooled his available resources, and purchased the St. Andrews Club in West Chicago. In 1951 he bought Cog Hill, adding his former employer to a growing list of golfing properties. By 1988 Jemsek owned five facilities and nine courses headed by Cog Hill's Dubsdread, the number four course and the site of many famous tournaments including the Motorola Western Open.

Q: Cog Hill is one of the most difficult courses around. Tiger Woods, playing as an amateur in the 1994 Western Open, shot a 74-75, missing the cut. He made the cut a year later but tied for 57th. What is considered to be the toughest hole on the course?

A: The 18th, averaging 4.296. The 452-yard par 4 is very long, and the green slopes downward to the pond.

"We tried to be the leader in making the public golf course just as good as the country club. We think we moved them all up in class."

JOE JEMSEK, 1988

1990

A record crowd of 45,000 poured into the Medinah Country Club on June 16, hoping to see Curtis Strange accomplish the near-impossible task of winning three consecutive U.S. Opens. Strange battled 45-year-old Hale Irwin and Mike Donald down to the wire, but in the end it was Irwin who prevailed in a sudden death playoff against Donald, claiming the winner's share of the $1.2 million purse. Hale Irwin was the oldest golfer to win the title, and the nine-day 1990 Open was the longest one on record.

1990-1991

Chicagoan Bill Pinkney became the first African-American to complete a solo sail around the globe. He began his journey on August 5, concluding the odyssey on June 9, 1991.

1995

The Rosemont Horizon hosted the third annual World Team Tennis All-Star Smash Hits to benefit AIDS research. Songwriter Elton John and Andre Agassi faced Billie Jean King and Martina Navratilova in a celebrity doubles match prior to the Philadelphia Freedoms (owned by Elton John) squaring off against Billie Jean King's Chicago Fyre. The celebrity event attracted 10,000 fans and netted Elton John's AIDS Foundation $10,000.

Q: What happened to the Chicago Fyre?
A: The original Fyre, long since disbanded, were reformed for this special event with Navratilova, Mark Woodforde, and Lindsay Davenport representing Chicago. The Freedoms, who songwriter John immortalized in his 1974 pop ballad "Philadelphia Freedom," defeated the Fyre 28-23 in five, one-set matches.

> *"It's Elton's idea—for his favorite cause, the fight against AIDS. He's loved tennis for years, and he wanted me to put together a match to raise money."*
>
> BILLIE JEAN KING

1997

OMC (Outboard Marine Corporation) and its rival Brunswick, located respectively in Waukegan and Lake Forest, retained their position as the largest players in the U.S. recreational marine industry.

Q: Which of these two companies is the oldest? Which sells the most outboards?
A: Brunswick is the oldest company, having been established in 1845 in Cincinnati, whereas OMC didn't get its start until 1909. Brunswick sold $2.3 billion worth of outboards in 1996; OMC, about $1.2 billion.

1997

On June 26 Olympia Fields hosted the 18th U.S. Senior Open, featuring 156 of the world's greatest over-50 golfers including

Arnold Palmer, Hale Irwin, Chi Chi Rodriguez, Lee Trevino, and 1996 defending champion David Stockton. The venerable cast of golfers competed for a top purse of $1.3 million with the champion receiving $232,500.

In preparation for this major tournament, the architecture firm of Cornish, Silva, and Mungeam renovated Olympia Fields' North course, reshaping the bunkers and restoring all 18 putting surfaces to what Willie Park Jr. created back in 1922.

Q: Who won the 1997 Senior Open?
A: Australian Graham Marsh claimed a one-stroke victory on the final hole despite seven bogeys. He finished with an even-par 280 total, besting John Bland.

"There's a calmness you get under pressure, when you know it might be your last chance."
GRAHAM MARSH, ON WINNING THE SENIOR OPEN

1997

Tiger Woods, golfing's newest glamor boy, captured the 1997 Motorola Western Open after posting birdie 2s on the 6, 12, and 14 holes at Cog Hill. For the tournament Woods posted a 4-under-par 68. A record crowd of 49,462 Tiger fans, including thousands of screaming children and young adults, charged up the 18th green to catch sight of their hero, who won a 3-stroke victory over Frank Nobilo on July 6. Not since the days of "Arnie's Army," the legion of Arnold Palmer admirers who followed their hero from tournament to tournament, had professional golf witnessed such an outpouring of affection for one man.

Q: Woods became the seventh golfer to win both the Western Amateur and the Western Open. Who were the other six?
A: Chick Evans, Jack Nicklaus, Tom Weiskopf, Ben Crenshaw, Andy Bean, and Scott Verplank

"When Tiger was 16 years old we were invited by the WGA to sit in the VIP suites over there. We stood in the back row when they brought out that huge check and presented it to the

winner [Ben Crenshaw]. Tiger hit me in the ribs and he said, 'Pop, one of these days I'm going to get one of those for you,'"

EARL WOODS, TIGER'S FATHER

"It's awfully flattering that the people think that highly of you. It really is. I could be an absolute nobody and nobody would care what I do out on the golf course. But people come out, support me, and root me on—and that means a lot to me."

TIGER WOODS, ON WINNING THE WESTERN OPEN

CHAPTER 6

A No-Tank Town: Boxing in the City of Big Shoulders

Man's instinct to survive evolved into mankind's earliest sport. Men depicted in pugilistic poses have been found etched on stones dating back to the fifth millennium B.C. The ancient Greeks and Romans staged matches during funerals to please the spirits. In early America boxers fought under the bare-knuckle London prize ring rules. These bloody spectacles were illegal in most areas, including Chicago, though statutes prohibiting them were not strictly enforced. In 1867 the Marquis of Queensberry rules were drawn up, establishing the three-minute round, the 10-second knockout rule, and the wearing of gloves.

The city of big shoulders always was a good boxing town, a place where matches were spiced by the ethnic rivalries—newspapers always noted the pugger's nationality in their coverage, and legions of followers of the same national origin would attend these events. Sometimes the fight would even spill over into the stands and continue outside the arena.

Some of boxing's greatest fighters entered the ring in Chicago, among them: John L. Sullivan, Jack Dempsey, Joe Louis, Rocky Marciano. These greats often put their title on the line in the Windy City. Chicago has also been part of boxing's sordid past—shady promoters and managers all had their hands in the cash register. Broken promises equaled the number of broken noses. A well-connected fighter could climb the ladder of success by hardly breaking a sweat.

Jim Norris was the big operator in town. The son of a multimillionaire, Norris established the International Boxing Corporation in 1949 with his father's partner Arthur Wirtz. The IBC established financial footholds at the Chicago Stadium and other sports arenas in the Midwest and promoted 36 of the 44 world title fights between 1949 and 1953. Norris's organization also featured weekly boxing matches on television, which killed small neighborhood boxing clubs throughout Chicago and other cities. In 1957 Norris and Wirtz were found guilty of monopolistic practices by a federal court in New York, and the New York and Chicago divisions of the IBC were dissolved.

Chicago is no longer the boxing center of the country. Today, boxing doesn't rely much on the live gate; cable television and pay-per-view put fans at ringside. The big matches are staged in desert oases such as Las Vegas, and women now fight in the Golden Gloves Tournament.

1885

The great John L. Sullivan fought local boxer Jack Burke at the Driving Park Racetrack. A gala crowd attended the program, which featured other boxing matches and a Greco-Roman wrestling bout. A 20-piece brass band entertained the crowd between fights.

Sullivan walked to the boxing ring; Burke ran to the ring. Before the festivities began, two Chicago policeman examined the combatants' gloves. Sullivan, who outweighed Burke by 60 pounds, put his adversary down during the first exchange. Burke then wisely became a cautious fighter. But John L. continued to dog him and sent him to the canvas seven more times—five times in the fifth and final round.

1894

Jimmy Barry of Chicago proclaimed himself the bantamweight champion of the world after knocking out Casper Leon. The fight was staged under a tent in a picnic grove at Lemont. At the time there was no governing body to dispute Barry's claim, and Barry made a strong case for himself having never lost a bout.

1895

Casper Leon was saved by the authorities instead of the bell in a rematch with Jimmy Barry at Chicago. Leon, fighting with one eye shut and bleeding profusely from the mouth, fell to the canvas after a four-punch barrage from Barry. Before the referee could finish counting out the hapless Leon, four police officers came through the ropes and halted the proceedings.

In a later bout in England, Barry KO'd Walter Croot in the 20th round. Croat died the next day. Barry was arraigned on manslaughter charges but he was later acquitted in court.

Q: On what grounds was Barry found innocent?
A: Death in a ring with gloves and rules could not be other than accidental. The decision established the principle for future boxing mishaps.

1900

In February Terry McGovern fought Eddie Santry of Aurora at Chicago for the featherweight title. Nine thousand people witnessed the match at the Tattersalls Athletic Association, located south of the Loop at 16th and Dearborn. Special trains were chartered from Aurora and Elgin for the event. The smaller but more experienced McGovern took the brunt of Santry's punches while administering some leather of his own. Halfway through the fifth round, McGovern had Santry seeing stars after a left and a right to the jaw.

In a nontitle match in December at Tattersalls, McGovern KO'd the great African-American boxer Joe Gans in the second round. The fight gave off a bad odor. Gans, who was known as a hard hitter, didn't even put up a fight. He was knocked down four times by some phantom punches. Both Gans and McGovern were pelted with cigar stubs and newspapers from the disgusted fans. After that sordid event boxing was banned in the Loop for years.

Q: Why did Gans throw the fight?
A: Probably for the money. But also there was an unwritten rule that black fighters were required to throw some matches to their white counterparts. After Chicago, Gans went on to dominate the lightweight division, going unbeaten for eight years.

"I had the barrow and I was pushing it, trying to pay a bet. I backed Santry and my failure to pick the winner resulted in my having to wheel that barrow in the street in the morning."
ALBERT STRAUSS, AFTER BEING ARRESTED FOR DISORDERLY CONDUCT AT THREE IN THE MORNING ON NORTH CLARK STREET

1903

Chicago newspaperman Lou Houseman invented a new weight class for prizefighters: the light heavyweight division. Houseman managed a fighter named Jack Root, who boxed in the middleweight division. But after Root had outgrown his class, the reporter conceived an "in-between" division when he realized that his charge was not big enough to qualify for inclusion in the heavyweight division.

Q: And what happened to Root, given his new lease on life?
A: Root outpointed Kid McCoy on April 22, 1903, but lost his title a year later to George Gardner in Buffalo, New York. Kid McCoy, one of the craftiest boxers of his age and inventor the "corkscrew punch," was convicted of manslaughter in 1924 for the alleged murder of his paramour Teresa Mors.

1904

Abe Attell, a stylish pugilist from San Francisco, KO'd Chicagoan Henry Forbes at St. Louis to win the featherweight title. Over the next eight years, Attell successfully defended his title 13 times. He also engaged in two nontitle bouts in the Chicago area.

Attell often bet on his own fights and once won $40,000 on a match; he could also carry a fighter for 10 rounds. Those fights would end in a no-decision, setting up a lucrative rematch.

"I was saving him for 'Frisco.'"
ABE ATTELL REMINISCING ABOUT A DRAW WITH JEM DRISCOLL

Q: What was Attell's biggest stakes game?
A: The fixed 1919 World Series. A stooge of gentleman gambler Arnold Rothstein, Attell acted as the intermediary between the eight Black Sox players and the high rollers.

1926

In the first fight held under the auspices of the newly formed Illinois Boxing Commission, Sammy Mandell used his five-inch height advantage to ward off Rocky Kansas at Comiskey Park. Stinging Kansas's jaw with left jabs, Mandell won a 10-round decision.

"He [Mandell] dodged in and out with faster footwork then a Charleston dancer."
DON MAXWELL, *CHICAGO TRIBUNE* SPORTSWRITER

In December at the Chicago Coliseum, Mickey "The Toy Bulldog" Walker defeated Theodore "Tiger" Flowers for the middleweight title. Flowers, who had become the division's first black champion, was a church deacon from Georgia who recited Scriptures in the dressing room before each match. During the bout the deacon might have smelled a whiff of alcohol on Mickey Walker's breath, as the hard-charging Walker often fought under the influence. Walker's corner men kept a water bottle laced with gin next to his stool.

Walker, who thrived on punishment, took two punches for every one that Flowers threw. Flowers scrambled Walker's face and shut his left eye. In the ninth round Walker caught a glimpse of his target from his one good eye and floored Flowers with a left hook to the jaw to seal the verdict.

After his win in Chicago, Walker moved up to the heavyweight division, which was an extraordinary leap for him considering his weight and height (5'7", 160 lbs.). His courage and stamina carried him to victories over some top-flight heavies.

> *"The decision was given to Walker after 10 bloody rounds, but it was one of the worst even handed down in the ring and caused the Illinois boxing commission to hold a special meeting the following day to investigate the verdict."*
>
> NAT FLEISCHER

> *"Sober or stiff, I belted the guts out of them."*
>
> MICKEY WALKER

Q: What endeavor did the brawling Walker take up after boxing?

1. Boxing promoter
2. Boxing referee
3. Artist
4. Professional wrestler

A: Artist. Walker became a noted landscape artist, working predominantly in oils. Many of his works were displayed in museums.

1927

Champion Gene Tunney and challenger Jack Dempsey met at Soldier Field in boxing's most controversial heavyweight bout: "The Battle of the Long Count." The fight was a well-anticipated rematch of two of the most popular boxers of the golden era of sports.

Tunney, the scientific boxer, had won the first meeting between the two combatants, out-slugging the brawling Dempsey at Philadelphia before 120,000 fans in boxing's first million-dollar gate. The Chicago fight became boxing's first two-million-dollar gate.

People all over the world listened to Graham McNamee's broadcast. At ringside were celebrities like George M. Cohan, Douglas Fairbanks, Tom Mix, and Irving Berlin. Sportswriters who covered the match included Ring Lardner, Grantland Rice, Walter Winchell, and Damon Runyon, who disliked Tunney—too slick, he thought.

From the onset the crowd never stopped roaring. As in their previous encounter, Tunney kept Dempsey at bay with sharp jabs.

A minute into the seventh round Dempsey suddenly knocked Tunney down with a right and a left hook. The referee, Dave Barry, before beginning his count motioned Dempsey to go to a neutral corner. But Dempsey stood admiring his work. Barry then grabbed Dempsey around the waist and pushed him away. The extra time allowed Tunney to regain his composure and he rose at the count of nine. Backpedaling, Tunney was able to make it through the round. Tunney controlled the fight the rest of the way and won the match by a decision.

Q: Why didn't Dempsey immediately go to the nearest corner?

A: The neutral corner rule was a new boxing concept. Previously, a fighter was allowed to hover over their fallen opponent, a tactic Dempsey used to get a jump on the other boxer. The referee did instruct both fighters before the bout about the new rule.

"Boxers always go by the referee's timing; whether 25 seconds had elapsed when the referee said 'nine' would have made no difference to me. My signal to get off the floor was the count nine."

GENE TUNNEY

1928

Chicago's version of the Golden Gloves was inaugurated, sponsored by the *Chicago Tribune.* Now in its 70th year, the bouts are held at St. Andrew's Gym.

Q: Name some famous boxers who competed in the Golden Gloves.

A: Barney Ross, Tony Zale, Sugar Ray Robinson, Sonny Liston, and Muhammad Ali.

1929

The new $7 million Chicago Stadium was christened on March 28 with a light heavyweight bout between Mickey Walker and Tommy Loughran. Only 5,000 people paid to watch Loughran take a 10-round decision. The opening was broadcast by WGN

Radio. Stadium owner Paddy Harmon blamed the poor attendance on an early-evening fire that had destroyed a small portion of the roof. There to be seen, the swells—wearing evening frocks, tuxedos and top hats—occupied the $16 ringside seats.

Chicago pugger Jackie Fields won a 10-round, hard-fought decision over Young Jack Thompson for the welterweight crown. The slam-bam affair, held before 9,000 fans at the Chicago Coliseum, provoked a small riot in the arena. In the eighth round a leather-clad fan directed a racial epithet at Thompson. Two Thompson supporters took umbrage and left their seats to do battle, one holding a gun, the other clutching a knife. People fled the area, overturning chairs in their wake. The stampede spread throughout the stadium, and some fans entered the ring while others crawled under the canvas apron. The fight was stopped and the lights were turned on. Order was finally restored and the match continued. One hundred and fifty people, one of whom died the following day, were admitted to area hospitals.

> *"We had no discussion of putting a ban on bouts between white and Negro boxers. The commission has never favored such matches, however."*
>
> Paul Prehen, chairman of the Illinois Boxing Commission

1929-1930

White Sox first baseman Art Shires decided to enter the boxing circuit after decking his manager, Lena Blackburne, on two different occasions. Shires KO'd his first opponent, one Dan Daly of Cleveland, 21 seconds into the first round at the Windy City Arena. In Shires's next match he lost a decision to Chicago Bears center George Trafton. For most of the fight, Shires and Trafton staggered around the ring in an impromptu wrestling match as the fans pelted the arena with ice cubes. But Shires always had bigger game in mind than a bear, he wanted a cub in the ring: the Chicago Cubs' barrel-chested outfielder Hack Wilson.

> *"Hack will lose sight of my gloves just as he lost sight of the ball in the [1929] World Series. But instead of looking at the sun, he'll be seeing more stars than there are in heaven."*
>
> Art Shires

Q: Who won the Cubs-Sox match?

A: After the Trafton-Shires debacle, Wilson declined the offer. Shires continued fighting pugs and again stirred up a bout with Wilson. Eventually baseball commissioner Kenesaw Landis intervened and drafted a memo disallowing any ballplayer from entering the ring.

1930

George Trafton, fresh from his triumph over Art Shires, continued plugging. Trafton, who had a reputation on the gridiron as a bone crusher, took on the giant Italian heavyweight Primo Carnera (6'6", 267 lbs.). Carnera sent Trafton to the canvas three times in the first 54 seconds of the fight.

Q: Was Carnera Trafton's toughest opponent?

A: No. Trafton's toughest opponent was his 115-pound wife. In divorce court he charged her with cruelty, complaining she had hit him with an alarm clock, a chair, and a bottle.

1930

The lights were turned on at Wrigley Field for . . . a wrestling match. Over 10,000 fans watched Jim Londos pin "Strangler" Lewis in a ring installed in the middle of the baseball infield. Wrigley Field was illuminated by portable lights.

Q: Prior to the installation of light standards in 1988, what other events besides wrestling were staged under the Wrigley Field lights?

A: Boxing and baseball. A Jake LaMotta-Bob Satterfield bout was staged in 1944. In 1954 the Harlem Globetrotters made a nocturnal appearance.

1931

English fighter Jack "Kid" Berg won the National Boxing Association's welterweight title in Chicago over Irishman Goldie Hess.

Q: Was Hess Irish?

A: Yes, for this particular bout. Mindful of the ethnic attraction of an Irishman in Chicago and the resulting bigger gate, Hess declared he was three-quarters Irish and one-quarter German. In a previous bout in New York Hess had fought as a German Jew. In a match in Los Angeles he had claimed Scottish origin.

1932

Jackie Fields, an Olympic gold medalist at age 17, successfully defended his world welter title against Lou Broullard in Chicago on January 28.

1933

At Chicago the Windy City's own Barney Ross beat Tony Canzoneri for Canzoneri's lightweight title. Ross grew up in the tough Jewish district on Chicago's West Side. As an amateur he won the Western Golden Gloves featherweight title. In the pros he claimed three different crowns: lightweight, junior lightweight and welterweight.

Barney Ross squared off three times with Jimmy "Baby Face" McClarnin for the welterweight title. In a period when ethnic rivalries were strong, the Irish-American McClarnin had built his reputation by beating the best Jewish fighters. Ross won the initial meeting, then lost the crown, then recaptured it. All three bouts were held in New York, and each match went 15 rounds. Ross's triumph made him a hero of Olympic proportions to his legion of fans.

Q: What did Ross do after retiring from boxing?

A: He served with the marines in World War II. He was wounded at Guadalcanal and became addicted to morphine. His recovery from drugs was depicted in the movie *Monkey on My Back*.

1937

The "Brown Bomber" Joe Louis won the world heavyweight title at Comiskey Park on June 22, defeating James Braddock. Forty-five thousand people squeezed into Comiskey Park for the match. Nine hundred policemen—one-sixth of Chicago's entire force—were on duty, and J. Edgar Hoover, Clark Gable, and George Raft were some of the luminaries at ringside. The journeyman Braddock, who had suffered 20 losses in his career, negotiated a sensible contract on his behalf. He received $300,000 for the match and 10 percent of each of Louis's future fights, which made losing almost as good a proposition as winning.

Braddock sent Louis to the canvas with a vicious uppercut in the first round. Louis got to his feet immediately. After peppering Braddock with left jabs for seven rounds, Louis finished him in round eight with a thunderous overhand right. It would require 23 stitches to close Braddock's cuts.

Q: How did Chicago's African-American population celebrate Louis's victory?

A: After the fight people bounded from their flats and swarmed onto the street. Bonfires were set and trolley cars were spun around. Some people jammed into taxicabs, and others went up and down the street chanting, "Joe Louis, Joe Louis."

"A sportsman, a gentleman and a citizen—that's Joe Louis, the Brown Bomber."

CHICAGO DEFENDER, JUNE 26, 1937

1938

On April Fool's Day at the Chicago Stadium Joe Louis knocked out Harry Thomas in the fifth round. It was Louis's third title defense in 10 months. In all he would make 25 successful defenses. With a dearth of top challengers in the heavyweight division, Louis's opponents were jokingly referred to as the "bum-of-the-month."

Q: Was Harry Thomas a typical bum?

A: Yes. Nicknamed Paul Bunyan, the Eagle Bend, Minnesota, native had compiled a 56-4 record against grade-B opponents. Moving up in class in a bout with Max Schmeling, Thomas hit the canvas seven times. Louis flattened Thomas six times—four times in the fourth round. After the fourth knockdown, Thomas sat down on his corner stool with 10 seconds left in the round.

1938

A new Chicago Stadium attendance record was set when 21,500 spectators turned out for the finals of the 11th annual Golden Gloves Tournament. C.Y.O. Boxer Jimmy O'Malley, who was presented with the Barney Ross Sportsmanship Trophy donated by the legendary Chicago fighter who began his career as a Golden Glover, won the welterweight crown amid thunderous applause. On hand for the festive evening was Joe Louis, the "Brown Bomber," who put up the heavyweight prize.

Q: What is a welterweight?

A: A weight class for boxers, typically 145-147 pounds. The term dates back to 1792 when English farmers began calling themselves "welters." The word was later applied to English horseracing.

"Many different sections of the country were represented, and Chicago sent its thousands to the ringside. It could not be described as a dyed-in-the-wool fiscal gathering. Rather, it was a pop-eyed, orderly but highly excited, crowd, amazed and delighted by the thrilling battles that Golden Gloves provided."

FRENCH LANE, *TRIBUNE* BOXING WRITER,
DESCRIBING THE MARCH 1938 TITLE ROUND

1940

On July 19 at the Chicago Stadium, Tony Zale stopped Al Hostak in the 13th round to win the National Boxing Association's middleweight title. Zale would go on to consolidate the title. An Indiana Golden Gloves champ, Zale lost the Chicago version of the amateur tournament. As a professional, Zale made Chicago his base.

Q: What made Zale unusual as a boxer?
A: His heart and grit earned him the nickname "Man of Steel," but Zale was a model-citizen type, a family man who attended church regularly. He interrupted his boxing career to serve in the navy during World War II.

1947

In Tony Zale's first title bout, after serving in the navy in September 1946, he knocked out Rocky Graziano at New York. A Zale-Graziano rematch took place in July at the Chicago Stadium. A near-capacity crowd of over 18,000 people attended the event, making it the biggest indoor gate in boxing history ($414,000). At ringside under the sweltering lights the temperature was over 100 degrees. Zale dropped Graziano to the canvas in the third round. Zale proceeded to open up cuts over both Graziano's eyes and was ahead in points entering the sixth round. But Zale got careless trying to pin Graziano on the ropes and was stunned by a right. Rocky followed with five straight unanswered punches, turning Zale around into the ropes. The referee hauled Graziano off the beaten champion.

Q: How did the two contestants differ from each other?
A: Graziano was the antithesis of the strait-laced Zale. Raised in New York's tough Hell's Kitchen, Graziano had spent time in reformatories and had been dishonorably discharged from the army for slugging an officer.

Q: When was the next installment of this great rivalry?
A: Two years later in Newark, New Jersey, Zale KO'd Graziano in the third round.

"This was no boxing match. It was a war and if there wasn't a referee, one of the two of us would have wound up dead. Today, I still can't look at the pictures of that Chicago Stadium fight."

Rocky Graziano

1948

At a Chicago Stadium bout held on February 20 Sam Baroudi, a 20 year-old lightweight boxer from Akron, Ohio, collapsed in a fatal coma after absorbing a low blow to the pit of the stomach administered in the 10th round by Ezzard Charles of Cincinnati. The finishing blow ignited a chorus of boos from 11,501 Windy City fight fans, but referee Tommy Thomas ruled it a fair punch. Baroudi, writhing in anguish, had to wait until the referee counted out Charles' victory before medics could remove him from the ring and administer first aid. The young fighter, who had joined the pro ranks after 50 amateur bouts, never regained consciousness. He died six hours later at Columbus Hospital. Meanwhile, Baroudi's trainer and manager pocketed the loser's purse of $4,000 and fled to the airport without so much as checking on the well-being of their client. Such was the nature of the fight game in the 1940s.

> *"The punch was fair; really it was fair! It landed in here, in the liver. I had used the same blow often during the fight."*
> EZZARD CHARLES, FEBRUARY 20, 1948

1948

Sugar Ray Robinson outpointed Bernard Docusen in a welterweight bout in Chicago on June 28.

1949

Joe Louis retired. Jim Norris and Arthur Wirtz, who had recently formed the International Boxing Club, enticed Louis to hang up his gloves. In exchange for the title Louis was offered a percentage of future fights. Plagued by tax problems, Louis was later forced to reenter the ring.

Q: What was the first fight under this new arrangement?
A: The next contest for Louis's vacant crown was between Ezzard Charles and Joe Walcott, which Charles won by a decision on June 22, 1949. A busy champ, Charles defended his title eight times over 19 months before Walcott finally

beat him. The last of Charles's successful defenses was in Chicago against Joey Maxim on May 30, 1951.

1949

Nelson Algren's grisly and powerful story of life in the saloons and boxing rings on West Division Street was published. Called *The Man with the Golden Arm,* the book so outraged the Polish-American Union that they asked for it to be banned from the Chicago Public Library.

Q: What Chicagoan starred in the movie based on Algren's book?

A: Kim Novak, of Polish origin herself, played Molly-O, the girlfriend of Frank Sinatra's starring role as Frankie Machine. Algren dismissed the movie as more a biography of Sinatra than his character.

1951

In a fight promoted by Jim Norris, up-and-comer Rocky Marciano knocked out 37-year-old Joe Louis at New York's Madison Square Garden. It was Louis's last official bout.

Q: What was another Chicago connection Marciano almost made?

A: Marciano had a tryout as a catcher for the Cubs. Marciano wasn't tendered a contract because he couldn't hit—a baseball!

1951

Two boxing legends—the dazzling Sugar Ray Robinson and the battling Jake LaMotta—met in Chicago for the middleweight title on February 14. It was the fifth match between the two combatants, which led Robinson to remark, "People think we're married." In their first encounter, LaMotta out-pointed Robinson, who suffered his first loss in 40 matches. Robinson won the next four engagements.

Q: What were the differences between these two masters?
A: Labeled the greatest fighter of all time, Robinson delivered the mail from his muscular legs and powerful shoulders. He could adapt to any style in the ring and fight in any fashion. LaMotta, who had used boxing to escape the slums of New York's Lower East Side, was a combative slugger. He had earned another middleweight title fight in 1949 by paying his mobster friends $20,000—and agreeing to throw another match.

Q: What was the Chicago match dubbed?
A: Sportswriters called it Day Massacre; Robinson's skillful hand and foot work dominated the early rounds. He then stepped up the attack and battered LaMotta until the referee intervened in the 13th round. LaMotta was against the ropes but still wanted to go on.

"I ran out of gas."

JAKE LAMOTTA

Later that year, a well-connected Chicago fighter named Johnny Bratton won Sugar Ray's vacant welterweight title with a decision over Charlie Fusari. Bratton, whose style featured a lunging right, had lost 16 times, including three of his previous seven fights. Two months later, Bratton was defeated by Kid Gavilan.

1953

In a May 15 fight held under the auspices of Jim Norris's International Boxing Club, Rocky Marciano dispatched Jersey Joe Walcott in the first round at the Chicago Stadium. Marciano's fabled "Suzi-Q" punch—a powerful right hand—made up for his sloppy decision win over Walcott eight months earlier in Philadelphia.

Q: How many more times did the Rock successfully defend his title?
A: He had five more title bouts before retiring undefeated in September 1955. Two days before he left the ring, the

federal government started antitrust proceedings against the IBC.

Q: Who were the only champions to retire undefeated?
A: Lightweight Jack McAuliffe (1884-1897), 41-0-9; bantamweight Jim Barry (1891-1899), 59-0-9; and Rocky Marciano (1947-1955), 49-0.

1953

Kid Gavilan, a Cuban-born boxer who was the foremost exponent of the bolo punch, defended his welterweight crown at the Chicago Stadium on February 11 when he bested Chuck Davey in the 10th round.

1955

Chicagoans got to see the great Sugar Robinson in the ring again; though he had retired in 1952, his tax problems forced his return to boxing. In this match he faced Bobo Olson, a pug from San Francisco who had won Robinson's vacant title. Though Olson had defended the title three times, he was no match for the smooth Sugar Ray. Robinson scored an easy second-round knockout; Olson was out cold for five 10-counts.

Over 12,000 people saw the match at the stadium, along with a national television audience. Besides Robinson and Olson, there were other parties interested in the gate receipts: Although Robinson had used a $25,000 IBC advance to pay an IRS writ, he remained a tax delinquent. Olson's estranged wife was also scrutinizing the purse.

> *"The knockout will put some sense into his head and he'll stop being a playboy."*
>
> BOBO OLSON'S WIFE

1956

In the last championship bout sponsored by the IBC, Rocky Marciano's vacant title was decided in Chicago in a match between Archie Moore and Floyd Patterson. The 21-year-old

Patterson, after beating Moore to the punch all night, knocked out his opponent. In his last bout Marciano had defeated Moore.

Q: How did the IBC figure in this match?
A: Jim Norris owned an option on Moore but not on Patterson. Gus D' Amato, who was Patterson's trainer, helped deliver the fatal blow to the IBC by staging non-IBC fights against handpicked opponents.

1956

The IBC's organization came under further scrutiny after a controversial match at the Chicago Stadium between Carmen Basilio and Johnny Saxton for the welterweight title. Saxton was managed by underworld boss Blinky Palermo, one of Jim Norris's pals. Because of his role in fixing a fight in New York, Palermo was prohibited from signing the Chicago contract.

The ultra-defensive Saxton won the match on points, but ringside opinion was that Basilio had won the fight. The brawling Basilio had taken the fight to Saxton. Then late in the third round Basilio delivered a left hook to Saxton's head, which buckled his knees. Saxton was saved by the bell. Early in the fourth round, the referee stopped the fight for 15 minutes to allow Saxton to change a glove after a mysterious slice appeared in it. The respite allowed Saxton to regain his composure, and he was declared winner in a questionable decision.

"I'll never fight in Chicago again."

CARMEN BASILIO, AFTER HIS BOUT WITH SAXTON

1957

Over 14,000 fans at the Chicago Stadium saw Sugar Ray Robinson revenge a previous loss to the brawling Mormon from Utah, Gene Fullmer. Robinson took Fullmer out with a sweeping left hook in the fifth round. The aging Robinson almost hadn't come out for the fifth round. He was ready to quit after absorbing some punishing body shots.

1958

In the tradition of the Tony Zale-Rocky Graziano bouts, Chicago hosted one leg of one of boxing greatest rivalries: Sugar Ray Robinson versus Carmen Basilio, despite the latter's vow never to fight in Chicago again. With the advent of closed-circuit television, the match drew the largest paid audience in the history of boxing.

In their first match at New York, Basilio had out-pointed Robinson in a bitterly fought duel: Robinson accused Basilio of putting an illegal substance on his glove, and Basilio charged Robinson with head butting. Their mutual dislike made for an exciting rematch at Chicago and was another great slugfest filled with moments of skill and courage, although marred at times by rabbit punches and other rough tactics. Robinson, relying on right uppercuts to catch the bobbing and weaving Basilio, closed Basilio's eye with a lifter in the sixth round. The courageous Basilio fought the next nine rounds with only one eye. The winner, Robinson, had to be carried to the dressing room, but Basilio walked from the ring on his own accord.

> *"I could have gone another 15 rounds."*
>
> CARMEN BASILIO

> *"Well, maybe he could have went another 15, but he wouldn't have went them with me."*
>
> SUGAR RAY ROBINSON, RESPONDING TO BASILIO'S REMARK

1960

The youngster known as Cassius Clay was every inch a champion, even in his teens. After disposing of Jimmy Jones from Gary, Indiana, in the 1960 Golden Gloves heavyweight class and thereby claiming the Joe Louis Prize, Clay and his Chicago teammates advanced to New York for the intercity finals held at Madison Square Garden on March 21. Clay's victory over Gary Jawish, an employee of the Washington Redskins football team, assured the Windy City its 16th team title against nine defeats and eight deadlocks since the New York-Chicago Golden Gloves competition began in 1928.

Q: Who was Cassius Clay?

A: Within a few years the world would come to know the Louisville youngster as Muhammad Ali.

Q: Why did Clay enter the 1960 tournament in the top heavyweight class?

A: Clay boxed in the 1959 matches, but not in the heavyweight division. He was Chicago's light heavyweight (175-pound) Golden gloves title holder, the champion of the intercity match and the National A.A.U. Tournament. In 1960 he agreed to step up in class in order to permit his younger brother, Rudy Clay, to compete as a light heavyweight. Rudy was eliminated in his second appearance.

"Clay, as shifty and clever as any of the heavyweights who preceded him since the tournament came into being in 1928, knew Jones was dangerous, but after feeling him out in the first round, went on to win the next two without much trouble. He had the Gary boy in trouble frequently while sensing Jones' heavy right-hand tactics."

MAURICE SHEVLIN, *CHICAGO TRIBUNE*

1961

The famed Chicago-New York intercity boxing rivalry known as the Golden Gloves Tournament made its last appearance in the Windy City until 1977. New York gained a 9-7 victory.

Q: Who originated the Golden Gloves Tournament?

A: The series of boxing benefits sponsored by Chicago Tribune Charities was launched by the *New York Daily News* in 1928, but the idea stemmed from a 1923 Chicago charity event. The *Tribune* began its sponsorship of the annual tournament pitting the top local boxers from the Windy City and the Big Apple in 1930.

1962

One crisp September evening at Comiskey Park, 18,894 Chicago boxing fans did not get their money's worth. The match that night was between Sonny Liston and Floyd Patterson for the heavyweight title, but a traffic snarl outside the park meant many fans hadn't arrived at their seats before the contest began.

It was a slaughter. After bullying Patterson around the ring, Liston hammered him to the canvas with a thunderous left hook at 2:06 of the first round. Patterson didn't even get up for seven minutes.

Patterson entered the ring a 7-5 underdog but was America's favorite in this battle of the beauty and the beast. One of 24 half brothers and sisters, Liston was an ex-con who had compiled a 33-1 record before and after prison terms. Patterson was a modest man who some said was in the wrong sport. Though he had won an Olympic medal and risen through the heavyweight ranks defeating the easier fighters of the division, he hadn't really faced a tough opponent until this match with Liston.

After the match the embarrassed Patterson slunk out of town wearing a fake beard and mustache and rode back to New York in an automobile.

> *"It was a terrible hoax. The people who paid to see that fight were burglarized—and shows like that one are rapidly killing boxing."*
>
> GENE TUNNEY

> *"I have trouble getting anyone to box with him. Even the local pros don't want to work with him. He makes every workout a fight."*
>
> SONNY LISTON'S FORMER GOLDEN GLOVES TRAINER MONROE HARRISON

1965

At the International Amphitheater Chicagoan Ernie Terrell won a decision over journeyman Eddie Machen for Muhammad Ali's vacant World Boxing Authority (WBA) title, which Ali had relinquished after giving Sonny Liston a rematch. Machen, fighting from a low crouch, was content in going the distance with the 6'6" Terrell. The underdog Machen was cheered on by the crowd, who booed the decision against him. Two years later Ali toyed with Terrell in a title fight.

"No one looks good against Eddie Machen."

ERNIE TERRELL

1969

Sportscaster Jack Drees and businessman Joe Kellman founded the International Boxing League, which had teams in eight cities. Chicago's entry was called the Clippers. Each team consisted of 15 boxers—three boxers for each of the five boxing divisions. Each match between boxers was six rounds. The concept didn't catch on and the league folded after one season.

Q: Why did the IBL fold?
A: Boxing is simply not a team sport. Other leagues featuring individual performances—bowling, tennis—have met the same fate.

Q: Name the other teams in the IBL.
A: Detroit Dukes, Louisville Pacers, New York Jolters, Miami Barracudas, Denver Rocks, Milwaukee Bombers, and St. Louis Saints.

1969

On August 31 Rocky Marciano boarded a single-engine Cessna 172 at Chicago en route to a party to be held in his honor in Des Moines. The former heavyweight champ never made it; his plane crashed and burned in a wooded area 30 miles east of Des Moines.

Q: Marciano was a ruthless attacker in the ring who was often accused of being a dirty fighter. But in 1952, at age 28, he became the first white boxer to claim the heavyweight title. Who was the last white champion?
A: James J. Braddock in 1935.

1977

The New York-Chicago Golden Gloves Tournament intercity bouts returned to Chicago after a 16-year hiatus. The Golden Anniversary featured a near-record 331 entrants assigned to two divisions—Open and Novice—with 11 Olympic weight classes in each division. Unfortunately, the New Yorkes prevailed.

1981

Chicago hosted its first championship bout in 16 years. At the Rosemont Horizon Mike Weaver successfully defended his WBA heavyweight title against Jim "Quick" Tillis. The fight, though, did not raise the public's fervor like a Sugar Ray Robinson-Carmen Basilio match of old. The weigh-in was a cheerful event, but the actual match was a tedious affair with both boxers exchanging more pleasantries in their too-numerous clinches.

1994

Following some legal challenges, women were allowed to compete in the Golden Gloves Tournament, and 30 entered the event. The women's matches were shortened to three two-minute rounds.

> *"The strangest thing is you can really like someone and get in the ring against that person and really want to hurt them. If you knock them down, it's better. If they bleed, it's even better. And then you can be friends again after it's over."*
>
> SARAH LAHALIH, WOMAN BOXER

CHAPTER 7

Cold Steel on Ice: Hockey South of the Border

The game of hockey, which likely developed in the cold Baltic countries and Russia, came south from Canada where it is less a casual pastime than an enduring source of national pride. It was on the frozen ponds of eastern Canada that the fastest game in the world took root, and by the late 1880s several amateur leagues flourished there. The sport began to spread into the United States in 1893, the year the first Stanley Cup was presented to the champions of the Canadian amateur competition.

The fabled Stanley Cup, a silver mug valued at only $48.67 when Lord Stanley lent his name to the prize, has been presented since 1912. Beginning in 1917, the year that the National Hockey League was formally incorporated in Montreal, the Stanley Cup has been awarded annually to the winning team in the NHL's Stanley Cup Play-Offs.

Hockey took root as an amateur attraction in the U.S. between 1895 and 1896. In the ensuing years it gradually gained momentum on the East Coast and in Chicago, where the Chicago Athletic Association sponsored the senior amateur hockey league. But not until the mid-1920s was serious attention given to organizing the city's first professional teams.

Chicago had evolved into one of the country's premier speed-skating centers. By 1926, a breakthrough year for hockey, the sport's popularity and the *Chicago Tribune*'s annual Silver Skates Competition convinced two local entrepreneurs that the time was right to introduce professional ice hockey to Chicago. Thus, coffee heir Frederic McLaughlin and another businessman named Edward Livingston established separate teams in Chicago just two years after the National Hockey League admitted the first U.S. team into its ranks—the Boston Bruins.

McLaughlin transplanted the Portland Rosebuds to Chicago and renamed them the Blackhawks. Livingston established his own team through the auspices of the rival American Hockey Association, but the odds were against him from the moment his team took to the ice. His Chicago Cardinals lasted only one season after losing a grim trade war with McLaughlin that eventually found its way into a district court.

After the AHA collapsed and the Cardinals disbanded, McLaughlin and Joseph Chesterfield Farrell, his ingenious marketing and promotions wizard, began building a strong base of fan support. Over the years "The McLaughlin Group" of owners and investors and its successor, the Arthur Wirtz family, have fended off all challengers to the Blackhawks hockey monopoly.

The conservatively run franchise has marketed its product to a mostly white, upper-income audience successfully. The merchandising of Hawk paraphernalia on television or billboards is minimized because its proud but aloof ownership understands that even during the leanest of times, it can count on that core constituency of 20,000 hockey enthusiasts showing up at game time to root for the team.

1917

Amateur speed-skating races on the city's rough, uneven lagoons and ice rinks were a popular winter pastime in Chicago around the turn of the century. Neighborhood skating clubs were organized for competition against rival teams from the ethnic fraternal societies across the city and for a chance to participate in the fabled annual Chicago Tribune Charities Silver Skates Derby, which offered prizes to the city's elite amateur speed skaters.

The first race was held in Humboldt Park on the city's near Northwest Side on January 28, 1917. More than 30,000 spectators lined the banks of the lagoon to encourage 128 racers.

As the years went by, the event steadily grew in popularity. In 1923 45,000 skating fans showed up at Garfield Park on the West Side to cheer on Harry Kaskey, who won the six-lap race by just five yards over Robert Reed.

The Silver Skates provided competition at various age and skill levels including junior boys, intermediate, and a senior class. Bernie Cannata, a prep football sensation at Austin High School in the early 1930s, won the Silver Skates competition at all three levels between 1933-1940 as a member of the C.Y.O. Skating Club.

Q: Who initiated the Silver Skates Derby?
A: *Tribune* sports columnist Walter Eckersall, who played collegiate football for Amos Alonzo Stagg at the University of Chicago during his own amateur athletic career.

Q: What prizes were awarded to the winning contestants?
A: Top winners received a pair of the coveted silver skates. Second-place finishers were awarded chromium skates, and the third placers received bronze skates. Specially designed trophies, medals, and a *Tribune* patch were given to winners in the different age brackets.

Q: Where was the Silver Skates competition held?
A: It all depended on the late-winter weather conditions in Chicago. If the ice ponds were melting, the competition was moved indoors. Otherwise it was held outdoors at Humboldt Park and Garfield Park. In later years it rotated between the outdoor ponds,the Waveland Avenue Ice Arena, and Westmont Ice Plaza.

1926-1927

On September 25, 1926, Frederic McLaughlin, a man who liked to call himself Major, an heir to the Manor House Coffee fortune, and the husband of famed dance impresario Irene Castle, paid the National Hockey League $12,000 for the right to operate a team in the Windy City.

The Major and a team of investors purchased the Portland Rosebuds of the Western Canadian Hockey League for $200,000, a staggering sum in those days. The newly formed Chicago Blackhawks took to the ice for the first time on November 17, defeating the Toronto St. Pat's in the smoky, humid Coliseum at 16th Street and Wabash Avenue by a 4-1 score.

Q: How did the Blackhawks get their name?

A: Contrary to popular belief, the team was not named after the tribe of Native Americans who once inhabited the Chicago area, but for the military unit McLaughlin served in during World War I. Originally a sergeant assigned to the First Illinois Field Artillery on the Mexican border in 1917, McLaughlin went overseas with the 58th Blackhawk Division as a major.

"A small group of men who have seen hockey and know it to be the best game on earth to watch decided some months ago that professional hockey would add to the pleasure of life in Chicago. The Chicago National Hockey League team was started and financed by men who had in mind solely the idea of sport . . . and with whom the thought of financial profit was in this case unimportant."

MAJOR FREDERIC MCLAUGHLIN, IN A 1926 MESSAGE TO THE FANS

1926-1927

The Blackhawks were not the only pro-hockey team to hit town during the 1926-1927 season. A rival league calling itself the American Hockey Association was organized in September 1926 from the remnants of the defunct Central Hockey Association. The league was essentially a midwestern operation with teams located in Chicago, Duluth, Detroit, St. Paul, Minneapolis, and Winnipeg. The rival Cardinal owner, businessman Edward J. Livingston, despite doling out thousands of free tickets, faced formidable odds luring fans to his team when it came to town in December.

To accompany the hockey games, Livingston scheduled a series of speed-skating events, and he did his level best to acquaint the public with his top stars: defenseman Teddy Graham, forward Marvin "Cyclone" Wentworth, and team captain and forward Ross Stephenson.

Then the Major claimed that Wentworth and Graham were illegally signed by an interloper league and filed a lawsuit against Livingston and the Cardinals to recover the players. He won, the American Hockey League folded, and the two disputed Cardinal players were returned to the Blackhawks for the next season.

Not until 1972 would another league challenge the supremacy of the National Hockey League.

"Chicago will be one of the best hockey cities on the North American Continent!"

EDWARD LIVINGSTON, ON ESTABLISHING THE CHICAGO CARDINALS

1926-1927

The infant Blackhawks finished in third place with a 19-22 record. Left-winger Dick Irvin, known as the "silver-haired fox," led the team in total points with 36 and delighted fans with his ambidextrous stick handling.

Q: What was the "Curse of Muldoon"?

A: Impatient to develop a winner and quickly turn a profit for his investors, McLaughlin hired and fired 13 coaches during his first 10 years in Chicago. Peter Muldoon coached the Hawks in their inaugural season, but the Major was not satisfied and fired him at the season's close. According to popular legend, Muldoon threatened dire consequences. "Fire me, Major, and you'll never finish first! I'll put a curse on this team that will hoodoo it till the end of time!" In truth, though, the curse was a cruel hoax perpetrated by *Toronto Globe and Mail* newspaper columnist James X. Coleman 15 years after Muldoon was fired. It wasn't until the 1966-1967 season that the Hawks finished a regular season in first place.

1929

On March 28 the Chicago Stadium, showcased as the "world's largest indoor arena," opened, but not until December 16 would the Blackhawks play the first game on the new ice. They defeated the lowly Pittsburgh Pirates 3-1.

Q: Who built the Chicago Stadium?

A: Through the efforts of the colorful but often reckless sports promoter Patrick "Paddy" Harmon, Chicago's major winter sports were eventually consolidated under the roof of the Chicago Stadium at 1800 West Madison Street. The facility cost Harmon $2,500,000 of his own money. On July 22, 1930, after he lost out to McLaughlin in a bid to purchase an expansion team for Chicago in 1926, Harmon was tragically killed in a traffic accident. In his pocket police found $2.50, all the money he had left in the world.

1930-1931

After winning two "total-goals" series against Toronto and New York in the opening rounds, the Blackhawks advanced to the Stanley Cup Finals for the first time in their history. The Hawks played a tough checking game in a best-of-five showdown against an injury-riddled Montreal team, but were stymied by bad officiating. Hawk coach Dick Irvin filed a formal protest accusing a referee of showing favoritism for the Canadians, who played magnificent defense throughout the series.

1933-1934

The Blackhawks won their first Stanley Cup on April 10, 1934, but no one had counted on the victory. The Hawks, as they would often demonstrate in future Stanley Cup encounters, were classic underdogs who staggered into the championship round after upsetting vastly superior hockey teams.

> *"Mass delirium seized the customers at the Chicago Stadium."*
>
> CHARLES BARTLETT, *CHICAGO TRIBUNE* HOCKEY WRITER

Despite the ravages of a season-long illness, Chicago's heroic goaltender and team captain, Charles Gardiner, put in a heart-stopping performance that allowed the Hawks to defeat the Detroit Red Wings three games to one in the best-of-five series. The finals all boiled down to a battle of two outstanding goalies, Gardiner and the Wings' Wilfred Cude, who stopped 53 shots on goal in the final game. Both men were superb, but in the deciding game Gardiner held his opponents scoreless until forward Harold "Mush" March drove the puck past Cude at the 10:05 mark of the second overtime, delivering the Stanley Cup to Chicago. More than 18,500 stadium fans roared their approval.

As maintenance crews cleared away the empty champagne bottles the next day, Gardiner collected on a bet. His teammate Roger Jenkins had wagered that if the Hawks ever won the cup he'd chauffeur Gardiner around a city block—in a wheelbarrow. Two other teammates acted as referees while the red-faced Jenkins made good on the bet. Sadly, Gardiner's follow-up wasn't nearly as lighthearted. The fearless little goalie died in his Winnipeg home that June from a head injury sustained earlier in his career.

Q: For the next three decades, Charlie Gardiner held the Blackhawks team record for most regular season shutouts with 42. Which two Chicago goaltenders eventually surpassed the mark?

A: Tony Esposito (1969-1984) heads the all-time list with 74 shutouts, followed by Glenn Hall (1957-1967) with 51. In 316 NHL games Charlie Gardiner's goals-against average was a stingy 2.02.

"Harold "Mush" March, a shrimp of a hockey player who matched his 140 pounds against all the heavyweights of the game is going home with the most valuable puck in existence this morning. He seized the little black disc out of the Detroit cage last night at the Chicago Stadium after having blazed it past Wilfred Cude."

CHICAGO TRIBUNE, APRIL 11, 1934

1934

Sometimes the crowds who came out to watch the annual Silver Skates Derby became unruly—often testing the patience of Chicago police. The 1934 event nearly erupted into a riot after the excited spectators broke through a police line obstructing the race judge's decision. Edwin Stundl of the Olympic Skating Club had closed to within six feet and was still gaining on Al Kucera of the Brekke Skating Club when the crowd ran onto the ice. The frazzled referee declared a tie—the only draw in Silver Skates history. The two men were each awarded a pair of silver-plated skates in a velvet-lined case.

The Silver Skates continued to attract the area's top speed skaters through the early 1980s. Many of them, like Anne Henning of Northbrook, Leah Poulos, and Dianne Holum, went on to compete in the Olympics.

Q: What was the final fate of the Silver Skates Derby?
A: The *Chicago Tribune* lost interest in the event and relinquished control to the Mayor's Office of Special Events, who carried on the tradition into the 1980s.

1937-1938

No sane sports fan would have wagered his last two bits on the laughable Blackhawks as they closed out the sluggish 1937-1938 season in next to last place in the American Division. Rookie coach Bill Stewart was gainfully employed as a National League baseball umpire from April until October. The Blackhawks featured more American-born players than any other team, placing them at a terrible disadvantage against the seasoned Canadian teams. The old Major was obsessed with the notion that Chicago fans would root only for a team composed of native sons. This admirable patriotism led to a dwindling number of victories.

Nobody counted on the Hawks to do much in the opening series against the Montreal Canadians, but they managed to make it to the Stanley Cup Finals where they faced the Toronto Maple Leafs. NHL president Frank Calder was so confident of the series outcome that he had the Stanley Cup delivered to Toronto so it would be there in time for the Leafs' postgame celebrations.

The Hawks' regular goalie, Mike Karakas, was injured and could not skate. Only minutes before game time the Maple Leafs' managing director, Conn Smythe, offered to provide Chicago with a substitute goalie.

As promised, at exactly 7:15 P.M. on April 5 Stewart was introduced to his new goaltender, dredged from the minor league Pittsburgh Hornets. The young man, alas, had quaffed one too many in a nearby tavern. Nevertheless he met the challenge bravely. He allowed an early first-period goal but was flawless the rest of the game. Smythe's surprise turned into Chicago's delight. The Hawks won 3-1 and went on to win two of the next three games to capture the best-of-five series and their second Stanley Cup in five seasons.

Q: Who was this young goalie who took to the ice three sheets to the wind?

A: Alfie Moore, born and raised in Toronto. His entire career included this one play-off game with Chicago and two games the following season with the New York Americans.

"We gave him a shower and poured him full of coffee but it looked like a sad night when the first Toronto shot went past him for a goal. We had something to cheer about later though when he got a save by accident. He thought the puck had gone into the net and refused to look, but he had been fooled by a fake."

JOHNNY GOTTSELIG, BLACKHAWK FORWARD AND LATER PUBLIC RELATIONS MANAGER, REMEMBERING ALFIE MOORE'S BIG NIGHT

1938-1939

A complete season ticket to all 24 Blackhawk home games cost $60; the mezzanine seats sold for $42.

1942-1943

Chicago Blackhawks home games were broadcast over the radio, but only a small portion. For the first time Jack Ryan and Lyall Smith, two sportswriters for the old *Chicago Daily News,* described the third period action of every home game on WIND. Their broadcast booth was an organ loft in the old Chicago Stadium.

1943-1944

While the Hawks valiantly tried to salvage at least one victory against heavy odds, the Canadians swept the Hawks in four straight games to win their fifth Stanley Cup. Unruly Montreal Forum fans littered the rink with garbage and debris.

Q: What change in hockey strategy did former Blackhawks forward Paul Thompson institute after taking over as head coach?

A: Thompson pulled the goaltender late in the game in order to put an extra player on the ice, a tactic he introduced in the final game of the 1940-1941 season when he yanked goaltender Sam Lopresti against Toronto.

> *"The Montreal spectators had demonstrated that Chicago's fervent fans have no monopoly on the practice of using the rink for a rubbish heap. Their pet weapons were rubber overshoes, and a bottle or two descended on the ice, but the game never was delayed more than a few seconds."*
>
> ED PRELL, *CHICAGO TRIBUNE*, APRIL 14, 1944

1944

The beloved but sometimes eccentric Major Frederic McLaughlin died at Lake Forest Hospital on December 17 following a long illness. He was still chairman of the board at the time of his death. In 1939 William J. Tobin, once a goalie for the Edmonton Eskimos of the Western Canada League, had succeeded him as president. McLaughlin was elected to the Hockey Hall of Fame in 1963.

Q: McLaughlin had given Chicago a hockey team that enjoyed the largest following of any in the U.S. or Canada at the time of his death, but he was interested in other sports as well. What were they?

A: He brought Chicago its first big-time polo matches at the Onwentsia Club and helped bring the Arlington Park Jockey Club into international prominence as its first president.

> *"The Blackhawks played and won from Detroit last night 2-1, but in deference to a man who had been unostentatious in his lifetime, there was neither a memorial service nor a eulogy at the Stadium. Each of the Hawks wore a three-inch band of black crepe on the left sleeve of his white shirt."*
>
> DAN DESMOND, HOCKEY WRITER,
> *CHICAGO HERALD-AMERICAN,* DECEMBER 18, 1944

1946-1947

On a frigid and miserable February 23, 1947, a record-setting crowd of 20,004 jammed into the Chicago Stadium, breaking the original stadium attendance record of 19,749, set in January 1946. Hawk management honored Boston Bruin coach Dit Clapper on his induction into the Hall of Fame before the game—then absorbed a humiliating 9-4 defeat. That surely could not have explained the attendance phenomenon.

> *"They're sure to bust every hockey attendance record in the books and when, in years to come, up in Saskatchewan and Ontario and Alberta, they gather the young sprouts around 'em they can always top off the story with: 'and folks came out to see us by the thousands even if we* were *a hopeless last.'"*
>
> DAN DESMOND, *CHICAGO HERALD-AMERICAN,* FEBRUARY 24, 1947

1948-1949

On November 3 the Chicago Stadium hosted its first All-Star Game, and 16,681 fans got more than they'd paid for when a dandy fistfight broke out between Gordie Howe of the Detroit Red Wings and Toronto's Gus Mortson. The All-Stars defeated the Toronto Maple Leafs 3-1.

Q: In what other years was the All-Star Game played in the Windy City?

A: The All-Stars defeated the Blackhawks 3-1 on October 7, 1961; the Western Division beat the East All-Stars 6-4 on January 29, 1974.

1951-1952

On March 23 Bill Mosienko, a diminutive right wing and one of the smartest players in Hawks history, scored three goals against the New York Rangers in a 21-second spurt, breaking a 14-year-old record held by Carl Liscombe of Detroit.

Q: What famous scoring line was Bill Mosienko a part of?
A: Mosienko teamed with center Max Bentley and his brother Doug Bentley at left wing to form the Pony Line, a potent scoring combination during the late 1940s.

1952

On September 11 the floundering Blackhawks, who'd finished in last place for three consecutive seasons, were sold by William Tobin to an investors' syndicate. The group included Arthur Wirtz, president of the Chicago Stadium, and James Norris Jr. and his brother Bruce, sons of the owner and president of the Detroit Red Wings.

Almost up to the moment of his death on December 4 that year, Norris Sr., who built the Red Wings into a hockey dynasty after purchasing the Motor City team in 1932, owned the Chicago Stadium with Wirtz. The resulting interlocking ownership of these NHL rivals and the rinks they played in is one of professional sports' curiosities.

Wirtz, who'd made his fortune buying and selling Chicago real estate, had joined with the elder Norris in 1933 to purchase the Detroit Olympia, the Red Wings' home ice.

This strange saga continued through two generations until James D. Norris Jr. passed away in February 1966 and Arthur's son, William Wirtz, took over as Blackhawks president.

"Racing is pure luck. In boxing the outcome has nothing to do with the promoter. But hockey, it's a team sport where psychology and desire are half the game."

JAMES D. NORRIS JR., A MEMBER OF THE HOCKEY HALL OF FAME DESPITE HAVING A FEDERAL COURT DECLARE HIS PRIZEFIGHTING OPERATIONS A MONOPOLY. TWO UNDERWORLD ASSOCIATES IN THE FIGHT GAME WERE SENT TO PRISON FOR CONSPIRACY.

1954

Rumors of an impending transfer of the Blackhawk franchise to St. Louis soured many Windy City fans. Facing total collapse, Wirtz and Norris spared no cost, "hiring" coach Tommy Ivan of the Detroit Red Wings to rebuild the tattered Chicago franchise. From 1947 to 1954 Ivan led the Wings to three Stanley Cups and six first-place finishes.

With brains and imagination Ivan rebuilt the Blackhawk farm system from scratch. He also had a little assistance from the league, which unveiled a "Help the Hawks" plan, bringing to Chicago several promising youngsters including right-winger Eddie Litzenberger and Eric Nesterenko. But charity could only go so far. When Ivan needed a certain minor league star to complement his ambitious five-year plan, he simply went out and bought the whole team. Thus in January 1955, in order to secure the services of defenseman Pierre Pilote, the Hawks' general manager purchased the Buffalo franchise for $150,000.

Q: Ivan's plan really worked out when the Hawks acquired the St. Catharine's, Ontario, Tee-Pees, a junior hockey amateur team that yielded a phalanx of future Hawk stars. Name some of the young St. Catharine's players who were so instrumental to the success of the team in the 1960s.

A: Elmer "Moose" Vasko, Phil Esposito, Dennis Hull, Chico Maki, Matt Ravlich, Pat "Whitey" Stapleton, Stan Mikita, and hockey's "Golden Jet" Robert Marvin Hull.

1957

On January 5 CBS telecast an NHL game nationwide for the first time, but the matinee contest between the Blackhawks and Rangers in New York's Madison Square Garden was blacked out in Chicago. The network could not sell the broadcast rights to a local sponsor because nobody was interested in the last-place Hawks and Arthur Wirtz didn't much care if his team was seen on television or not.

Q: What was the score of that game?

A: As a historical footnote, the Hawks lost it 4-1.

Q: Has the Wirtz family changed its attitude about televising games?
A: No, it has remained rigid on this issue for decades. Only selected road games appear on the Sports Channel in Chicago.

1957

In July the shuttle bus from the Motor City delivered Red Wing goalie Glenn Hall and left-winger Ted Lindsay to the Blackhawks in exchange for John Wilson, Forbes Kennedy, Bill Preston, and Hank Bassen. Though Lindsay was an inconsequential player, Glenn Hall—"Mr. Goalie" and one of the true legends of the game—was pivotal to the Hawks' success throughout the 1960s. This great net-minder experienced bouts of frequent nausea prior to the dropping of the puck, the result of pregame jitters.

Q: For seven consecutive seasons Glenn Hall led the NHL in minutes played. He still holds the record for consecutive games played. What years did he play and what is his record-setting total?
A: From the beginning of the 1955-1956 season up until November 8, 1962, when he was forced out of action with a pinched nerve, Hall played in 502 consecutive games, still an NHL record.

Q: Why had Lindsay overstayed his welcome in Detroit?
A: He'd attempted to organize the National Hockey League Players Association.

1957

Bobby Hull, a terrifying force whose slap shot was clocked at 115 miles per hour at the height of his legendary career, signed his first professional contract with the Blackhawks in October 1957. At age 18 he was the youngest player ever in Chicago hockey history.

Spotty play during his first two campaigns reflected his

youthful inexperience, but in the 1959-1960 season he blossomed into a full-fledged star, scoring 39 goals.

> *"When I think of Hull, I think of Gordie Howe, the all-time great I had with the Detroit Red Wings."*
>
> TOMMY IVAN, MOMENTS AFTER SIGNING HULL TO A CONTRACT

1958

Joseph Chesterfield Farrell, the Hawks' longtime publicity director who sold Chicago's sporting public on the game of hockey in the early years, passed away at his Michigan home on September 25. For 27 years the tall, striking man with a clear, resonant voice had been known around town as the voice of the Blackhawks. He retired after the Wirtz family bought the club from Bill Tobin in 1952. If not for his exceptional marketing and promotional skills the Hawks might not have survived.

Q: Farrell's legacy is recalled each and every time the Hawks take the ice. What is this lasting contribution to Blackhawks history?

A: Farrell wrote the lyrics to the famous stadium fight song, "Here Come the Hawks."

Q: What had Farrell done before hooking up with Major McLaughlin in 1926?

A: Farrell had been a Broadway songwriter and president of Charles Comiskey's White Sox fan group known as the Woodland Bards.

1960-1961

In their first winning season in 15 years the Blackhawks finished a distant third with a less-than-sparkling 29-24 record in the regular season, but it was just a prelude to the glories that lay ahead for this young team.

Q: What shocking upset was proof that the Hawks would defy some very long odds in their latest cup quest?

A: In the tradition of the great over-achieving Hawks teams of the 1930s, the 1961 edition moved past the defending champion Montreal Canadians four games to two in the semifinal round of the play-offs, then won the Stanley Cup in six games against the Detroit Red Wings.

Until the arduous rebuilding process began in 1957, the Hawks had finished in the NHL basement nine times in 11 seasons and were a collection of spare parts and second- and third-year men put together by Coach Rudy Pilous and General Manager Tommy Ivan. Thirteen of the 18 regular players who were with the Hawks this season came from other teams.

Q: Pilous had known some of the Hawks' young players earlier. How?
A: From his days coaching the St. Catharines Tee-Pees.

Q: What traits endeared Pilous to his players, though they may not have helped him get along with boss Tommy Ivan?
A: The players appreciated Rudy's keen sense of humor and easygoing nature and knew they might not have escaped Montreal without him.

Q: Which former Blackhawks bad boy scored the pivotal tying goal in game six of the Stanley Cup Finals, which provided Chicago with the necessary momentum to outlast the Wings?
A: Forward Reggie Fleming.

"That's when we won it! That goal only tied the game but it took the starch out of them and gave us the zip we needed. What more could you ask than to score a goal when you're shorthanded?"

REGGIE FLEMING, AFTER THE HAWKS' STANLEY CUP VICTORY OVER THE RED WINGS ON APRIL 16

1963-1964

At Tommy Ivan's direction, former Maple Leafs coach Billy Reay replaced the easygoing Rudy Pilous, who left an undisciplined Blackhawks unit desperately searching for direction.

Coach Reay, who had been discharged by the Leafs after only a year and a half on the job, was more successful with the Blackhawks and led them to six first-place finishes in 14 years.

Q: What coaching record does Reay still hold?
A: He coached the Hawks longer than anyone else has before or since, winning 516 games against 335 losses.

A reserved, taciturn individual, Reay quickly adapted to changing conditions and rebuilt his teams accordingly.

Q: Who are the top five winning coaches in Blackhawks history?
A: (1) Billy Reay (1963-1977), 516 wins; (2) Rudy Pilous (1958-1963), 162 wins; (3) Bob Pulford (1977-1979, 1982, 1985-1987), 157 wins; (4) Mike Keenan (1988-1992), 153 wins; (5) Darryl Sutter (1992-1995), 110 wins.

1964-1965

Third-place finishers during the regular season, the Blackhawks surprised the Detroit Red Wings in the opening round of the NHL play-offs to advance to the Stanley Cup Finals against the Montreal Canadians. The seven-game showdown boiled down to a home ice advantage for both teams, with Montreal taking the last four on their own ice.

Q: Only eight players from the 1961 Stanley Cup champions were still playing for the Hawks in the 1964-1965 season. Who were they?
A: Goalie Glenn Hall; defensemen Elmer Vasko and Pierre Pilote; centers Red Hay and Stan Mikita; and wingers Bobby Hull, Eric Nesterenko, and Kenny Wharram.

"The contrast between the Chicago crowd and the fans in Montreal is marked. About 80 percent of the Forum's ticket-holders are French-Canadians, traditionally sports lovers. They know their hockey. A clever pass or a delaying tactic is appreciated as much as a goal. At the Stadium every goalward move

by the Hawks brings down the house. Every blocked shot by the Hawks causes an immediate cheer."

GERALD ESKENAZI

1965-1966

For the first time the entire Chicago Blackhawks road schedule was telecast over WGN-TV. A new generation of hockey fans would come of age listening to the golden tones of the Blackhawks' new voice.

Q: Who was the dapper gentleman commentator whose trademark call—"A shot . . . and a goal!"—became a household phrase?

A: Lloyd Pettit, who had been hired as a staff announcer by WGN in 1956 after broadcasting the Braves over WTMJ Radio in Milwaukee.

1965-1966

Like Babe Ruth's home-run record, the 50-goals-per-season record had withstood the test of time until shattered with customary flair by arguably the greatest player to don the Indianhead jersey. The goal came during a Saturday matinee game at the Chicago Stadium on March 12 against the fifth-place New York Rangers. The Hawks finally broke from a streak of three scoreless games and dented the net against an opponent. Working a power play, Bobby Hull, "The Golden Jet," drilled one of his patented slap shots at the Rangers' hapless goalie, Cesare Maniago. The puck sailed past his pads into the right side of the net and history was made.

Q: How many seasons had passed since the earlier record was set?

A: Twenty-two seasons earlier, Maurice "Rocket" Richard of the Montreal Canadians scored 50 goals in a season.

Q: The record had been tied twice. When and by whom?

A: Bernie "Boom Boom" Geoffrion tied it on March 16, 1961, and Bobby Hull also hit the mark in the 1961-1962 season.

Q: When did "The Golden Jet" break his own mark?
A: In the 1968-1969 season he scored 58 goals, which is still a Hawks single-season record.

Q: Who are the only other Blackhawks to score 50 or more goals in a season?
A: Al Secord, 54 (1982-1983); Jeremy Roenick, 53 (1991-1992); and Roenick again in 1992-1993 with 50. Bobby Hull did it five times as a member of the Blackhawks.

"I started up the center. Their defense and their wingers kept backing. I stopped about 10 feet inside the blue line and I saw they were still backing up. I shoved the puck out a little in front of me to get a good shot. But the ice was a little sticky and it didn't go out as far as I wanted. I didn't get really a good shot. It hit just inside the post. I stood there for just a minute. I wasn't sure. I knew it had gone in, but I wasn't sure. It might have hit one of our guys first."

Bobby Hull, March 12, 1966

1966-1967

The seasoned Blackhawks unburdened themselves from "Muldoon's curse" forever by finishing first in the last year of the old six-team setup. The following year six new U.S. teams would join the league, comprising the Western Division. After easily outdistancing runner-up Montreal, the Hawks faltered in the play-offs and were eliminated in the first round by the Toronto Maple Leafs.

1967

It has been described as the worst trade in Blackhawks history—or one of the very best. The jury is still out 30 years later.

Moments before the NHL trading deadline on May 14, Tommy Ivan traded three seasoned pros to the Boston Bruins for three defensemen, all of them 25 years of age or younger and all untested.

Phil Esposito had performed dismally in the 1967 play-offs, and this may have had something to do with Ivan's decision to trade the unproven player. But in Boston with a team in the process of rebuilding, Esposito blossomed into one of the all-time greats. A great loss.

Pit Martin, but not Gilles Marotte, paid long-term dividends for Chicago. Not quite up to Esposito's achievements, but maybe Phil would not have enjoyed the same success had he remained in the Windy City.

Q: How many goals did Phil Esposito score for the Hawks? What was his career total?

A: Esposito scored 74 goals as a member of the Blackhawks and a total of 778 goals during his 18-year National Hockey League career.

"We think that in Marotte we landed one of the best defense-men in hockey. Martin and Esposito are about equal in talent."

TOMMY IVAN, MAY 14, 1967

1969-1970

From worst to first in one year. After finishing the 1968-1969 season in the basement of the NHL Eastern Division, the Blackhawks defeated the Montreal Canadians 10-2 in the last regular season game of the 1969-1970 campaign to clinch the division and win only their second Prince of Wales Trophy. The big improvement was due to the new net-minder in town—rookie Tony Esposito, who led the league with the lowest goals-against average—a miserly 2.17. "Tony-0," number 35, heads the Blackhawk list with 74 shutouts, 418 wins, and 51,839 minutes played.

Q: Who minded the Blackhawks net the year before Tony Esposito arrived?

A: Denis DeJordy, who spent most of his 11-year career riding the Blackhawks bench as the backup goalie to Glenn Hall. DeJordy appeared in 53 games during the 1968-1969 season but only 10 games the following year.

"No team in my lifetime has given me the thrill this team has."

BILLY REAY, CHICAGO BLACKHAWKS COACH

1970-1971

The bitter taste of defeat marred a season of perfect team play and a Western Division championship.

Hopes for a Stanley Cup were running high on West Madison Street, but hopes quickly faded to dust when the Montreal Canadians and their brilliant young goaltender Ken Dryden overcame a 2-0 third-period deficit in the decisive seventh game of the NHL Finals to wrest away the Cup from the Hawks.

The Montreal hex was never more apparent than in this pivotal series, when victory was clearly within Chicago's grasp. Billy Reay's team, powered by the potent "MPH Line" (Pit Martin, Jim Pappin, and Dennis Hull), sensed victory and might have wrapped it up in the Montreal Forum on May 16, 1971, if not for a late flurry of action around the Hawks net. The "Habs" prevailed 4-3, setting up the final showdown in the Stadium on May 18.

The air-conditioning system in the Chicago Stadium broke down with the Hawks ahead 2-0, and visions of a Stanley Cup danced in the heads of the 18,000 who had faithfully attended hockey games inside this ancient rink on Sunday nights for so many years.

When play resumed Montreal relentlessly peppered Tony Esposito. The valiant Chicago goalie did the best he could in the foggy mist, but by the third period he simply ran out of gas. Henri Richard, the "Pocket Rocket," scored the winning goal in a 3-2 Montreal victory that sealed yet another doom for the Blackhawks at the hands of this wrecking crew from Canada, who must be ranked with the New York Yankees as the second most successful sports team in history.

Q: The Blackhawks have faced the Montreal Canadians 17 times in the Stanley Cup Play-Offs, dating back to 1930. In all but five of the series Montreal has prevailed. Can you name the years the Hawks slid past the Habs?

A: The 1934 quarter finals, 1938 quarter finals, 1941 quarter finals, 1961 semifinals, and 1962 semifinals. The last time these two teams met in the postseason was in 1976.

1971-1972

A new semipro team named the Chicago Cardinals—a ragtag collection of weekend warriors, NHL has-beens, and college recruits—began play at the Oakbrook Twin-Ice Forum. One of the owners played right defense. The players earned $25 per game, and the 800 or so shivering fans who showed up at the rink for Saturday evening contests loved every minute of it despite poor ventilation and lack of heating.

The following season the Cardinals joined the seven-team United States Hockey League and moved into more pleasant surroundings—the Willow Ice Chalet in Willow Springs, Illinois.

Q: What former Chicago Blackhawks forward coached the Cardinals?

A: Gene Ubriaco, who played 21 games for the Hawks in 1969.

"I was a drunk for 12 years and should have been in the clink all along. All the time I was in the NHL, people kept giving me breaks, but I never took advantage of them. I just kept going out and getting bombed. I never went out with the idea of having one drink. I went out with the idea of getting blasted. Hockey was always good to me, so finally, I decided to be good to it."

GENE UBRIACO, CARDINALS COACH

1972

Twenty-year-old Dianne Holum of suburban Northbrook won the bronze medal at the Women's Speed Skating Championships in Heerenveen, Netherlands, on March 5.

Spirits soared on the American side as Dianne broke the Russian postwar dominance of this annual tournament that tested the skills and stamina of the world's premier female skaters. She carted home four metals (gold in the 500-meter, bronze in the 1,500 and 1,000 overall), and was honored by Chicago sports fans on the opening night of the baseball season at Comiskey Park. Dianne threw out the first ball.

Q: Who was the only other American skater to win a metal at this event since 1945?
A: Dianne Holum in 1967.

1972

Olympian Ann Henning set two world records in the 1,000-meter speed skating international competition at Davos, Switzerland. She skated the 1,000 meters in just 1:27:03. It was a perfect tune-up for the 1972 Winter Olympics.

Q: Who finished in second place?
A: Friend and fellow Northbrook neighbor Dianne Holum.

1972-1973

With high hopes for the future of a growing sport, two West Coast sports entrepreneurs named Gary Davidson and Dennis Murphy organized the 12-team World Hockey Association (WHA), promising to give the NHL a fight to the finish. It was the first serious attempt to challenge the NHL monopoly since the ill-fated American Hockey League was launched in 1926.

Davidson's blueprint strategy for long-term success was geared toward luring established NHL stars into the new league with the promise of boxcar salaries and teams located in major metropolitan areas with new existing arenas in place or in the developmental stages.

The Chicago franchise was granted to a consortium headed by A. John Syke, developer of the Twin-Ice Forum in suburban Oakbrook, but lack of funds delayed the completion of that project and imperiled the future of the team they nicknamed the Cougars. Short on cash and with no adequate facility for the Cougars to play in, Syke sold his interest to six Chicago-area businessmen, including a 34-year-old attorney named John Ladner, who was named team president. It was announced that the Cougars owners had entered into preliminary discussions for the services of several unhappy Blackhawks including Jim Pappin, Pit Martin, and Stan Mikita.

However, the underfinanced Ladner group was no more prepared for the responsibilities of ownership than Syke.

Accordingly, the Cougars were sold to real estate developers Walter and Jordan H. Kaiser in June 1972. It was the third ownership change in less than six months, and the Cougars had not yet skated together as a team!

The Cougars went ahead and signed former Hawks bad boy Reggie Fleming to a WHA contract, invested heavily in local advertising, then negotiated a lease with the International Amphitheater for use during the upcoming season. The washed-up Fleming was the only recognizable name on the opening-night roster. The Kaiser brothers did not have the time or the financial wherewithall to go after a Bobby Hull or any other NHL superstar, but they did invest in a good oral surgeon. The owner believed that having a full-time dentist on staff was essential if you were to succeed in the hockey business.

Just getting through the first season proved to be the toughest challenge of all. The Cougars, outfitted in their colorful gold-and-green uniforms, finished last in the WHA Western Division under the direction of Coach Marcel Pronovost.

Q: In addition to WHA hockey, what other sports novelty did the Kaiser brothers bring to Chicago?

A: World Team Tennis. Kaiser's money bankrolled the Chicago Aces, one of the 16 teams comprising the first professional tennis league inaugurated in May 1974 at the Lakeshore Racquet Club.

"Either the WHA is going to be a going venture or it isn't. We have no question that it will be a successful league, and in a successful league franchises have a substantial value. So it really isn't too important how much you make or lose in the short term. But we're in this as a long-term thing primarily for the development of sports centers."

JORDAN H. KAISER, DECEMBER 1972

1972

Almost single-handedly the "Golden Jet," Bobby Hull, revived a dormant franchise and a game that had been relegated to the back pages of the sports section in the 1950s. His good-natured charm and courage in the face of adversity made him a hero to his legion of followers in Chicago. Unfortunately, his employers took him for granted. After Billy Reay shifted the emphasis more toward the defense in the early 1970s, the Wirtz family decreed that Bobby should begin to play a more disciplined brand of hockey. The World Hockey Association began bargaining for Bobby's services, and on June 27 he came to terms with the new league's Winnipeg Jets. Hull signed a 10-year contract valued at $2.75 million.

The loss of Hull was a devastating blow to the Blackhawks, and it signaled a downturn in the franchise's fortunes for years to come.

Q: Who was the most electrifying sports figure to play in Chicago prior to the arrival of Michael Jordan?
A: In the opinion of many it was Bobby Hull.

Q: What scoring milestone did Bobby Hull and his son Brett accomplish during their respective NHL careers?
A: Brett and Bobby Hull are the only father-son combination in history to record 500 goals each. Brett Hull became the 24th NHL player to top the coveted 500-mark when he completed a hat-trick against the Los Angeles Kings on December 22, 1996.

"The whole thing has made me wonder what the hell they were thinking. They must have thought I was bluffing or they must have thought they'd gamble that the Winnipeg offer would fall apart. If anything I made their side of it easier when I said publicly at the start of all this that I wanted to stay in Chicago and I didn't expect them to come close to matching the Winnipeg offer. They didn't need me as much as the new league did and I knew that."

BOBBY HULL, JUNE 27, 1972

1972-1973

The Hawks won the Western Division crown, advanced through two rounds of play-offs, and then encountered the Montreal Canadians standing at the end of the road. Led by Yuan

Cournoyer, who scored a freak goal in the third period of game six, the Canadians won the Stanley Cup . . . again.

> *"This one is tougher to take than 1971. I've had teams here in my 10 years with more talent than this one, but I've never had one that was willing to work harder or sacrifice more for the team."*
>
> COACH BILLY REAY AFTER HIS HAWKS BOWED OUT OF THE STANLEY CUP FINALS IN 1973

1973-1974

Disenchanted Hawks fans began calling themselves the "Cougar Standbys" and the "Rafter Rats," when a trio of Blackhawks—Pat Stapleton, Darryl Maggs, and Ralph Backstrom—jumped their contracts and signed with the Cougars for their second season.

The hustling new team brought spasms of joy to the 6,000 fans who filed into the creaking old International Amphitheater each night to root for this Cinderella-like upstart. In the last two days of the season the Cougars gained the fourth and final spot in the WHA play-offs.

After surprising victories over the New England Whalers and the Toronto Toros, the Cougars advanced to the championship round against the mighty Houston Aeros, led by hockey legend Gordie Howe and his two sons.

That the Cougars might be playing for the WHA Championship Avco Cup was considered so unlikely that the management of the International Amphitheater had not only scheduled another event but had gone ahead and melted the ice before the outcome of the Toronto series had been determined.

The Kaiser brothers bickered with the Amphitheater's owners, but despite threats of a lawsuit, the latter refused to break their other commitments, forcing the Cougars to consider moving their play-off home games to another city. Then the team struck a deal with the Randhurst Twin-Ice Arena, a suburban rink that seated only 3,000 people.

Unable to short-circuit Houston's power play, the Cougars quietly bowed in four straight games to a far superior hockey team. Despite the unhappy outcome, the fortunes of the

Chicago franchise seemed to be on an upswing. Maybe the city could support two teams after all. But then again, maybe not.

Q: What Amphitheater event forced the Cougars to move their play-off games to Randhurst?

A: The musical *Peter Pan,* which was being revived as an extravaganza and was traveling around the country. Peter Pan not only caused the Cougars problems, but the Aeros also had to play their first two games in Randhurst because the same show had just opened a limited engagement in Houston.

"Chicago is our home and we feel our fans deserve to see the games here. We're proud of our team and are pleased to bring Chicago an Avco Cup contender in our second year in the WHA"

WALTER KAISER, AN APOLOGY TO THE FANS, APRIL 1974

"Maybe we could play a game in every other town, like a traveling circus."

PAT STAPLETON

1974-1975

Dwindling attendance at the rickety Amphitheater had the Cougars skating on thin financial ice, so on December 27 the Kaiser brothers sold the team to a partnership of three players: Pat Stapleton, Ralph Backstrom, and Dave Dryden, along with their attorney Jeff Rosen.

Fending off league pressure to move the team to Baltimore, the new owners vowed to stay in Chicago—a promise that depended upon negotiations for a new northwest suburban stadium that had been on the drawing board for several years.

Despite Pat "Whitey" Stapleton's valiant efforts, interest in the Cougars fell off. The new owners could not make a go of it at the Amphitheater, and the new stadium was still several years away. At season's end, the team was dissolved. Reduced to only seven teams, the WHA folded at the end of the 1978-1979 season.

Q: Where did Whitey Stapleton wind up the following season?

A: He was playing for a new team, the Indianapolis Racers.

Q: What was the name of the new stadium the Kaiser brothers desperately wanted?

A: It was the Rosemont Horizon, which eventually opened, but not soon enough to rescue the Cougars, who were promised that the facility would be ready in time to start the 1975-1976 season. The team filed a $13 million lawsuit against the village of Rosemont charging a "lack of good faith," but that didn't get the stadium built quickly enough to save the Cougars or the WHA.

"Everything we did was predicated on the arena in Rosemont. We programmed for an arena and we spent accordingly. We spent a lot. Stapleton, Ralph Backstrom, Dave Dryden . . . and all the others. In three years we built a club which was equal to 90 percent of all the others in hockey and that includes the other team in Chicago. We couldn't go on and on pouring money down the drain. There's not enough money in the world to make the team go without an arena."

JORDAN KAISER, NOVEMBER 1974

1976

Despite the arrival of Bobby Orr, who signed as a free agent on June 24, Hawks attendance fell off, and a series of injuries spiraled them into the bottom tier of their division. When Orr could not play because of his bad knees, somebody had to take the fall for this unexpected disaster.

At 4:00 A.M. on the morning of April 22, 1976, Reay returned to his apartment after an evening out and found an envelope under the door. The note from William Wirtz advised him of his immediate termination as head coach of the Hawks. True to his credo of honor and integrity, Reay refused to publicly criticize his former employer for this typically heartless act. Instead, he wished his successor the best of luck. His replacement, former Hawk defenseman Bill White, would need a whole lot of luck in the coming weeks.

Q: The only other NHL coach who exceeded Billy Reay's career victory total once played for the Blackhawks. Who was he?

A: It was Dick Irvin, who'd won 690 games between 1930 and 1956 coaching the Hawks, Maple Leafs, and Canadians. Reay's total was 542 from 1964 through 1977.

"My son Billy has complete authority over the hockey operation, and he's entitled to make any moves he sees fit. Just remember that we don't shoot from the hip and that we don't make a practice of making quick decisions."

ARTHUR WIRTZ

1980

On October 19 the Blackhawks retired Stan Mikita's #21 jersey. Mikita hung up the skates after 22 seasons with the Blackhawks. Born in Czechoslovakia, adopted by Canadian parents at age eight, and scouted by the Blackhawks when he was only 13, "Stosh" Mikita was second on the all-time Blackhawks scoring list with 541.

The ceremonies marked the first time Blackhawks management had honored a player.

Q: Stan Mikita won three major postseason NHL awards in consecutive years. What were the awards, and when did he win them?

A: Stosh won the prestigious Hart Trophy for most valuable player in 1966, the Lady Byng Trophy for most gentlemanly player in 1965, and the Art Ross Trophy for highest point total in 1968.

"I got a two-year contract for $8,520 a season from the Blackhawks and I was very satisfied with it. I thought it was fair at the time."

STAN MIKITA, RECALLING THE FIRST BLACKHAWKS CONTRACT HE SIGNED IN 1959-1960

1981-1982

The Blackhawks were in the Stanley Cup Play-Offs, and only the Vancouver Canucks stood in the way of a conference trophy and a shot at the Cup, but in the end when it really counted, Chicago fired blanks at Vancouver goalie Richard Brodeur who shut the Hawks down in five games. Getting that far wasn't a bad accomplishment for a team laboring under a 30-48 regular season record and trying to find the rhythm for general manager and coach Bob Pulford.

> *"What is a Canuck? A Canuck is a guy in an ugly uniform who drinks champagne from the Clarence Campbell Bowl and looks forward to playing the New York Islanders for the Stanley Cup. . . . A Canuck is a little guy in goaltender pads bouncing around making impossible saves, grabbing hold of a game and turning it around."*
>
> MIKE PERRICONE, *CHICAGO SUN-TIMES,* MAY 7, 1982

1984-1985

Led by the great Wayne Gretzky, the Edmonton Oilers denied the Hawks a Campbell Conference championship for the second time in three seasons.

Q: Forward Darryl Sutter, one of five Sutter brothers to play in the National Hockey League, set a new Blackhawk team record by scoring 12 goals in a play-off year. His 27 playoff points also established a new postseason record. Who held the original record and who has broken it since then?
A: Bobby Hull. The "Golden Jet" scored 11 goals and 14 assists in the 1970-1971 play-offs. Denis Savard broke it in the 1984-1985 season.

> *"Edmonton has Gretzky, but Chicago has fans!"*
>
> THE INSCRIPTION ON A BANNER DRAPED OVER THE RAILING OF THE SECOND BALCONY SUMMED UP THE FRUSTRATIONS OF THE CHICAGO BLACKHAWKS FAITHFUL HOPING FOR A MIRACLE IN THE FACE OF SUPERIOR MANPOWER

> *"Not many players get as far as we did. We were only two games away from playing for the Stanley Cup. This year we were pounding the door down. Next year we're going to get in."*
>
> EDDIE OLCZYK, 18-YEAR-OLD BLACKHAWKS ROOKIE FORWARD

1990-1991

Coasting through the season, Chicago's 49-23 record and 106 points was the best in the National Hockey League and earned the club its first President's Trophy. It was a season of all-around superlatives for the team. Jeremy Roenick, Steve Larmer, and Michel Goulet combined for 112 goals. Eddie Belfour shattered Tony Esposito's single-season total for victories by a goalie (38), which had stood since the 1969-1970 season. "The Eagle" won 43 games en route to his first Vezina Trophy.

For the fourth time in six years, Chicago bowed out in the first round of the play-offs when the Hawks were out-skated, out-scored, out-checked, and otherwise humiliated in six games by the Minnesota North Stars.

Q: Who was the last team to finish first overall only to lose in the first play-off round?

A: The 1971 Boston Bruins won 57 games but were defeated in seven games by Montreal.

"Our game is forechecking, hitting, hard work. You didn't see any of that. You never like to go out this early. This is my first experience with it. I hate it."

JEREMY ROENICK, BLACKHAWKS FORWARD, APRIL 14, 1991

1991-1992

After 19 bad years the Hawks returned to the Stanley Cup Finals. Powered by Jeremy Roenick's 53 goals, Chicago stormed through the first three rounds, knocking off St. Louis, Detroit, and Edmonton in short order.

The Hawks were on a roll, and they looked like champions after building a 4-1 lead against the Pittsburgh Penguins in game one. At their opponents' home rink, known as the Igloo, the Hawks encountered a formidable adversary and hopes quickly evaporated. The Penguins stormed back and won 5-4, then went on to take the series. After winning a dramatic 6-5 shoot-out at the Chicago Stadium the Penguins took home the Stanley Cup on June 1, 1992.

The game was also Mike Keenan's last as the Blackhawks'

head coach. A prodding, strident presence behind the bench, Keenan demanded constant perfection from his players. Many Chicago sportswriters blamed him for the team's latest failure.

Q: What happened to Mike Keenan after the Blackhawks fired him?
A: He was hired by the New York Rangers on April 17, 1993, becoming the highest-paid coach in NHL history. He led the Rangers to their first Stanley Cup in 55 years.

Q: What sarcastic nickname had the Chicago media bestowed on Keenan because he pulled players off the ice at unexpected moments?
A: He was known as Captain Hook.

"You can't afford to give up a game in a Stanley Cup Final. Not to be disrespectful, but I thought the series was closer than [a sweep]. They were just more prepared."

MIKE KEENAN, JUNE 1, 1992

1993-1994

The Blackhawks played their final game at the Chicago Stadium on April 28, 1994, inauspiciously bowing out of the Western Conference quarter-finals to Toronto 1-0.

Q: For how many years had the Hawks made hockey history at 1800 West Madison Street?
A: They'd played at the old stadium for 65 years.

Q: What marketing theme was conceived to attract fans to the stadium for the farewell season?
A: The marketing plan, "Remember the Roar," wasn't quite enough to propel Coach Darryl Sutter's team to victory.

Q: Stadium organist Frank Pellico had a particular treat for the last game. What was it?
A: Pellico whipped the partisan Hawks crowd into a pregame frenzy by playing one of the loudest renditions of the National Anthem ever heard.

Q: Who scored the final goal in the last hockey game played at the stadium?

A: It was Mike Gartner of the Toronto Maple Leafs who had tipped Dave Ellett's slap shot past Eddie "the Eagle" Belfour at 10:49 of the first period.

> *"There have been wondrous players here, even Stanley Cups, if you're old enough to know we're not lying. But what made the scene work were the fans. Generations of Chicagoans grew up in the Stadium. And most importantly they passed down the way to act in the Stadium. Be loud. Be crazy. Drink, hopefully in moderation. And make the damned building quiver. Make the other team shiver. Turn it into the most rousing spectacle imaginable, the heartbeat of a city."*
>
> JAY MARIOTTI, *CHICAGO SUN-TIMES,* APRIL 29, 1994

1994-1995

The Rosemont Horizon finally hosted a hockey game when the Chicago Wolves of the International Hockey League began their first season of play there. Former Blackhawk Grant Mulvey joined with Don Levin, Buddy Meyers, and Wayne Messmer in this risky new venture promising to deliver "alternative," hard-nosed hockey at a reasonable price. The Wolves were one of four new expansion teams to join the 49-year-old IHL for the 1994-1995 season. Mulvey had tried unsuccessfully for two years to bring a hockey team into the Horizon, and his timing could not have been better for Chicago's hockey-starved fans, who were toughing out a four-month NHL player strike when the Wolves made their debut. By drawing a league-leading average of 11,500 fans per game into the Horizon, the Wolves dispelled the myth that Chicago was a one-team hockey town. The team finished third in the IHL Northern Division with a 4-2 win over the Detroit Vipers on October 14, 1994. A standing-room-only crowd of 16,623 roared their approval.

Q: The Wolves' executive vice president, Wayne Messmer, who sang the National Anthem with dramatic intensity at the Chicago Stadium for 13 years, made a dramatic comeback that night. How?

A: Six months earlier Messmer had been shot in the throat by an armed robber, but this night he returned to sing the national anthem as he'd done for 13 years at the Chicago Stadium.

"No one can imagine how I felt. I guess I'm the only guy who can experience this. If the ice would have melted, I felt I could walk on water. To work so hard and make this thing come together . . ."

WAYNE MESSMER, ON HIS OPENING NIGHT JITTERS

Q: Who won that first game?
A: Almost 17,000 fans watched the Wolves win over the Detriot Vipers.

Q: What former Hawks player coached the Wolves in their debut season?
A: The ubiquitous Gene Ubriaco coached seven start-up teams during his nomadic hockey career, including the Wolves.

Q: What was Ubriaco's first taste of coaching a professional hockey team?
A: It came in 1976 when former TV announcer Lloyd Pettit bought the Milwaukee Admirals of the U.S. Hockey League and asked Ubriaco to go up there and help out.

Q: How long did he last?
A: With only 20 games left to go in the 1995-1996 season, Ubriaco was bounced as head coach. Grant Mulvey replaced him behind the bench.

1995

In a strike-shortened season, the Blackhawks inaugurated hockey at the new United Center on January 25, 1995, with a 5-1 victory over the Edmonton Oilers before 20,536 fans. In the first year the Blackhawks averaged 20,833 fans per game, making them the first NHL team to average more than 20,000 or more in one season. Hawk ownership, as was their want, made no special arrangements to promote their spacious, fan-friendly new home. Instead they adhered to the Wirtz credo: Sell the seats with minimum effort and they will come, because they have to.

Q: Who scored the first goal in the new building?
A: Forward Joe Murphy, assisted by Jeremy Roenick, at 11:33 of the second period.

"When Bob Pulford came here in 1977 to be the team's general manager, he came from Los Angeles and sat down with my grandfather (Arthur Wirtz) and had all these ideas for marketing. My grandfather told him the only marketing he believed in was putting fannies in the seats."

PETER R. WIRTZ, BLACKHAWKS VICE PRESIDENT OF MARKETING, 1993

"The old place was like a classical arena, a place for war. This is not."

HAWKS FAN, ON THE NEW STADIUM

1996

Unwilling to meet his $5 million-a-year salary demands, Blackhawks president Billy Wirtz traded star forward Jerry Roenick to the expansion Phoenix Coyotes.

Roenick purchased a $30,000 billboard banner at Orleans Street and the Kennedy Expressway to thank Blackhawk fans for all their support during his eight-year run in Chicago, but it was pulled down after only one day because "someone influential" in the city told the owners of the Computer City Building where the sign appeared that it had to go.

Q: Who did the Hawks get in return for Roenick?
A: Alexei Zhamnov, Craig Mills, and a draft choice.

CHAPTER 8

Gridiron Afternoons: Stagg, Sweetness, and the Sting

Chicago used to be a baseball town, but now it's a football town. Even the die-hards, the baseball purists who cling to the flickering hope that the summer game will once again occupy center stage in the hearts and minds of local sports fans, reluctantly concede that the gridiron game has become a year-round entertainment in the Windy City.

The city loves its heroes of autumn. Win, lose, or draw, the Chicago Bears are on everyone's mind, judging by the volume of calls to the local sports talk-show hosts, even in midsummer when the Cubs and White Sox should rightfully be the only game in town.

Before the Bears there were the Cardinals, and before the Cardinals there were the collegiate games. For 30 years (1890-1920), when Chicagoans thought of football—if they thought of it at all—it was the Maroons and the Wildcats (otherwise known as the "Purple"). The storied University of Chicago and Northwestern teams filled their stadiums on game days and monopolized the editorial space of the newspaper sports sections from early October until Christmas. In the first 25 years of this century the University of Chicago, Harvard, and the University of Michigan were the three dominant forces in college football nationwide. Because of their geographical proximity the two great universities of the University of Chicago and Northwestern begat a natural rivalry—a rivalry that captivated Chicago sports fans for years until both teams went into long, almost irreversible, declines in the 1930s.

The charismatic Amos Alonzo Stagg, the nation's most venerated college athlete before he accepted an appointment to guide the University of Chicago athletic program in 1892, propounded the opinion that amateur competition was the purest, most noble calling in the realm of athletics. Coach Stagg fought long and hard to block the professional "pay-for-play" leagues from compromising the integrity of football.

Those who subscribed to his conservative theories, like University of Illinois coach Bob Zuppke, formed a powerful lobby against George Halas, Edward "Dutch" Sternaman, and John "Paddy" Driscoll when these former college stars got together in 1920 to organize the nucleus of a professional association that would soon evolve into the modern National Football League.

Coach Stagg and his disciples ultimately failed to check the ambitions of Halas and Chicago Cardinal owner Chris O'Brien, who helped found the pro league. However, it would take another 35 years and the advent of television before the NFL supplanted college football. The disappearance of the University of Chicago's football program in 1939 and Northwestern's string of futile, losing seasons that followed hastened the popularity of the pro game locally.

The Bears, always a hot ticket even during their dreadful years in the late 1960s and the early 1970s, completed their conquest of the local sports world by winning a Super Bowl in 1986 under coach Mike Ditka, a force of nature whose solid work ethic, manner of dress, and sarcastic "in-your-face" attitudes appealed to legions of Chicago's blue-collar fans. The Halas team—wealthy, successful, and a local monopoly—drove the

Chicago Cardinals out of town in 1960 and fended off challenges from other local entrepreneurs who naively assumed there was room for two teams in town.

In the realm of soccer, promoters have tried and failed over the years to integrate the professional game into the city's conscience. However, despite strong interest in amateur soccer (four Chicago teams—the Sparta ABA [1938]; the Vikings [1946]; the Falcons [1953]; and the Eagles [1990]—won the U.S. Open Cup), the European game just never caught on locally.

On the other hand, Chicago takes its football very seriously, and a Bear loss on Sunday sparks seven days of second-guessing and week-long depressions for thousands of armchair quarterbacks. Those who subscribe to Mike Ditka's philosophy of life will surely agree with "da Coach" when he said, "I have no philosophy other than whip the other guy."

Chicago football. Indeed, it has always been "in your face."

1882

Collegiate football began at Northwestern University. The NU team played only two games that year, winning one and losing one.

1892

The University of Chicago, led by player/coach Amos Alonzo Stagg, inaugurated intercollegiate football in a historic game against Northwestern University on October 22. The contest was played at the 39th Street Grounds, future home of the Chicago White Sox, and it ended in a nothing-to-nothing tie.

Q: Where did Coach Stagg play collegiate football?

A: Stagg played right end for Yale before graduating from its divinity school in 1888. He was named to the nation's first All-American team in 1889, three years before being hired by William Rainey Harper of the University of Chicago at an annual salary of $2,500 per year.

"Our profession is one of the noblest and perhaps the most far reaching in building up the manhood of our country."

CREDO OF AMOS ALONZO STAGG

1893

On December 16 Chicago's first indoor football game was played at Tattersall's Riding Academy at 16th Street and Dearborn. The University of Chicago defeated their traditional rival, the Northwestern Wildcats, 22-14 on a tanbark flooring measuring 65 x 30 yards.

1894

The University of Chicago Board of Trustees agreed to meet on May 5 for the purpose of selecting a team color and a name for the football squad, which played its games at Marshall Field, named in honor of the Chicago retailer whose fortune helped build the wooden grandstand surrounding the gridiron.

Q: How did the University of Chicago football team become known as the Maroons?

A: University treasurer Charles L. Hutchinson, inspired by the mass of goldenrod growing wild on the field, initially selected yellow as the team's color, but after the mud and the slop of a football game all but obliterated that hue, a member of the athletic department purchased a selection of maroon and purple ribbons for the trustees to consider. They made their selection, and thereafter the U of C team was known as the Maroons.

1898

A gathering of neighborhood toughs organized a football squad in the South Side Morgan Park community. The young lads, predominantly of Irish extraction, played a series of "pickup" games against rivals from various Chicago neighborhoods under the banner of the Morgan Athletic Club. In 1901 Chris O'Brien, a South Side painting and decorating contractor, organized the boys into a semipro team and found a permanent home for the club at Normal Park, which was located at 63rd and Racine. Originally called the Normals, the team later changed its name to the Racine Cardinals, for their neighborhood affiliation. Thus were the humble beginnings of the National Football League's oldest and most venerable franchise, the Chicago-St. Louis-Phoenix Cardinals.

Q: How did the Cardinals acquire their name?
A: According to legend, Chris O'Brien purchased some faded maroon jerseys from the University of Chicago for his boys to wear during games in order to provide them with an identity.

"That's not maroon! It's Cardinal red!"
CHRIS O'BRIEN, NAMING THE CARDINALS

1899

Coach Stagg led the University of Chicago Maroons to their first championship season. The team completed a perfect 16-0 run, which included a 76-0 pasting of Northwestern.

Q: Who did the U of C play for the Western Conference championship?
A: The University of Wisconsin. The Badgers were one of three teams who refused to play in Chicago due to a dispute over gate receipts. However, Wisconsin, anxious to defend its honor, agreed to play the championship round in Madison on December 9. They lost 17-0.

1903

Northwestern won the first of their six Big Ten titles. The Wildcats posted a 9-2 record under Walter McCormack.

Q: In what other years did Northwestern prevail in the Big Ten?
A: 1926 (7-1); 1930 (7-1); 1931 (7-1); 1936 (7-1); 1948 (8-2); 1995 (10-2).

1904

Coach Amos Alonzo Stagg organized the Order of the C, the first football letterman's club in the nation.

"We hereby denote ourselves as members of the Order of the University of Chicago men, avow our steadfast loyalty to our alma mater, and pledge our enduring support of her athletic honor and tradition."

LOYALTY OATH TO THE ORDER OF THE C

1905

Coach Stagg called his 1905 Maroons the greatest team he had ever coached. Led by all-American quarterback Walter Eckersall, a graduate of Hyde Park High School, the Maroons breezed to a 10-0 record for their third Big Ten championship.

Q: Eckersall was a renown athlete in other sports. In 1903 he set a 10-second 100-yard-dash record that stood for 25 years. What noted Chicago-born Olympian shattered that mark in 1928?

A: Future U.S. congressman Ralph Metcalfe, who also starred in the 1936 Olympics in Berlin.

"Eckersall, Eckersall,
Running with the ball—
You will get an awful fall!
Eckersall! Eckersall!
Eckie! Eckie! Break your neckie!"

UNIVERSITY OF MICHIGAN STUDENT CHANT, 1905

1912

The Notre Dame Fighting Irish played a rare "home game" in Chicago's Comiskey Park on Thanksgiving Day, defeating Marquette University 69-0. The Irish appeared in Comiskey two more times in the next 30 years.

1913

The University of Chicago Athletic Field, otherwise known as Marshall Field, was renamed Stagg Field at the urging of the *Chicago Tribune* and the University of Chicago Alumni Club.

Q: What famous nonathletic event from history occurred on the squash court under the west grandstand at Stagg Field on December 2, 1942?

A: The first nuclear chain reaction was achieved by a team led by physicist Enrico Fermi, thus ushering in the atomic age. Today the Regenstein Library and Bartlett Gym occupy the site where the Maroons once played football.

1919

On New Year's Day a team from the Great Lakes Naval Base defeated the Mare Island Marines in the fifth annual Tournament of Roses Association Game in Pasadena by a 17-0 score. The Great Lakes Naval squad, led by three Chicago boys who later achieved National Football League notoriety, was the only noncollegiate eastern team to ever play in the Rose Bowl.

Q: Who were the three teammates who attained fame in the NFL?

A: Navy recruit George Halas scored a touchdown for Great Lakes and was awarded MVP honors; John "Paddy" Driscoll, who would play for the Cardinals and the Bears in the years to come, kicked a field goal; and Jimmy Conzelman, who coached the Chicago Cardinals to their 1947 championship, were the keys to the Great Lakes' surprise victory.

1920

There were two professional teams playing football in Chicago in 1920: the Chicago Tigers and Chris O'Brien's Racine Cardinals from 63rd Street, which joined the American Professional Football Association in 1920. In order to rid himself of unwanted competition, O'Brien challenged the Chicago Tigers, a charter member of the newly formed professional league, to a one-game "winner-take-all" proposition. The victor would henceforth represent Chicago. The loser would quietly disband. The Cardinals, coached by Marshall Smith, won the game 6-3 and claimed the city as their own—for the time being.

Q: Who scored the only Cardinal touchdown?
A: The great Northwestern halfback, Paddy Driscoll, a superior runner, dropkicker, and blocker; he'd been signed to a $3,000-a-year contract.

1920

Twenty-five-year-old George Halas went to work for A. E. Staley, the sports-minded owner of a corn products company based in Decatur, Illinois. Staley asked Halas to play for the company baseball and football teams because he believed that athletic participation molded productive, loyal employees. Later that year, Halas agreed to split coaching duties with former University of Illinois running back Edward "Dutch" Sternaman. Just before the Decatur Staleys kicked off their season, Halas and representatives from nine other football teams from the greater Midwest met at Ralph Hay's Hupmobile Showroom in Canton, Ohio, on September 17. Their goal was to organize the American Professional Football Association (APFA), forerunner of the modern NFL. The entire meeting lasted just two hours.

Q: What famous Native American track-and-field Olympic star who played football and baseball was named president of the APFA?
A: Jim Thorpe, the Sac and Fox Indian who was a star back for the Canton Bulldogs, one of the original 10 teams.

"To give the new organization an appearance of stability, we announced that the membership fee for individual clubs had been set at $100. However, I can testify that no money changed hands. Why, I doubt there was a hundred bucks in the whole room."

GEORGE HALAS

1921

Financial hardships beset the Decatur Staleys. The owner handed George Halas $5,000 in seed money and told him to go to Chicago to operate the team in a larger market—if he agreed to keep the original name for one year. The agreement papers were hastily signed. George Halas and Dutch Sternaman took the train to Chicago; as their first order of business, they paid a call on the president of the Chicago Cubs, who agreed to lease his North Side ballpark to the Staleys in return for 15 percent of the gate receipts and 100 percent of the concessions revenue. Playing in Cubs Park, the Staleys won the APFA title with a 9-1 record.

Q: Who was the Cub president who opened up the Chicago market for George Halas?
A: William Veeck Sr., father of beloved showman and future White Sox owner Bill Veeck.

1922

The American Professional Football League changed its name to the National Football League at the behest of George Halas, who said quite plainly, "The other name stunk!" At the same time Halas divested his ties to the Staley Company and renamed his team the Chicago Bears on January 28.

Q: Halas had a way of speaking his mind bluntly. As the Bears' coach this manifested itself in battles with referees. What did referee Jim Durfee do when Halas yelled "You stink!" for a 15-yard penalty?
A: Durfee penalized them another 15 yards and yelled back to Halas, "How do I smell from here?"

Q: Why did Halas name his team the Bears?
A: In order to remain consistent with his Wrigley Field landlord, the Chicago Cubs, Halas personally selected Bears because of his love of baseball and his affinity for Chicago's National League team. Team colors were blue and orange, the same colors as those of the University of Illinois.

1922

The Chicago Cardinals moved their home games to Comiskey Park, beginning an off-and-on-again and sometimes strenuous relationship with their landlord, the Chicago White Sox.

1925

Pro football came of age when the Chicago Bears signed University of Illinois halfback Harold "Red" Grange to a $100,000 contract. Grange was arguably the most famous collegiate player of the first quarter of the century, and the boxcar-sized deal was negotiated by his agent, theater owner C. C. Pyle.

Pyle also lined up a sum of $50,000 for Grange to endorse products such as a soft drink, shoes, sweaters, hats, and dolls.

Q: What was Grange's manager C. C. Pyle's nickname, and how did he get it?
A: The C. C. stood for "Cash and Carry." As he negotiated the cash, Grange carried it away.

Q: What famous sportswriter of the day nicknamed Grange "the Galloping Ghost?"
A: Grantland Rice.

"This tour will make you so wealthy, Halas, that next year, you'll be able to afford two sets of uniforms!"
C. C. Pyle to George Halas, just before the Bears launched their coast-to-coast, 16-game tour on November 26

"Football isn't meant to be played for money."
Bob Zuppke, coach of both Grange and Halas at the University of Illinois

1925

On Thanksgiving Day Red Grange was finally unveiled to the Chicago fans. The Bears and Cardinals met for their traditional holiday game at Wrigley Field, but the contest ended in a nothing-to-nothing tie because Paddy Driscoll, the great Cardinal halfback who played collegiate ball at Northwestern, stifled Grange's ground game by punting the ball away from him the entire game. The Galloping Ghost was held to only 36 yards.

The Cards opened the season as a dark horse directed by former Harvard coach Arnie Horween, who was replaced after the first game of the season by Norman Barry (who went on to become a noted Chicago judge). The Cardinals won the 1925

NFL championship by default; the Pottsville (Pennsylvania) Maroons were declared ineligible after violating league territorial rights by playing a game outside Philadelphia in defiance of league rules. The Cards were instructed to play two additional games. They whipped the Milwaukee Badgers 59-0 and the Hammond Indians 13-0 in the span of two days to claim the disputed title.

Q: Paddy Driscoll set a Cardinal record by scoring four touchdowns in a 60-0 rout of Rochester on October 7, 1923. What Chicago Cardinal broke Driscoll's team record when he scored six touchdowns of his own against the Bears on November 28, 1929?

A: Running back Ernie Nevers, an all-American out of Stanford, was coaxed out of retirement to serve as a Cardinal player/coach. The six touchdowns and four extra points scored by Nevers that day remain an all-time NFL single-game record.

"Mr. [Chris] O'Brien desires it to be known that his team isn't afraid of the Bears even now when they have Grange, and calls attention to the fact in his telegram to [George] Halas that the Bears haven't yet crossed the Cardinal goal line."

JIM CRUSINBERRY, *CHICAGO TRIBUNE* SPORTSWRITER, REPORTING ON CHRIS O'BRIEN'S DEMAND FOR A REMATCH AGAINST THE BEARS AND RED GRANGE. GEORGE HALAS DECLINED.

1926

Dyche Stadium, a 45,000-seat enclosure and the new home of the Northwestern Wildcats, opened for business. The facility was constructed on the site of the original wooden grandstand erected by the university in 1905. The original stands seated only 10,000 spectators.

Q: In whose honor was Dyche Stadium named?

A: Former Evanston mayor William A. Dyche, a Northwestern alumnus who spearheaded construction of the $1,425,000 stadium in 1926.

"I am obliged to you for setting the public straight in regard to the pronunciation of my name as D-I-K-E. It is commonly called Dish and Dysh and one Frenchman already addressed me as Deeshay. A friend suggests that on occasions when our boys are not successful, someone may speak of Ditch Stadium. I fear some trustees have let future generations in for a hard tussle with the name of Dyche Stadium."

William A. Dyche, in a letter to *Tribune* sports editor Harvey Woodruff, 1926

1926

The building of the monumental Soldier Field, a lakefront sports arena originally conceived by architect Daniel Burnham in his fabled 1909 "Plan of Chicago," was completed in October after nearly two years of construction. The $6 million stadium, with its classic columns and ornamentation, hosted many famous athletic events over the years: boxing matches, football games, bicycle races, and track-and-field events of all kinds.

Q: What was the original name of Soldier Field?
A: Grant Park Stadium. It was renamed in honor of the veterans of foreign wars.

1926

On November 27 the largest crowd in the history of football (up to that point in time) poured into Soldier Field to witness the annual Army-Navy Game. The two teams played to a heart-stopping 21-21 draw before 111,000 chilled fans and the vice president of the United States, Charles Dawes. It marked the first time the historic showdown was played in the Midwest.

Q: What other years did Chicago host the Army-Navy Game?
A: None

"The republic's two academies of the art and science of war delivered a great entertainment and drove straight and clean to

the hearts and minds of their delighted countrymen a great lesson in courage and fair play."

JAMES BENNETT, *CHICAGO TRIBUNE* REPORTER
COVERING THE GAME

1926

In order to make money off of his protége Red Grange, promoter C. C. "Cash and Carry" Pyle organized the American Football League. The Chicago entry, one of six teams comprising the AFL, was nicknamed the Bulls. They played their home games in Comiskey Park, which forced Chris O'Brien to make alternative arrangements for his champion Cardinals. The Big Red moved back to tiny Normal Park, where they stumbled and fumbled their way into ´10th place. Meanwhile, the American Football League disbanded early in 1927 after the Red Grange hysteria finally died down.

Q: Who owned the Chicago Bulls football team?
A: Former Chicago Bear halfback and University of Illinois star Joey Sternaman, whose brother Dutch was George Halas's business partner.

1929

In July 1929 Chris O'Brien sold the financially troubled Chicago Cardinals to David Jones, a noted sportsman who was part-owner of the Chicago Bruins, George Halas's professional basketball team. The price was $25,000, which is a fraction of what the modern NFL player makes in a single season.

Q: Where did the Cardinals play their home games that year?
A: Jones moved the team back to Comiskey Park, their home field for the next 29 years.

1930

The lyrics of the Chicago Bears fight song tells us how the "Bears thrilled the nation with their T-formation." In 1930 the Bears were the only NFL team to utilize this seven-man formation with three backs stationed behind the quarterback, forming a "T." George Halas is often credited with inventing the formation, but several other early innovators pioneered the "T."

Q: Who really invented the "T" formation?
A: Football historians believe Coach Bob Zuppke at the University of Illinois introduced the play in 1912. Others credit Ralph Jones, who coached at Lake Forest Academy during the 1926, 1927, and 1928 seasons before joining the Bears in 1930.

"The "T" formation is the shortest path to the goal line."
Bob Zuppke

1930

The Bears and Cardinals played an exhibition game to aid the unemployed victims of the Great Depression. The teams met on an abbreviated 80-yard field inside the Chicago Stadium. On December 15 a crowd of 10,000 watched the Bears down the Big Red 9-7.

Q: Indoor football was a 1930s novelty. In fact, a title game played indoors involving the Bears occurred two years later. What was the outcome?
A: Bronco Nagurski's two-yard touchdown pass to Red Grange wrapped up the 1932 title as the Bears downed the Portsmouth Spartans 9-0 before 11,198 fans on December 18. Because of inclement weather the game was played indoors at the Chicago Stadium.

1933

Upon attaining the mandatory retirement age, and after forty years of unbroken service on the Midway, Amos Alonzo Stagg was let go as head coach and athletic director at the University of Chicago. The Old Man, as he was known to the student body, was not quite ready to retire, however.

Q: Where did Stagg go after leaving Chicago?
A: He accepted an appointment to coach California's College

of the Pacific at Stockton. Stagg served in this capacity for the next 14 years.

1933

On October 24 Dr. David Jones peddled his Chicago Cardinals to Charles W. Bidwell, a wealthy and famous sportsman, for $50,000. Close associates believed that Mr. Bidwell felt greater pleasure at seeing victories by the Chicago Bears, his first love, than by building a champion on the South Side. Thirteen more years would pass before the Cardinals finally turned the corner and regained a semblance of respectability for an owner who purchased his team more as a civic duty than as a sporting venture.

Q: What other sporting venture was Charles Bidwell involved in?

A: He was part-owner of Sportsman's Park racetrack in suburban Cicero.

1933

The Bears emerged as the victors of the National Football League's Western Division. Playing in the first prearranged NFL championship game, the Miracle Bears defeated the New York Giants 23-21 before 26,000 fans at Wrigley Field on December 17.

Q: Why were they called the Miracle Bears?

A: A succession of last-minute victories earned the 10-2 Bears the 1933 title.

1934

George Halas's Chicago Bears and a team of college all-stars coached by Noble Kizer of Purdue dueled to a nothing-to-nothing draw in the first College All-Star Game, played on August 31 at Soldier Field. More than 165,000 fans cast their votes for the team of collegians who challenged the reigning National Football League champions in the annual charity event conceived by *Chicago Tribune* sports editor Arch Ward. The

College All-Star Game was one of the most anticipated and highly publicized sporting events of its day.

Q: Which Illinois university sent the most college players to the All-Star squad?
A: Through 1970, 60 Northwestern Wildcat teams participated in the College All-Star Game. The Wildcats ranked third for participation behind Notre Dame and Ohio State.

"The Tribune promotes this game not with the idea that it serves as a test of the merits of college and professional football but rather to provide a few hours of wholesome recreation for those who wish to see the best talent American football can present."

Arch Ward, 1936

1934

That year Halas's team won all of its regular season games only to lose the NFL title game to the New York Giants 30-13. The Bears were actually leading 10-3 at halftime when the Giants retreated to their locker room to formulate a new strategy; they switched to rubber-soled sneakers. When they returned to the slippery, frozen field, they regained their traction and ran wild.

Q: How much did a season ticket cost that year?
A: To see all six Chicago Bear home games at Wrigley Field cost only $13.20.

"We had a great undefeated team that year, and then got beaten by a Nor'easter that blew into New York and froze the Polo Grounds turf. I'll never forget it. . . . Giants Coach Steve Owne had his trainer raid the Manhattan College locker room for rubber-soled shoes. The Giants got traction out of the shoes, while we were skidding around on our cleats the second half, and we lost. The sneakers beat us."

George Halas, proving that it was the shoes all along

1935

University of Chicago halfback Jay Berwanger won the first John J. Heisman Memorial Trophy, presented annually to college football's most valuable player. Berwanger, who struck a characteristic pose for a famous photo of the day, is believed to have been the sculptor's model for the trophy.

Q: Berwanger is one of two U of C alumni named to the All-Time All-American Team in 1969. No other college football team can claim this distinction. Who was the other Maroon to be honored?
A: Quarterback Walter Eckersall.

1939

Intercollegiate football was discontinued at the University of Chicago on December 21 by a unanimous vote of the board of trustees. University president Robert Maynard Hutchins, worried about declining endowments in the academic realm, explained that the student body "derives no special benefit" from a football team. Thus Coach Stagg's beloved "Maroons" faded into the pages of history.

Q: What was the U of C's record in their final season?
A: The Maroons won only one of eight games. In their final appearance on November 25 they were routed 46-0 by the University of Illinois.

"Lonnie Stagg still thinks football at Chicago could have been saved. I don't believe so."

GRANTLAND RICE

"There is no doubt that, on the whole, football has been a major handicap to education in the United States."

ROBERT MAYNARD HUTCHINS, PRESIDENT OF THE UNIVERSITY OF CHICAGO, ON DISMANTLING THE UNIVERSITY'S FOOTBALL PROGRAM IN 1939

1940

Revenge was sweet for George Halas and the Bears. After losing 7-3 to Washington on November 17 the Bears were ridiculed by Redskins owner George Preston Marshall as "quitters . . . and a bunch of crybabies." To add insult to injury, Marshall added, "They fold up when the going gets tough!" Three weeks later the Bears returned to Washington intent on squaring accounts. At stake: the NFL championship. The result? The Bears turned Sid Luckman, a halfback on defense in his rookie year, into an outstanding "T-formation" quarterback and handed Washington their most devastating loss in team history, a 73-0 rout. Fifteen Bears scored points that day before a stunned crowd of 36,034.

Q: George Halas called Sid Luckman the greatest quarterback he had ever seen. What team records does Sid Luckman still hold?

A: During his 11-year Bear career (1939-1950), Hall of Famer Sid Luckman established individual career records for most yards gained (14,686); touchdown passes (137); consecutive 300-yard games (2, 1947); and most touchdown passes in one game (seven, against the New York Giants on November 14, 1943).

"George Preston Marshall, the mettlesome laundryman who owned the Redskins, looked on from the stands except when he charged up the aisle and threw a punch at a dissatisfied customer and when his ordeal was over, every hair in his raccoon coat had turned white."

RED SMITH, SYNDICATED *NEW YORK TIMES* SPORTS COLUMNIST

1941

The Chicago Bears became the first National Football League team to repeat as champions. The 1940s were truly their "Golden Age," beginning with the 1940 championship and continuing in 1941 when they stormed past the Green Bay Packers in a tie-breaking showdown for the Western Division title. The championship game against the New York Giants at Wrigley Field was a cakewalk. The Bears, dubbed the "Monsters of the Midway" won 37-9, but only 13,341 fans showed up for the game. The Japanese had just bombed Pearl Harbor, and there were more pressing concerns to address.

Q: Why were the Bears called the Monsters of the Midway?
A: A New York sportswriter mistakenly believed that the Bears practice field was located on the University of Chicago's Midway Plaisance. George Halas liked the name and it stuck.

1941

"Bear Down, Chicago Bears!" the popular team fight song, was published in sheet music.

1942

Forty-seven-year-old George Halas joined the navy. Upon completion of his four-year hitch in 1946, he retired as a full captain in the Naval Reserve and was presented the Distinguished Citizen's Award, the highest honor the navy can bestow upon a citizen. Minus George Halas, the Bears lost the NFL title game to Washington 14-6.

Q: Who coached the Bears while Halas was serving his country?
A: Former Chicago Bear Heartley "Hunk" Anderson handled the defense. Former Northwestern end Luke Johnson coached the offense.

1943

Northwestern quarterback Otto Graham set a College All-Star Game record with a 97-yard run against the Washington Redskins after intercepting a Sammy Baugh pass. The All-Stars defeated the Redskins 27-7 at Dyche Stadium.

Q: What other College All-Star Game record does Graham hold?
A: Following his retirement as a professional player, Graham coached more All-Star and professional squads than any other head coach who participated in the game. Otto led the All-Stars every year from 1958 to 1965 and again in

1969 and 1970. In addition, he coached the Cleveland Browns to a 33-0 win in the 1951 game.

1943

The wartime rosters of the professional teams were sorely depleted, but the Bears persevered and won their third NFL crown in four years. The championship game at Wrigley Field reunited the Bears and archrival Washington and featured a classic rematch of the league's top two quarterbacks—Sid Luckman against Sammy Baugh of the Redskins. The game belonged to Sid, who threw five touchdown passes. In all, Luckman's magic arm accounted for 286 total yards. Bears 41, Redskins 21.

Q: What famous Chicago Bear from the 1930s came out of retirement in 1943 to lead the Bears into the championship game?

A: Fullback Bronco Nagurski, retired since 1937, carried the ball 16 times and led the Bears past the crosstown Cardinals 35-28 on the last day of the season to sew up the title.

1944

As a wartime emergency measure, the Chicago Cardinals and Pittsburgh Steelers temporarily merged into one team representing two cities under the name "Card-Pitt." Chicago's top passer, receiver, and lineman—Johnny Clement, Bill Dewell, and Joe Kuharich—were all lost to the service. Card-Pitt, a neutered team with a ridiculous name, lost all 10 of its games that season.

Q: Who shared the coaching duties for Card-Pitt?

A: Phil "Motz" Handler and Walter "Kies" Kiesling were former Cardinal teammates for four seasons before joining the coaching ranks. They were recognized as two of the greatest NFL guards of the early 1930s.

1946

Sportswriter Arch Ward, the originator of baseball's All-Star Game, the College Football All-Star Game, and the International Golden Gloves Tournament, called the first meeting of prospective franchise owners for a new professional football league he had in mind on June 4, 1944. Despite dire predictions that a new league could not possibly succeed against the National Football League monopoly, the All-America Football Conference began play in 1946 after 115 NFL players "jumped" their contracts.

Ward's ingenuity and a willingness to lure established college coaches into the AAFC ranks spelled initial success for the league everywhere except in the Windy City. The newly christened Chicago Rockets, playing in Soldier Field, sputtered under the direction of coach Dick Hanley, a former marine colonel who inspired neither the respect nor trust of his players. The Rockets, thought to be the cornerstone franchise of the new league, finished dead last in the Western Division.

Q: How did the Rockets acquire their name?

A: Owner John L. Keeshin was inspired by the dawning of the jet age and the rocket-propelled missiles he believed would traverse outer space one day. No doubt the development of the atomic bomb at the University of Chicago during the war influenced him.

1946

George Halas returned from the war, and the Bears resumed their winning ways with another championship run. The high-octane Bears won the Western Division and then glided past the New York Giants 24-14 in the Polo Grounds on December 15 before 53,346. The victory was not without controversy. In fact, the game was anticlimactic to what transpired off the field that year.

Q: What event nearly wrecked the NFL in 1946?

A: The day before the Bears-Giants title game, NFL commissioner Bert Bell suspended Merle Hapes of the New York Giants after rumors surfaced that he had agreed to fix the outcome of the contest for gambler Alvin Paris in return for $2,500. Paris was arrested. A potential Black Sox scandal was narrowly averted by an NFL commissioner who acted with dispatch.

1947

Illness claimed the life of Chicago Cardinals owner Charles Bidwell at the very moment his beloved Big Red stood on the threshold of their first NFL championship. Charley Bidwell had finally built a winner. This club had his imprimatur all over it, but he did not live long enough to enjoy the fruits of his labor. However, his willingness to out-spend the fledgling AAFC in a bidding war for all-American halfback Charley Trippi from the University of Georgia salted away the 1947 title for the South Siders.

Trippi formed the nucleus of a million-dollar dream backfield that also included halfbacks Elmer Angsman, Marshall Goldberg; former University of Missouri quarterback Paul Christman, and fullback Pat Harder, who scored 102 points to lead the league. The Cardinals, always the underdog and never a bona fide champion until 1947, trounced the Chicago Bears 30-21 in Wrigley Field on December 14 before 48,632 chilled fans to wrap up the Western Division championship. It was the first time since 1922 that the Big Red defeated the Bears twice in the same season.

The Cardinals squared off against another former also-ran, the Philadelphia Eagles, in the league's title game, which was played on the frozen baseball diamond at Comiskey Park on December 28. Conzelman's team donned sneakers to offset the slick turf. Then, with Trippi and Angsman scoring two touchdowns a piece, the Cards ran wild against the stunned Eagles. They won the NFL championship, for only the second time in their history, 28-21.

Q: What famous College All-Star Game record did Trippi set during his collegiate and professional careers?

A: He was the only player to appear in the annual College All-Star Game at Soldier Field five times—four as a member of the College All-Stars and once as a Cardinal.

"My guys look good, but I don't think they're grim enough. I wish I could see a little more blood in those calf-brown eyes."

JIMMY CONZELMAN, ON PSYCHOLOGICAL MOTIVATION BEFORE THE BIG GAME

1947

WBKB-TV televised all six of the Chicago Bears home games from Wrigley Field. George Halas was paid $900 a game by station executives for the broadcast privileges.

Q: Who were the first TV announcers to narrate the Bears games?
A: Former Bear great Red Grange did the play-by-play. Russ Davis provided commentary.

1947

The AAFC realized its hopes for long-term success hinged on the well-being of its large-market teams. The disappointing Chicago Rockets of 1946 were placed in the competent hands of Jim Crowley, who resigned his $25,000-per-year salary post as AAFC commissioner in order to take over as head coach of the struggling franchise. Crowley purchased the team with several of his boyhood chums and set out to mold a champion. He instituted a highly geared "T" formation revolving around his 210-pound halfback Elroy "Crazy Legs" Hirsch and the speedy quarterback Bob "Hunchy" Hoernschemeyer. They looked good on paper, but Crowley's Rockets kept losing the close ones. A poor defense accounted for their dismal 1-13 record.

Q: What famous college line did Crowley play on in his younger days?
A: He was a member of the famed Four Horseman backfield (Crowley, Elmer Layden, Harry Stuhldreher, and Don Miller) for Knute Rockne's 1924 Notre Dame squad. Crowley went on to become the head coach at Fordham University in New York.

"Probably no team in the history of football, professional or college, has fielded so powerful an offense and yet met with such proportionately small success."

PRESS NOTES ON THE ROCKETS, OCT. 31, 1947,
CHICAGO ROCKETS VS. BROOKLYN DODGERS

1948

With the death of Chicago Cardinals owner Charles Bidwell, ownership of the club passed into the hands of the widow, Violet Bidwell, who married St. Louis businessman Walter Wolfner shortly afterward. The fortunes of the Big Red plummeted in the coming years, but in 1948 Conzelman's team closed out the regular season at 11-1, a high-water mark for the franchise never to be duplicated in the Windy City. The NFL championship game was a rematch of 1947, only this time the Cardinals played in a blinding Philadelphia snowstorm and lost to the Eagles 7-0 after assisting the grounds crew in clearing away the snow in order for the game to begin. While the Cards shoveled, the Eagles played gin rummy in the comfort of their dressing room. The only touchdown occurred late in the game after the Cardinals fumbled the ball on their own 14-yard line.

Minus the steadying hand of Charley Bidwell, the Cardinals quickly went into the dumper. Mrs. Bidwell and her husband were just not capable of reversing the trend or re-creating the 1947-1948 magic.

Q: The Cardinals managed only two more winning seasons before moving to St. Louis in 1960. In what years did the South Siders come out ahead?

A: In 1949 Chicago finished 6-5. In 1956 they won seven and lost five.

1948

How is it possible for a professional football team to lose 13 of 14 games two years in a row? The Chicago Rockets defied logic and accomplished the impossible. They were even worse than their 1948 1-13 record indicated. At season's end, "Crazy Legs" Hirsch, one of the fastest and most elusive halfbacks in football, joined the Los Angeles Rams, where he became one of the game's true immortals. Unaccustomed to losing, owner Jim Crowley abandoned hope and put the club up for sale.

1948-1949

Trailing by a point with less than three minutes left to play in the 1949 Rose Bowl Game, the Northwestern Wildcats, coached by Bob Voigts, snatched victory from the jaws of defeat and upended the University of California 20-14. The Wildcats' defense made the difference against the undefeated Golden Bears, who were led by Coach Lynn Waldorf. Left halfback Frank Aschenbrenner's record-setting 73-yard run from scrimmage opened the scoring for the Cats in the first quarter.

Q: What did these two rival coaches have in common?
A: Bob Voigts played right tackle for the Wildcats in 1936, the year Lynn Waldorf coached the Cats to a Big Ten title. Two years later Voigts was named an all-American.

"Anyone who makes Northwestern a seven-point favorite is a crazy, unfit to handle money, or both."
BOB VOIGTS, NU COACH, DISPLAYING PREGAME MODESTY

1949

James C. Thompson and two business associates purchased the hapless Rockets from Jim Crowley and desperately tried to make a go of it in Chicago's overheated, thinly stretched pro-football market. Thompson changed the team's name to the Hornets. He hired a new coach who was no stranger to long-time Chicago Bear fans. He undercut ticket prices charged by the Bears and Cards and assembled a team that was 400 times better than the crew of misfits who had opened the 1948 season. Indeed, Thompson did many things in a very short period of time, but without fast-moving halfback "Crazy Legs" Hirsch on the squad, the Hornets' modest 4-8 record failed to convince Chicago fans of his sincerity.

In December 1949 the AAFC threw in the towel and agreed to a merger with the National Football League. The Hornets were purchased by the NFL and the team was quietly disbanded. Arch Ward's dream of a second professional football league was over, for the time being.

Q: What former Bear nemesis coached the Hornets in their final season?

A: Former New York Giants end Pat Flaherty, who suggested to his teammates that they switch to tennis shoes in the 1934 NFL play-off game in order to counter the slick, frozen turf at the Polo Grounds. The strategy worked, and the Giants downed the Bears 30-13.

"We are out to prove rather than claim that sports fans in the Chicago area will see all the rough, tough, fast, furious, and fighting major league football they want at prices that make good sense. In proving our point, we are going the whole way to bring to Soldier Field a Chicago Hornets football team that's manned by top gridiron stars and coached by a staff of experienced grid mentors who have proven their ability to build champs."

JAMES C. THOMPSON, OWNER'S STATEMENT TO THE FANS

1956

Ara Parseghian, a legendary college coach and member of the Football Foundation Hall of Fame, succeeded Lou Saban as head coach of the Northwestern Wildcats. Improvement was immediate and dramatic. Winless in 1955, the Cats played .500 ball in 1956, winning four and losing four. During the "Ara Era" Northwestern won 36 and lost 35—a mark of achievement considering the long, losing seasons that were to follow.

Q: Who replaced Parseghian as NU coach?

A: Parseghian lasted until 1963, when he took over head coaching duties at Notre Dame. Alex Agase, a three-time all-American at the University of Illinois and Purdue replaced Parseghian.

1956

George Halas was on the sidelines again after announcing his third "retirement" from the game on February 2. He turned the ball club over to his friend and former Bear star "Paddy" Driscoll, who guided the team to a 9-2 record and a shot at the NFL championship. The Bears played the New York Giants for the title on December 30 at Yankee Stadium in near sub-zero temperatures. Proving that history sometimes repeats itself, the Bears were soundly defeated 47-7 in a game that brought back haunting memories of the 1934 debacle that also cost them the championship.

Q: How did the Giants defeat the elements and whip the Bears for a second time?

A: To overcome the slick, ice-covered field, the New York players donned rubber-soled sneakers—just as they had done in 1934.

> *"Even though Halas has transferred himself to the sidelines and no longer will permit the public to see those anxious tugs at his hat, the man who originated the Bears will continue to pull most of the strings."*
>
> CHICAGO SPORTSWRITER, FEBRUARY 2, 1956

1960

Pro football's oldest continuous franchise severed its ties with Chicago on March 13, 1960, when Violet Bidwell Wolfner announced that the beloved Chicago Cardinals were transferring to St. Louis. The embattled Cardinal ownership broke their Comiskey Park lease after the 1958 season because of their dissatisfaction with the rental terms, but drew only 160,438 customers into Soldier Field to see them play in 1959. Two of the "home games" were actually played in Minneapolis.

The NFL was eager to have the Cardinals vacate Chicago. George Halas, it was reported, helped pay their moving expenses after successfully blocking the Cards' move into Northwestern's Dyche Stadium in Evanston—by invoking a 40-year-old clause in the NFL agreement awarding him exclusive territorial rights north of Madison Street. The rich and prosperous Bears emerged the victor in the local football wars fought inside the corporate suites, while the city suffered a much greater loss—the departure of a legendary and historic team that introduced the professional game to Chicago.

Q: Who coached the Chicago Cardinals in the final year?
A: Frank "Pop" Ivy, a former Cardinal star from the 1940s. His team finished 2-10 for the season.

"It's just a lot of bleating in the wind. We've got the same letterhead as always. The Chicago Cardinals will remain the Chicago Cardinals."

WALTER WOLFNER, MANAGING DIRECTOR, DENYING THE REPORTED MOVE TO ST. LOUIS, MARCH 10, 1960

"There has been long, constant pressure from within the league for us to move. The purpose was to open up Chicago for TV."

WALTER WOLFNER, THE DAY AFTER THE MOVE WAS ANNOUNCED, MARCH 14, 1960

1963

Seventeen years had passed between Chicago Bear championships. George Halas was still around, but the supporting cast had changed markedly since 1946. Assistant Coach George Allen implemented a zone defense, and suddenly Chicago had the strongest defense in the league. The Bears twice defeated their archrivals, the Green Bay Packers, fulfilling George Halas's preseason objective: Beat Vince Lombardi's team twice and the championship is for the taking.

The 11-1 Bears edged Green Bay to wrap up the Western Conference, then played the New York Giants for the NFL championship in frigid eight-degree weather on December 29. Quarterback Bill Wade keyed the title run by scoring two touchdowns. The stingy Chicago defense intercepted five Y. A. Tittle passes and held on for a 14-10 victory in frozen Wrigley Field.

Mike Ditka, a 1961 first-round draft choice out of the University of Pittsburgh, was quarterback Bill Wade's favorite target that season. The young tight end caught 59 passes.

Q: Why was the 1963 Bears championship a watershed event for Chicago sports?
A: It would be Chicago's last championship—of any kind—until 1981, when the Chicago Sting would win the North American Soccer League title.

"People who live in the past are cowards—and they're losers. And it's the same for people who write about the past—they're losers and they're cowards."

MIKE DITKA, KNOWN AS "DA COACH," EXPRESSING HIS PHILOSOPHY

1965

Kansas running back Gale Sayers launched his pro career with the Chicago Bears. George Halas had to come up with big money in order to secure the services of the talented Sayers—reportedly $150,000 in bonus money. He did not disappoint. Sayers won Rookie of the Year honors in his first year. He went on to set 23 team records and seven National Football League records during his brief seven-year career. At thirty-four he was the youngest player ever inducted into the Pro Football Hall of Fame in Canton, Ohio.

Q: Who did the Bears draft ahead of Gale Sayers in the 1965 college draft?

A: Middle linebacker and future Hall of Famer Dick Butkus from the University of Illinois was the third pick in the rich 1965 college harvest. Sayers was the fourth player selected by Chicago that year.

"He looks no different than any other runner when he's coming at you, but when he get's there, he's gone."

GEORGE DONNELLY, SAN FRANCISCO 49ERS DEFENSIVE BACK, ON SAYERS, THE BALL CARRIER

1967

Two rival professional soccer leagues, organized in the fall of 1966 by a consortium of multimillionaires who believed that the European game was finally ready to take off on U.S. soil, began play the following spring.

The Chicago Spurs, owned by William Cutler and Al Kaczmarek, represented the Windy City in the North American Soccer League (NASL). Soccer stars from 12 European nations played on the Spurs team, including the famed "Three Musketeers of Germany"—Wolfgang Glock, Gerd Ziemann, and Heinz Banschewitz. The Spurs were coached by Alan Rogers, a Brit who had difficulty communicating with his foreign-speaking players. The language barrier contributed to a morale breakdown midway through the season that was impossible to overcome. After Rogers was demoted to assistant coach because of his lack of fluency in German, he sued the owners.

The floundering Spurs played their home games at Soldier Field before tiny crowds. They were aired locally on WGN-TV.

The Chicago Mustangs of the 12-team United Soccer Association (USA) played an up-tempo style of game and enjoyed greater success in Comiskey Park than the Spurs in their cavernous Soldier Field home. John Allyn, the eternally optimistic younger brother of White Sox owner Art Allyn, organized the rival USA league with other big money sportsmen from across the U.S. including William Clay Ford, scion of the Detroit automotive fortune; Jack Kent Cooke of Los Angeles; and Lamar Hunt of Dallas. The vigorous and skillful Mustangs were no more successful than the pitiful Spurs in luring fans into the stadium to witness professional soccer—a doomed sport despite occasional flourishes of success in the early 1980s.

Q: The Chicago Mustangs were an existing team imported from another country. They were given a new nickname by John Allyn. Where did the Mustangs come from, and what was their original name?

A: The famous Unione Sportiva Cagliari team of Sardinia represented Chicago as the Mustangs.

Q: The Spurs inaugurated pro soccer in Chicago with a 2-1 victory over the St. Louis Stars on April 16, 1967, before a tiny gathering of 4,720. What future Chicago Sting coach scored both goals for the Spurs in their debut?

A: Willy Roy, the German centerman whose last name means "king" in French.

"We'll probably average six or seven thousand a game for the first few years, but we figure to be able to put our operation in the black in five years."

LAMAR HUNT

1968

The North American Soccer League and the United Soccer Association folded after just one year of competition. The NASL announced that it was suspending play for three years on November 2, in order to support one national touring team representing the U.S.

1970

Chicago Bear running back Brian Piccolo, suffering the ravages of cancer, passed away on June 16. The four-year veteran was only 26 years old. The Bears retired his number and established the Piccolo Fund, which has raised $2 million for cancer research to date.

Q: Who starred in *Brian's Song,* the movie adaptation of Brian Piccolo's life?

A: James Caan portrayed Piccolo, and Billy Dee Williams played Gale Sayers in the 1970 film.

1970

The Bears played their final home game at Wrigley Field on December 13, defeating archrival Green Bay 35-17.

1971

The Chicago Bears moved into spacious, but outdated Soldier Field. The stadium's seating capacity of 55,000—approximately 6,000 more than Wrigley Field—appealed to George Halas. However, he was never satisfied with the lack of amenities, the parking situation, or his arrangements with the Chicago Park District. Through the next two decades the Halas heirs would lobby the state of Illinois, the city of Chicago, and the taxpayers to build a modern new stadium to play in. The issue remained unresolved, and was still a bone of contention, 25 years later.

Q: Soldier Field was the Bears' second choice. Where did they originally intend to play future home games after leaving Wrigley Field?

A: Dyche Stadium in Evanston. Discouraged by resident complaints following a regular season game played against Philadelphia in Dyche Stadium on September 27, 1970, Halas "settled" for Soldier Field. They have remained there ever since.

1974

Chicago builder Tom Origer bought into a fragile dream. Like others before and after him, he gambled that Windy City football fans were ready to support a second professional team in a rival league, in this case the Chicago Fire of the World Football League (WFL), which was inaugurated in October 1973. Origer was the first man standing in line to purchase a WFL team when franchise applications became available, the first one to hire a coach, the first to hire a general manager . . . and his team, tragically, was the first one to fold.

Ticket sales were brisk in the early weeks of the season. The Fire won their first four games and were drawing an average crowd of 26,600 fans into Soldier Field. But then the team lost 10 games in a row, the Bears, Blackhawks, and Bulls began their seasons, and interest in the Fire dwindled. Origer tried to mortgage his team to pay outstanding bills, but the league rejected the plan and ordered him to dissolve the franchise on January 20, 1975. Tom Origer lost $1.2 million pursuing his dream.

Q: Who was the Fire's number one draft pick?
A: Bill Kollar, who signed with the Cincinnati Bengals. Origer tried to sign Notre Dame quarterback Joe Theismann as well, but Theismann wanted a $50,000 bonus and a $100,00-per-year salary, which the Chicago Fire could not afford to pay.

"It doesn't look good at all for the league. I've had a few people express interest in the Fire but I'm not about to sell them a lemon. All they would be buying is another season of losses. Smart businessmen won't be buying losses the way the economy is now."

Tom Origer, January 1975

1974

On Halloween day Lee Stern, a Chicago commodities broker and part-time White Sox investor, founded the Chicago Sting, the newest entrant in the revived North American Soccer League. Under the direction of Coach Bill Foulkes, the outdoor team narrowly missed winning the division title in its first season.

Q: How did the Chicago Sting acquire its nickname?

A: One of Lee Stern's sons suggested naming the team the Chicago River until Cub announcer Jack Brickhouse gently reminded Stern that the Chicago River runs *backward.* Acting on the suggestion of NASL commissioner Phil Woosman, the owner christened his team the Sting after the Oscar-winning motion picture of the same name starring Robert Redford and Paul Newman.

1975

After a brilliant career at Jackson State, the Chicago Bears drafted Walter Payton, who became one of the all-time great running backs in team history. Walter holds 28 team records, and he played for 13 seasons and only missed one game during that time. The amazingly durable Payton played when he was sick and injured and with an intensity uncommon for most athletes in the modern era.

Q: Walter's #34 is one of 13 uniform numbers retired by the Bears. Can you name the other 12 Bear immortals and their numbers?

A: Bronco Nagurski (#3); George McAfee (#5); George Halas (#7); Willie Gallimore (#28); Gale Sayers (#40); Brian Piccolo (#41); Sid Luckman (#42); Dick Butkus (#51); Bill Hewitt (#56); Bill George (#61); Clyde "Bulldog" Turner (#66); and Harold "Red" Grange (#77).

"Well they call me Sweetness—
And I like to dance,
Runnin' the ball is like makin' romance
We've had the goal since training camp—

To give Chicago a Super Bowl champ
And we're not doin' this
Because we're greedy—
The Bears are doin' it to feed the needy.
We don't come here to look for trouble.
We just come here to do
The Super Bowl Shuffle."

WALTER PAYTON, SINGING ABOUT HIMSELF IN THE CHORUS OF THE 1986 "SUPER BOWL SHUFFLE"

1975

The WFL refused to give up on Chicago, and suburban insurance executive Eugene Pullano believed he could succeed where Tom Origer failed.

Pullano was awarded a franchise in the restructured league. He nicknamed his team the Chicago Winds and lured several wealthy out-of-town investors into a shaky partnership. But when two of the club's California backers withdrew their $175,000 investments, the WFL suddenly and without warning revoked Pullano's franchise on September 2, 1975. The Winds were "gone with the wind" after playing only two exhibition games and five regular season games. Only 3,502 fans had witnessed the Winds one and only victory in rain-soaked Soldier Field. The World Football League collapsed less than two months later on October 22.

Q: Who coached the Chicago Winds in their abbreviated season?

A: Former Chicago Bears head coach Abe Gibron.

1976

The College All-Star football game, a midsummer tradition along the Chicago lakefront for 43 years, was discontinued by Chicago Tribune Charities because of rising insurance costs associated with escalating player salaries. The yearly event raised $4 million for charitable causes since the game was first played in 1934.

"The College All-Star game played a major role in promoting the growth of the National Football League. I regret that it is no longer practical economically for Chicago Tribune Charities to sponsor it."

PETE ROZELLE, NFL COMMISSIONER, DECEMBER 21, 1976

1976

Anything for a headline.

The Chicago Sting drafted Marilyn Lange, *Playboy* magazine's 1975 Playmate of the Year. The comely Ms. Lange had actually played soccer for a women's team in Hawaii and had done some promotional work for Lee Stern prior to being selected in the player draft by General Manager Jim Walker.

"We had a nationwide hookup for the draft and we came down to the last round. I said Marilyn Lange from Hawaii. The commissioner got madder than hell. He made me repeat her name six *times."*

JIM WALKER

1981

The Chicago Sting fulfilled destiny's long overdue call and won the NASL Soccer Bowl in Toronto after downing the New York Cosmos before 36,971 in a shoot-out at Exhibition Stadium on September 27.

The winning goal was driven past Cosmo goalie Hubert Birkenmeier by Rudy Glenn. It was Chicago's first sports championship since 1963, when the Bears captured the NFL title. Thousands of delirious soccer fanatics turned out at O'Hare Airport to hail Coach Willy Roy and his conquering heroes as they stepped off their plane.

There was a certain hustle and pizazz to this team lacking in the other sports operations around town. Call it showmanship. The nightly giveaways and "sign-up parties" engineered by Charlie Evranrian, the director of operations, went over big with younger fans. Professional soccer in Chicago was on the rise . . . for the time being.

Q: The high-scoring Sting led the NASL in goals. But what defender was named the Soccer Bowl's Most Valuable Player in 1981?

A: Franz Mathieu, who was also a first-team all-star that season.

"We had more fans here than we used to draw at home. It's a far cry from the days we used to draw 2,945 and round it off to 3,015."

LEE STERN, WHO STILL LOST A MILLION DOLLARS ON THE STING IN 1981

"Hurrah for the Chicago Sting! How fitting it is that our youngest major sports franchise should be the one to give Chicago its first professional championship in 18 years!"

CHICAGO MAYOR JANE BYRNE

1980-1981

The Chicago Horizons, belonging to the three-year-old Major Indoor Soccer League (MISL), inaugurated play at the Rosemont Horizon. They folded at the end of the year, leaving behind a trail of unpaid bills and lawsuits.

1982

On August 19 the Chicago Sting announced that it had joined the Major Indoor Soccer League (MISL) after the North American Soccer League dropped indoor soccer from the schedule. The Sting elected to remain in the NASL for the outdoor season, despite the league's mounting economic woes.

Soccer purists derided the high-scoring indoor game as little more than a silly variation of pinball. However, the Sting had enjoyed tremendous success the year prior when the NASL game first went indoors. They made it to the league finals after finishing with the best regular-season record in the league.

Q: Where did the Sting play its indoor season?

A: At the Chicago Stadium, where they averaged 13,300 fans and out-drew both the Bulls and the Blackhawks.

> *"I wouldn't say it is Rollerball. But I'm a little scared of what might happen to the game. Yet the American players like this. It's more . . . I guess . . . American. My hope is that the World Cup can come here in 1986 so that people can see how beautiful the best kind of soccer can be."*
>
> INGO PETER OF THE CHICAGO STING

1982

Longtime Chicago favorite Mike Ditka was hired to coach the Chicago Bears on January 20, 1982. The fiery Ditka, intense in his approach to life, played for George Halas from 1961 to 1966. He was only the 11th Bear head coach since 1920.

Q: Name the only two players who caught more passes in their Chicago Bear career than Mike Ditka.
A: Walter Payton (356, 1975-1987) and Johnny Morris (356, 1958-1964).

> *"Again and again, you are confronted with visions of him throwing clipboards and cursing officials when he should be sending in the next play on offense and calling the next defense. He is after all, a creature of brute force, the quintessential Midway monster, and as such is not the stuff head coaches are made of."*
>
> JOHN SCHULIAN, *CHICAGO SUN-TIMES* COLUMNIST, JANUARY 5, 1982

1983

George Halas, Chicago's Papa Bear, passed away on November 11 at age 88. The Bears' founding father was a towering figure in Chicago football and an endless contradiction. At times he was a visionary, a ruthless mercenary, a builder of champions, pioneer, and the man most responsible for the demise of the Chicago Cardinals. George Halas was inducted into the Football Hall of Fame in 1963.

Q: George Halas retired from coaching on May 27, 1968, with a career record of 324-151-31. His win total was the best in the NFL for many years. Who finally bettered the mark?

A: Don Shula shattered the record with his 325th coaching victory on November 14, 1993.

"I suppose some people think an interest in sports is frivolous, but not for myself. I've loved sports since I was old enough to cross a Chicago street by myself . . . I haven't aged in my outlook on life. Maybe, I even scored a victory over the generation gap they keep talking about."

GEORGE HALAS, FEBRUARY 2, 1971

1983

Ted Diethrich, one of the most famous heart surgeons in the country, purchased a majority interest in the Chicago Blitz of the new United States Football League (USFL), the latest pretender to the NFL football throne. Diethrich would have preferred to operate his team in sunny Phoenix, where he conducted his medical research at the Arizona Heart Institute, but someone else had already been granted the local franchise rights. So, in the interest of becoming a national sports celebrity in his own right, Diethrich jumped at the chance to enter the saturated Chicago sports market.

Preseason forecasters expected big things from the Chicago Blitz, but the team lost two of its first three games, including a 16-13 drubbing to the Denver Gold in the home tilt at Soldier Field on March 20, 1983. The game was played in a blinding snowstorm before a disappointing turnout. But after this inauspicious beginning the talent-laden Bltiz won 11 of the next 14 games and advanced to the USFL semifinals, where they were defeated by Philadelphia.

Q: Who coached the Blitz during their first season?
A: Dr. Diethrich hired George Allen, an NFL legend who molded the defense of the champion 1963 Bears.

Q: Who was the starting quarterback for the Chicago team in 1983?
A: Greg Landry, the silver-haired, former Detroit Lions quarterback who starred in the 1968 College All-Star Game against Vince Lombardi's Green Bay Packers.

"I think pro football is a national sport, more so than baseball, and there isn't enough of it. The long-term idea of spring football is appealing. There's nothing more beautiful than [sitting in Soldier Field] on Lake Shore Drive in Spring."

CHICAGO BLITZ OWNER TED DIETHRICH

1983-1984

The prognosis for Chicago was grim after Dr. Diethrich announced his purchase of the Arizona Wranglers on September 27, 1983. Because the Phoenix heart surgeon was not permitted to own two USFL teams at the same time, the good doctor cleverly avoided a thorny legal complication with the league's governing body by exporting the hapless Arizona Wranglers—a 4-14 doormat in 1983—to Chicago, where they opened the 1984 spring season. Meanwhile, he *imported* all of the Blitz' top players—and Coach George Allen—to the Valley of the Sun and rechristened them the Wranglers.

It was a shifty scheme foisted onto the football fans of Chicago by a carpetbagging owner from the West Coast solely concerned about his own selfish interests. It was indicative of the caliber of ego-charged men who were getting into professional sports in the 1970s and 1980s.

Worse, Diethrich sold the neutered Blitz to an underfinanced investment group headed by a colleague from the medical profession named Dr. James Hoffman, who made a cash down payment of $500,000 to Diethrich and then ran out of money.

Unable to meet his financial obligations, Hoffman relinquished control of the Blitz to the USFL before the season even started. Playing before meager gatherings of four and five thousand fans at Soldier Field, the ownerless football team managed to win only five of 18 games in 1984.

Despite hopeful indications that White Sox co-owner Eddie Einhorn would step in and rescue the troubled franchise from extinction, the pathetic Blitz played their last game on June 24, 1984—bowing out quietly to the Michigan Panthers 20-17 before 5,557 sun-worshiping fans who came to pronounce the last rights on USFL football in Chicago. A year later the USFL went the way of buggy whips and button hooks.

Q: What famous NFL coach guided the Blitz to a last-place finish in their final season?
A: Marv Levy, a graduate of Chicago's South Shore High.

Q: Who replaced Greg Landry as the starting quarterback in 1984?
A: Former Chicago Bear castoffVince Evans.

"I was against this moving all along. If it was my decision I'd stick it out in Chicago. No way I'd move. I have a warm feeling for Chicago fans. [But] I had to go with my players. I worked 90-100 hours a week to build up this team last year, and I'm not going to start from scratch again."

GEORGE ALLEN, APOLOGIZING TO CHICAGO FANS

1984

In the final year of outdoor play, the Chicago Sting won the 1984 Soccer Bowl after defeating the Toronto Blizzard 3-2 before 16,482 rowdy Canadian fans who hurled smoke bombs and water balloons at the Chicago players all through the game. Unlike the raucous but happy celebration that accompanied the Sting's 1981 title run, this latest soccer superlative was barely noticed by the media or the apathetic Chicago fans whose infatuation with this team was obviously coming to an end.

As his victorious team walked off the field, Lee Stern announced that he was pulling out of the NASL, but his Sting would continue, for a few more years at least, to operate as an MISL indoor team.

Six months later the NASL collapsed after league president Howard Samuels died of a heart attack.

Q: Who was named the 1984 Soccer Bowl MVP?
A: Forward Pato Margetic, who scored two goals in the game.

1984

Walter Payton broke the National Football League all-time career rushing record against the New Orleans Saints on October 7. For his 12-year career Walter rushed for 3,838 yards.

Q: Who was the legendary NFL player whose record Payton shattered?

A: Hall of Fame Cleveland Brown fullback Jim Brown.

1985-1986

Bridesmaids no more. After two consecutive Central Division titles the Chicago Bears finally broke through and made it to Super Bowl XX. Mike Ditka's team won their first 12 games of the season en route to a 15-1 regular season mark, tying a record for the most wins in NFL history. In their first-ever Super Bowl appearance, the Bears annihilated a vastly inferior New England Patriots team 46-10, which set a host of league records including most points by a team and the largest margin of victory.

The colorful Bears, who recorded the "Super Bowl Shuffle" on the eve of the big game, were led by Jim McMahon, the "Punky Q. B.," who defied social conventions, league rules—and Commissioner Pete Rozelle—by wearing a headband that advertised a well-known athletic company. William "the Refrigerator" Perry, a 325-pound defensive tackle out of Clemson, scored a Super Bowl touchdown and was "the best thing to happen to fat since the invention of bacon," according to *Chicago Sun-Times* columnist Ray Sons.

Q: When Mike Ditka appeared in Super Bowl XX in New Orleans, he became only the third man in NFL history to have appeared in the postseason event as both player and coach. Who were the other two?

A: Quarterback Tom Flores played with the Kansas City Chiefs in Super Bowl IX and coached the Raiders in two other Super Bowl games. Forrest Gregg of the Green Bay Packers appeared in the first two Super Bowls and coached Cincinnati in Super Bowl XVI.

"There are teams that are fair-haired and there are teams that aren't. There are teams named Smith and teams named Grabowski. The Rams are a Smith. We're a Grabowski."

MIKE DITKA, IDENTIFYING THE BEARS AS A "BLUE-COLLAR" TEAM IN THE MOLD OF LINEBACKER JIM GRABOWSKI, WHO BRIEFLY PLAYED FOR THE BEARS IN 1971

1988

Mike Ditka's team whipped the Philadelphia Eagles 20-12 at Soldier Field in round one of the NFL play-offs on December 31. Bear fans called it the "Fog Bowl" because of the unusually mild temperatures and pea-soup fog that enveloped the stadium during the game. Playing for a berth in the Super Bowl, the Bears were pounded 28-3 a week later by the San Francisco 49ers in the National Football Conference championship game.

Q: Nineteen eighty-eight was the final year in a string of five consecutive winning seasons, duplicating an earlier record of success by the "Monsters." When was the last time the Bears put together five winning seasons?

A: 1946-1951.

1988

After 14 tumultuous years and many millions of dollars lost, Lee Stern finally threw in the towel and folded the Chicago Sting. Declining attendance, the failure to attract new sources of revenue, and an ill-conceived league marketing strategy that placed national television exposure above the interests of the local affiliated stations doomed the Sting to oblivion. Stern was understandably bitter over the strange unfolding irony.

The same week Stern was forced to withdraw from a sport he had worked so hard to promote for more than a decade, it was announced that the United States would host the 1994 World Cup, with several games scheduled to be played in Chicago.

> *"They didn't pay attention to the mistakes of the NASL. In 1982 when we first played in the MISL, I got up and said I'm hearing the same things that gave the NASL a problem. I don't think we paid attention to history. In 1984 I told [MISL founder] Earl Foremen that we should merge the NASL and MISL. He wouldn't listen. If we would have done that, I don't think we'd be talking about the death of professional soccer in this country."*
>
> LEE STERN, JULY 9, 1988

1988

Lou Weisbach, a former investor in Lee Stern's operation, organized the remnants of the Chicago Sting into a new indoor team: the Chicago Power. The team joined the five-year-old American Indoor Soccer Association (AISA), playing a limited 20-game home schedule at the Rosemont Horizon. In their first season of play, the Power advanced to the league championship round but lost a best-of-five series to the Canton Invaders. The team averaged just over 4,000 fans per game.

Q: The Power was actually Chicago's fifth professional indoor soccer team since the fad began in the late 1970s. Can you name the four predecessors?
A: The Shoccers, Horizons, Vultures, and Sting.

Q: Who coached the Power in its maiden season?
A: The colorful and controversial former Chicago Sting striker Karl-Heinz Granitza.

"This league has the formula for success. It's fiscally responsible."

LOU WEISBACH, OWNER OF THE POWER

1990-1991

The Chicago Power won the National Professional Soccer League (NPSL) title.

Q: Who was general manager of the Power during their title season?
A: Peter Wilt, who was named general manager of Chicago's new Major League Soccer (MSL) franchise, awarded to Denver-based Philip Auschutz in 1997.

1994

A billion people, spanning the four corners of the globe from sub-Sahara Africa to southeast Asia, witnessed the opening ceremonies of professional soccer's famed World Cup on June 17 through the medium of television. Chicago exhibited warm midwestern hospitality and was a gracious and pleasant host to the more than 250,000 visitors and tourists who converged upon the Windy City to witness five second-round games played at spruced-up Soldier Field.

On balance, the festivities were a rousing success for the city, though attendance fell well short of the projected goal of 400,000 spectators the World Cup USA Organizing Committee counted on when Chicago was added to the list of cities scheduled to host games.

Q: Which nation emerged the victor in the second round at Chicago?

A: Defending World Cup champion Germany recorded a pulsating 3-2 victory over Belgium on July 2.

> *"From the surprised reactions of the tourists who roamed our streets, parks, and lakefront to the glowing reports sent back home by foreign journalists, Chicago has a new identity. We are now the city that put on the best World Cup celebration in the United States. . . . what I have learned from this World Cup experience is something I had known but never seen so clearly. Chicago, like no other city, is able to bring the public and private worlds together and unite behind a common goal. We are in fact, a city that works."*
>
> JAY A. PRITZKER, COCHAIR, CHICAGO HOST COMMITTEE

1994-1995

The Chicago Power ended its unhappy seven-year run after playing 10 "home games" at Rockford's MetroCentre. The NPSL operated the franchise on a shoestring budget after the local ownership withdrew its financial backing. Things really unraveled for the team after Howard Balson, the radio voice of Chicago soccer through 1,000 Sting and Power games, announced his retirement in order to attend to his north suburban Mexican restaurant. The team was transferred to Edmonton, Canada.

The Power-outage offered further proof that professional soccer as a spectator sport in the Windy City has limited appeal.

1995-1996

The Northwestern Wildcats, rumored to be on their way out of the Big Ten because of chronically poor performance, climaxed an unbelievable comeback season with a trip to the Rose Bowl for the first time in 37 years. Success was credited to the inspired leadership of Coach Gary Barnett, who had launched an ambitious recruiting program in the Chicagoland area that paid immediate dividends.

The Cats, given up for dead and a laughingstock for so many years, registered their first winning season since 1971. On November 18 the Purple captured the school's first Big Ten Conference title in 59 years after knocking off Purdue 23-8 and then squared off against the University of Southern California Trojans in the Rose Bowl. Quarterback Steve Schnur passed for 336 yards, good enough for fifth place in Rose Bowl history, but it wasn't quite enough to overcome the seasoned Trojans. USC prevailed 41-32. Despite the disappointing outcome, all in all, NU's success in 1995-1996 was the sports story of the decade.

Q: Before coming to Northwestern in 1992, what was Gary Barnett's only other collegiate head coaching assignment?
A: Barnett guided Fort Lewis College in Durango, Colorado, through two losing seasons, 1982-1983. His combined record there was 8-11-1.

> *"What he has really done is he has changed the attitude. People don't understand how hard that is. Defeatism had set in. He's been able to sit in a room with those kids and convince them that they can win. He built up something."*
>
> ARA PARSEGHIAN, ON GARY BARNETT

1996-1997

A 34-9 loss to the Penn State Nittany Lions cost the Northwestern Wildcats a return trip to the Rose Bowl. Northwestern had to settle for a New Year's Day engagement at the Citrus Bowl, where they were paired against the 9-2 Tennessee Volunteers. The magical ride to the big-time bowl games turned out to be a bumpy ride for the second year in a row.

The injury-stricken Cats, who spent their week in the Florida sunshine touring Disney World instead of concentrating on the game, were ripped 48-28 by a stronger, faster Tennessee team.

Q: What NU all-American had to sit this one out?
A: Running back Darnell Autry, who suffered from a case of the flu.

"It's been a fun run. When I came here it was pretty bleak, so it was a great ride."
PAT FITZGERALD, NU MIDDLE LINEBACKER, LOOKING BACK ON HIS COLLEGE CAREER IN EVANSTON

1997

Old ideas die hard. The historic failure of professional soccer in the Windy City did not deter the promoters of the two-year-old Major Soccer League (MSL) from placing an expansion team in Chicago to begin the 1998 season, The new team announced a schedule of home games at Soldier Field and promised to recruit the top European talent in order to made the product attractive to Chicago's large ethnic population—an idea Lee Stern dismissed as far-fetched. "We had that mixture and it didn't draw flies," grumbled the former Sting owner who tried every gimmick in the world to make soccer viable in Chicago, but with only fleeting success.

"It was absurd for us to consider ourselves a national league without Chicago."
COMMISSIONER DOUG LOGAN, APRIL 9, 1997

CHAPTER 9

Slamming and Jamming: Windy City Round Ball

Before the Chicago Bulls had the good fortune to sign Michael Jeffrey Jordan to his first contract, professional basketball was strictly a losing proposition in the Windy City. The Bulls had played to empty houses night after night, raising doubts about the franchise's long-term future.

"Chicago? No chance! It's a graveyard!" the rap went. "College games score, but the pro game will never take off—not like it did on the East Coast!"

The Bruins, Gears, Stags, Zephyrs/Packers, Hustle, and several lesser-known semipro teams had collapsed after only a few years, and nobody mourned their passing. The Chicago media relegated the Bruins and Gears to page five. Except to the owners, the demise of the hardwood game mattered little.

The game of basketball, which incorporated elements of soccer, football, and hockey, was invented in 1891 by James Naismith, an instructor at the Young Men's Christian Association Training School in Springfield, Massachusetts, where the Basketball Hall of Fame opened in 1959. Played back then by both men and women, the game quickly gained popularity after a number of U.S. colleges added the game to their athletic curriculum beginning in 1893. Girls' high school basketball games were played in the Chicago area as early as 1896, when Austin High and Oak Park squared off in a contest that was won by Austin 16-4.

During the first decade of the century, the University of Chicago dominated the college game nationally and locally. Loyola played only limited schedules prior to the 1920s, and the DePaul Blue Demons didn't get going until 1921. But it wasn't until the advent of important postseason pairings—the National Invitational Tournament (NIT) begun in 1938 and the National Collegiate Athletic Association (NCAA) elimination contests begun a year later—that the game began to pick up momentum and gain a national following.

Colorful personalities, flamboyant coaches, heart-pounding games where the outcome remained in doubt until the closing seconds, plus local prep and collegiate heroes like George Mikan of DePaul and "Wibs" Kautz of Loyola, cemented a place for college basketball in the minds of Chicago sports fans during the Depression and World War II. The famous college double-headers played at the Chicago Coliseum in the 1930s and at the Stadium beginning in 1941 became yearly traditions.

Thus things remained for many years. In the late and early 1980s the winning Blue Demons, not the lackluster Chicago Bulls, were the basketball fans' preferred choice in the Windy City. In fact, many believe that a few more years of stadium crowds falling consistently below the nine- to 10-thousand mark, and the Bulls would have been forced to abandon Chicago.

And then came Michael—the resurrection and the light of pro basketball in Chicago. Round ball's renaissance was at hand.

1907

The University of Chicago Maroons basketball team finished the season in a first-place tie with Wisconsin and Minnesota in the Western Conference, the forerunner of the Big-Ten Conference. Each team compiled a 6-2 record. The U of C's 78-12 record spanning the years 1900-1909 was by far the best in collegiate basketball during this era.

Q: What was the big crosstown rivalry in these years?
A: Though it is almost impossible to imagine today, the University of Chicago basketball program dominated college hoops for nearly a decade. Its contests with Northwestern were some of the most intense in the college game.

Q: The Maroons' top scorer, 6' 3" center John Schommer, is credited with what major contribution to the game?
A: A long-forgotten figure, Schommer—a Helms Foundation all-American—is credited with inventing the backboard.

Q: Before the University of Chicago officially withdrew from the Big Ten in 1946, the Maroons won five more Big-Ten Conference titles and three straight Helms Foundation Championships. What years did the U of C prevail?
A: The Maroons won five Big-Ten titles in 1908 (8-1); 1909 (12-0); 1910 (9-3); 1920 (11-2); and 1924 (8-4, tied for first with Wisconsin and Illinois). The Helms Foundation of Los Angeles declared the University of Chicago to be the national champions in 1907 (22-2); 1908 (21-2); and 1909 (12-0).

1907-1908

In a two-game play-off with heavily favored Penn, the eastern champions, the Maroons handily defeated their opponents in both games behind guard/center Joseph E. Raycroft.

Q: What unique place does Raycroft hold in college basketball history?
A: He served a dual role as player and coach and was one of the first basketball coaches to draw a salary from the university. He steered the Maroons to three straight national championships (1907-1909), according to the Helms ratings.

1923

Leonard Sachs took over as head coach of the Loyola Ramblers. During the next 19 years he guided Loyola to its longest unbeaten streak (32 straight games between 1928-1929). Sachs was elected to the Basketball Hall of Fame in 1961 before thousands of fans at the Chicago Stadium who had come to pay tribute to one of the game's true pioneers. Sachs helped introduce the zone defense to basketball.

Q: How did the Ramblers acquire their famous nickname?
A: Prior to the 1920s they were called the "Maroon and Gold," after the school's colors. In 1925 Loyola's student newspaper sponsored a contest to name its football team. The wining entry was "Grandees," but that nickname never caught on. A year later Chicago sportswriters began calling the team the "Ramblers" because an extensive road trip that year had taken them all over the United States.

1924

Loyola's Alumni Gym, affectionately known to generations of Chicago basketball fans as the "Old Brown Box that Rocks" opened. Built at a cost of $500,000 and partly financed by 12 Loyola alumni calling themselves the Bugs, the 3,000-seat lakefront arena was a real showcase in its day. Over the years many famous athletes made use of it—including Chicago native and Olympic champion Johnny "Tarzan" Weissmuller, who was the first person to swim in its pool.

Q: Two legendary Chicago college coaches were on opposing sides in the 1932 National Catholic Interscholastic Basketball Tournament, an annual high school tournament staged at Loyola's Alumni Gym from 1924-1941. Who were they?
A: Future DePaul coach Ray Meyer played for St. Patrick's that year and against future Loyola coach George Ireland, who was then star of the Campion (Wisconsin) team. St. Pat's beat Campion in the semifinals and Chicago's St. Mel's in the final round to claim the Cardinal Mundelein Trophy.

"I loved Alumni Hall. Fans were so close, so intimate, so excitable, so gung-ho. They screamed from the rafters. The gym was a tremendous edge for the home team."

RED RUSH, RADIO AND TV COMMENTATOR WHO COVERED THE RAMBLERS FROM 1962-1970

1925-1926

George Preston Marshall, a Washington, D.C., laundry tycoon and owner of the football Redskins, had organized a basketball team there. He then persuaded Cleveland department-store owner Max Rosenblum and Chicago Bears owner George Halas to help him launch a professional basketball league headed by former NFL president Joe Carr. The idea intrigued Halas, and he bankrolled the city's first pro team, which he called the Chicago Bruins. They joined the newly formed American Basketball League (ABL). Nine teams headquartered in Brooklyn, Washington, Cleveland, Buffalo, Rochester, Detroit, Fort Wayne, Boston, and Chicago comprised the new league.

Q: Where did the Bruins play?
A: The Bruins briefly found a home in the cramped Broadway Armory building on Chicago's North Side. They edged the Philadelphia Quakers 28-27 in their debut game on December 9, but were a dismal failure all the way through their first season despite promoting the talents of two local Chicago boys who started at forward: Mike Wickhorst and Jack Tierney.

Q: What were some of the innovations introduced by the ABL that modernized basketball?
A: In order to conform with the guidelines of the Amateur Athletic Union, ABL organizers eliminated the two-handed dribble, which was popular on the East Coast. Further, players were disqualified after committing five fouls in a game. Backboards, invented two decades earlier by Maroon John Schommer, were now required, and the cages were banned.

1926-1927

After John "Honey" Russell, a top defensive star for Cleveland, had a falling-out with Mat Rosenblum, George Halas purchased him. But even with this great player on board, the Bruins showed no signs of improvement, and they lost over half their games that season. Seton Hall's "Honey" Russell, who was eventually elected to the Basketball Hall of Fame, was the one bright spot. He finished ninth in the league in scoring.

Q: What was Russell's points-per-game average?
A: It was just 6.4. Basketball games were low-scoring affairs until the players abandoned the two-handed set shot. The one-handed jump shot, slowly coming into vogue in the early 1950s, revolutionized the game of basketball.

1927

Chicago merchant Abraham Saperstein organized an all-black basketball team from a South Side semipro team known as the "Savoy Big Five." He called them the Harlem Globetrotters. A man of vision who recognized the universal appeal of razzle-dazzle basketball, Saperstein showcased the team's talents all over the world. The team's first road trip took them only as far as tiny Hinckley, Illinois, a distance of eight miles from Chicago, on January 7, 1927.

Q: Where did Saperstein discover many of his star players?
A: At Wendell Phillips High School on the South Side. Inman Jackson, Toots Wright, and Runt Pullins were Phillips alumni.

Q: Over the years, some of the finest stars to grace the hardwood were Globetrotters before they were anything else. Name some of these players.
A: Ted Strong, Babe Pressley, Reece "Goose" Tatum, Honey Taylor, Josh Crider, Curly Neal, Meadowlark Lemon, and Sonny Boswell all played for the Trotters.

Q: What is believed to be the largest crowd to ever witness a basketball game?
A: In 1951 the Trotters played before 75,000 fans at Berlin's Olympic Stadium.

Q: What's the name of the famous Globetrotter theme song used as a warm-up routine?
A: "Sweet Georgia Brown." Five of the most famous Trotters—Bill Brown, Leon Hilliard, Clarence Wilson, Josh

Crider, and Babe Pressley—performed the routine before Pope Pius XII in Castel Gandolfo in 1952.

"I won't let my team fake games and out-and-out clowning is no good. The only answer is a blend of basketball and entertainment. I am the only one in the business who seems to realize this."

ABE SAPERSTEIN, ON THE ENTERTAINMENT VALUE OF BASKETBALL

1927-1928

The Bruins finished last in the ABL's Western Division with a 13-36 record, but they acquired future Hall of Famer Johnny Beckman from the Detroit Cardinals when the Motor City team went under.

Q: What was Beckman known as?
A: Some called him the Babe Ruth of basketball.

1928-1929

Nat Hickey, one of the game's early stars and a member of the Original Celtics, was sold to the Bruins in December 1928, and the Bruins finally were able to provide their fans with a few thrills. Hickey was traded in an attempt to achieve some competitive balance.

Q: What was the strategic reason for this transaction?
A: The Cleveland franchise had dominated the league in its first few years, but this greatly worried the ABL's financial backers, who believed that a basketball monopoly in Cleveland was bad for business elsewhere.

1929-1930

George Halas took advantage of the ABL's various financial woes and brought to Chicago Nat Holman, a play-making 5'11" guard and one of the league's top ball handlers and outside shooters. Then Halas moved the team into the Chicago Stadium, where they hoped the attraction of a spacious new arena and the league's top talent would finally lure people to the games.

After posting a .500 record in the first half of the season, the retooled Bruins claimed third place in the second half of the season, with a 17-13 record. When the dust had cleared, they trailed league-leading Rochester by only two games.

> *"I hired John 'Honey' Russell of New York to coach and signed a great player, Nat Holman, for $6,000 for half a season, more than I could afford. Hope, hope, what can be accomplished without hope! Hope carried me through the next two years. Hope led me into taking the team into the vast Chicago Stadium, giving up half of the gate as rental. It was a sporting success but a financial disaster."*
>
> GEORGE HALAS, MEMOIRS

1930-1931

The onset of the Depression crippled the American Basketball League beyond repair. Several teams, including Cleveland, folded in midseason. Players were put on the auction block and the schedule of games was cut back.

In these inauspicious times, with the league teetering on the brink of failure, it figured that the Chicago Bruins would suddenly mount a title threat. With Loyola cage star Charley Murphy on board and the tandem of Benny Borgmann, Lloyd Kintzing, and Ralph Miller setting up the plays, the Bruins rolled to an 11-5 second-half record that matched league-leading Ft. Wayne. Then the Indiana team defeated the Bruins in a one-game play-off 20-16 to claim the title.

At year's end all the ABL's clubs folded, with the exception of the Original Celtics, who became a barnstorming team. During the season the Bruins had also been forced to abandon the Chicago Stadium because of its steep rent.

Q: What famous Chicago Bruins player would coach the Boston Celtics in 1946, the inaugural season of the Basketball Association of America (later the NBA)?

A: John "Honey" Russell, who had played for the Bruins two years earlier.

1930-1931

The Northwestern Wildcats, coached by Arthur Lonborg, sat atop the Big Ten for the first time in their history with an 11-1 record (16-1 overall). Their only loss was a 35-28 drubbing to the University of Illinois.

Q: Did the Wildcats ever win another Big Ten crown?
A: Two years later Lonborg's team finished in a first-place tie with a 10-2 record. No other Wildcat team has ever come close to duplicating these numbers.

1933-1934

DePaul's Blue Demons posted a perfect 17-0 record and claimed a share of the national championship. For their 13th win, the Demons narrowly avoided an upset by topping Armour Tech (the Illinois Institute of Technology) 43-41.

Q: What was distinctive about the Blue Demons' record that year?
A: It was the only Blue Demons team in history to go undefeated.

1935-1936

A new semiprofessional team belonging to the Midwest Basketball Conference and known locally as the Chicago Duffy Florals began play at the Chicago Teacher's College Gymnasium at 68th and Stewart on the South Side.

Q: How did the team acquire this unlikely name?
A: It was sponsored by Duffy Florists, a sports-minded company that also backed a semipro baseball team and bowling team bearing the same name. The basketball league folded after two years.

1938-1939

The *Chicago Herald American,* a Hearst afternoon newspaper, sponsored the first annual World's Professional Basketball

Championship. An invitational round-robin tournament, it featured the top pro and touring teams from across the nation, which included the two premier black ball clubs, the Harlem Globetrotters and the New York Rens. The field of 11 also included the Original Celtics, but the Rens emerged the victor the first year, downing Oshkosh 34-25.

Q: Where was this popular tournament held?
A: During the war years, this annual event played to enthusiastic crowds at the Madison Street Armory and the Chicago Coliseum.

1938-1939

The undefeated Loyola Ramblers squared off against the Long Island University Blackbirds for the championship of the National Invitational Tournament (NIT) before more than 18,000 fans on March 22, 1939.

Q: What was this game's place in basketball history?
A: It was the only time in major college history that two undefeated ball clubs faced each other in a national postseason tournament. Unfortunately, the Ramblers played tight and were routed 44-32 by the Blackbirds at Madison Square Garden. Long Island ended the season at 24-0; Loyola finished up at 21-1.

Q: Rambler coach Lennie Sachs ranks number two in the school's history for most victories. His Loyola teams posted a 223-129 record spanning 19 years. Who holds the record for most wins as the Ramblers head coach?
A: George Ireland, who coached the team during the 1960s, leads with 321.

1938-1939

On March 27, 1939, the very first NCAA Championship game, just a footnote event in those days of NIT dominance, was played at Patten Gym on Northwestern's campus.

Pacific Coast Conference champs, the University of Oregon,

defeated the Ohio State Buckeyes 46-33 before a crowd of 5,000 fans. The fans seemed more interested in the pregame entertainment, which featured two squads of Northwestern Wildcats playing an unusual exhibition game using the original basketball rules drawn up by James Naismith in the 1890s.

Q: Can you name the losing Ohio State coach who took over the reins of the Chicago Stags in their maiden season of 1946?
A: Harold "Ole" Olsen.

1939-1940

In order to capitalize on the growing popularity of college basketball, three large midwestern corporations organized the National Basketball League (NBL) in 1937. A lineal ancestor of the NBA, it was an attempt to sell the concept of professional pay-for-play basketball to the sporting public.

Q: What were the three teams?
A: Goodyear Rubber Company of Akron, Ohio; General Electric of Fort Wayne, Indiana; and Firestone.

With a collection of rookies and veterans drafted from the rosters of existing NBL teams, George Halas tried to resuscitate the Chicago Bruins for the 1939-1940 season. Home games were played at the 132nd Armory Building at Madison and Rockwell. The Bruins were frequently forced to share top billing with the local junior colleges in weekend double-headers.

The new basketball Bruins played a tougher, more aggressive, style of game than their predecessors; as a result, they finished third in the Western Division behind Oshkosh and Sheboygan. Thanks to the inspired play of two sensational Loyola all-Americans, the Bruins remained in a dead heat with the two Wisconsin teams for much of the season.

Q: Who were these two rebounding and shooting whiz kids out of Loyola?
A: Six-foot nine-inch guard Wilbert "Wibs" Kautz and Mike Novak, a 6' 9" center, from Tilden Tech.

1939-1940

In overtime the Harlem Globetrotters defeated the Chicago Bruins 31-29 in the championship game of the World Tournament, a victory that helped put Saperstein's team on the map. After that the Trotters played in the best sports arenas across the country and the world. On November 29, 1940, with the memory of the World Tournament fresh in their minds, 22,000 fans packed the Chicago Stadium to watch the Harlem Globetrotters play their first game against the nation's College All-Stars.

Q: Name the Globetrotter starting five who burned the Bruins to become world champions that year.

A: Bernie Price, forward; Sonny Boswell, forward; Ted Strong, guard; Babe Pressley, guard; and Inman Jackson, center.

1940

The success of the World Tournament convinced the editors of the *Chicago Herald-American* to sponsor a championship game pitting the nation's top collegiate all-stars against the number one cage team from the pro ranks. Thus was born the All-Star Basketball Classic, a yearly charity event with proceeds going to the Herald-American Benefit Fund.

The college players were more than up to the task. In the first eight years the collegians whipped the pros six times.

Q: Who coached the college all-stars?

A: Arthur "Dutch" Lonborg, the veteran basketball coach at Northwestern University who guided the Wildcats through 23 seasons (1927-1950). Only the Fort Wayne Zollners in 1944 and 1945 were able to master Dutch and his boys.

1941-1942

The lackluster Bruins finished sixth in the NBL after losing two of their stars to the war effort. At the end of the season George Halas, fed up with basketball and convinced that the game had no future outside of the college circuit, folded his team.

1942-1943

Twenty-nine-year-old Ray Meyer, an assistant coach at Notre Dame under George Keogan during the previous two seasons, began his career as head coach of the DePaul Blue Demons. He signed a one-year contract. George Mikan, a 6' 8" center out of Quigley Prep, who in 1950 was voted the greatest player of the first half of the century, made his college debut that same season.

Q: Ray Meyer won 724 games and lost 354 as head coach of the Blue Demons from 1942-1984. Which DePaul basketball coach has the highest career winning percentage?
A: Jim Kelly. His .820 winning percentage (100 games won, 22 lost) spanned seven seasons, 1929-1936.

1942-1943

NBL stars Mike Novak and Dick Evans and United Auto Workers members at the local Studebaker plant who were doing wartime production got the union to sponsor a replacement team, a group that included Sonny Boswell, Duke Cumberland, and Bernie Price of the Harlem Globetrotters.

This precedent-shattering and noble experiment ended on a sour note, however, when the players split into two hostile camps. Torn by racial strife, the team played well below its potential and won only eight of 23 games. The team was disbanded at the end of the season.

Q: What was the name of this one-year wonder?
A: The Chicago Studebaker-Flyers.

1944

Intercollegiate basketball double-headers on January 8, 1944, pitted the DePaul Blue Demons against the University of Chicago Maroons in game one and the Northwestern Wildcats against the Wisconsin Buckeyes in the second. The first game, an unremarkable one, was followed by a special between-games ceremony.

Q: Where were these legendary double-headers played and how long did they last?

A: They were originally played at the 132nd Infantry Armory on West Madison Street and the Chicago Coliseum in the late 1930s; in the early 1940s they were moved to the Chicago Stadium. These legendary matchups continued into the 1960s.

Q: What Wildcat was honored that evening?

A: All-time great Wildcat quarterback Otto Graham, who happened to play forward for the basketball team, was about to be inducted into the navy air corps. He was presented with the Silver Football Most Valuable Player Award for the previous season by the *Chicago Tribune* to acknowledge his achievements.

Q: What other legendary figure was on hand for the festivities?

A: Former University of Chicago football coach Amos Alonzo Stagg was given the famed Order of the C Award for his 42 years in the field.

Q: How did Graham do in the game that night?

A: The honored quarterback notched three field goals and played an outstanding defensive game as the Cats downed Wisconsin 60-38.

Q: What became of Graham in later years?

A: Drafted by the Cleveland Rams (later Browns) in 1946, he went on to a distinguished 10-year career, leading the Browns to four championships in the National Football League before being inducted into the Hall of Fame. At Northwestern Graham won eight varsity letters in football, basketball, and baseball while majoring in music.

Q: What role did future Chicago Stags president John Sbarbaro play in these double-headers?

A: A longtime basketball promoter, he was instrumental in moving the collegiate double-headers from the Chicago

Coliseum and the Madison Street Armory to the Chicago Stadium in 1941.

"I've had a lot of fun in intercollegiate football the last few years. If I should be called upon to make the same sacrifice as [Nile] Kinnick, it's all right with me!"

OTTO GRAHAM, COMMENTING ON HIS IMPENDING WARTIME SERVICE AND THE DEATH OF IOWA STAR NILE KINNICK IN THE PACIFIC THEATER A YEAR EARLIER

1944-1945

Just two years after advancing to the NCAA Final Four for the first time in the school's history, Meyer's Blue Demons swept all three games of the National Invitational Tournament (NIT) at New York's Madison Square Garden. The NIT was the nation's first prestigious tournament.

Q: What teams did the Demons route that year?
A: West Virginia, Rhode Island State, and Bowling Green; overpowering center George Mikan had set a school record by scoring 53 points against Rhode Island State in the NIT semifinals.

Q: How many postseason tournaments did Ray Meyer's DePaul teams participate in during his 42-year stint as head coach?
A: The Blue Demons made 13 trips to the NCAA and seven NIT appearances. Meyer coached three teams to the NIT championship game in 1944, 1945, and 1983.

1944-1945

The Chicago American Gears, sponsored by the American Gear Company, joined the National Basketball League playing home games at the Chicago Stadium with a cast of college athletes—some of whom played under assumed names in order to protect their amateur status. U of I forward Stan Patrick and all-American DePaul guard Dick Triptow contributed a lethal offensive punch, and Patrick set a league record on the last day of the season by scoring 38 points against Pittsburgh.

Q: What happened to the Gears after this glorious start?
A: They made it to the first round of the play-offs after finishing 14-16 during the regular season, but dropped two of three games to Sheboygan.

Q: What pro career did guard Triptow go on to?
A: The Chicago Cubs signed him up to play baseball.

1945-1946

In an otherwise so-so .500 season, the Gears stunned the basketball world by signing DePaul star George Mikan to a whopping five-year contract valued at $60,000. As soon as his collegiate year ended Mikan donned jersey number 99 and made his Chicago Stadium debut during the annual World Tournament series, scoring 100 points during the series and getting named the most valuable player.

Q: How did Mikan change the game of basketball?
A: DePaul coach Ray Meyer instructed big man Mikan to position himself under the basket and swat away shots that were certain to land in the net. Goaltending was still legal in those days, but Mikan forced a rule change. Maximizing the advantage of his 6'10" frame, he became the greatest practitioner of the emerging "inside game."

Q: What experiment was tried briefly in order to slow scoring sensation George Mikan?
A: In a 1953-1954 game between the Minneapolis Lakers and the Milwaukee Hawks the basket was actually raised to 12 feet in height. The experiment lasted only one game.

1946-1947

The National Basketball League, essentially still a midwestern operation after nearly a decade of existence, got some new competition. Eleven teams began play in the Basketball Association of America, which was formed by *New Yorker* sportswriter Max Case and promoter Ned Irish.

Its Chicago entry was nicknamed the Stags and outfitted in

red, white, and blue. Owned by attorney Arthur Morse, the new team was coached by Harold "Ole" Olsen, who'd won five Western Conference titles at Ohio State before taking a shot at the pros. He led the Stags through a 30-game home schedule that season, en route to a Western Division title, but lost to Philadelphia in the championship round.

> *"It's going to be a team rather than a galaxy of individual stars and that takes plenty of running!"*
>
> HAROLD "OLE" OLSEN, OCTOBER 1946

> *"We intend that the Stags will measure up in every way to the highest standards of Chicago's professional sports operations. No effort will be spared to attain that goal, to give Chicago an outstanding team as its first major basketball representative."*
>
> JUDGE JOHN SBARBARO, CHICAGO STAGS TEAM PRESIDENT

1946-1947

The Chicago American Gears survived financial setbacks and the near-loss of top star George Mikan, who became angry and sat out six weeks after owner Maurice White tried to cut his salary below the $12,000 specified in the star center's contract. White finally mended his fences with his great star, and added veteran guard Bobby McDermott to the team.

The talented Gears finished third in the Western Division, but they edged the Anderson Packers for the division play-off spot. Then they stormed past Indianapolis and Oshkosh and squared off against the Rochester Royals in the championship round. After dropping the first game they won the next three to claim the NBL crown.

Q: This NBL championship featured a classic matchup between Mikan's inside power game and the expert ball-handling, pattern offense of the Royals. What renowned future NBA coach played against Mikan's Gears?

A: Red Holzman, who would lead the New York Knicks to championships in 1969 and 1972.

1947-1948

Rookie Andy Philip, a former member of the Illinois Whiz Kids and one of the best play-makers in the Big Ten, made his pro debut with the Stags.

Q: What free agent signed by the Stags that year became the only Chicago professional player—other than Michael Jordan—to lead the league in scoring?

A: Guard Max "Slats" Zaslofsky completed an outstanding sophomore season by winning the league scoring title, but averaging only 21 points per game.

Q: Which future Hall of Famer, later drafted by the Stags, ended up with the Boston Celtics instead?

A: Guard Bob Cousy out of Holy Cross. Boston Celtics coach Red Auerbach hoped to draft Max Zaslofsky, but instead drew Cousy's name out of the hat—the one guy he didn't want.

1947-1948

Maurice White attempted to break away from the National Basketball League and form a confederation of 16 teams that would revolve around his Gears and their marquee attraction George Mikan. Financing for the risky new venture was put up by White's company, which had attracted some lucrative military contracts for supplying gears to the navy during World War II. Called the Professional Basketball League of America, this group collapsed in November just two weeks after the start-up date. White lost $600,000 and wound up in the hospital with a nervous breakdown.

Q: In the dispersal draft that followed, where did the Gears' leading players wind up?

A: Mikan was awarded to the Minneapolis Lakers, Bobby McDermott wound up with Sheboygan, and Dick Triptow was assigned to the Tri-Cities.

1948-1949

In 1949 the Basketball Association of America merged with the remnants of the old National Basketball League and changed its name to the National Basketball Association (NBA).

1949-1950

The Stags were shifted into the NBA's Central Division, and despite another fine season by Max Zaslofsky and Andy Philip, professional basketball just wasn't catching on with Chicago fans. The team played the final game of their brief existence on March 25, 1950, before 10,852 dejected fans. The Minneapolis Lakers, led by former DePaul great George Mikan's 34 points, downed the Stags. The Chicago Stadium had hosted the last NBA game that would be played in Chicago for 11 years. The team was disbanded over the summer. Max Zaslofsky was claimed by the New York Knicks in the dispersal draft.

1952-1953

The Northwestern Wildcats, without a home arena since 1940 when Patten Gym was torn down to make room for the Technological Institute, moved into their new field house, McGaw Memorial Hall, named in honor of Reverend Francis A. McGaw, a Presbyterian minister who died at his mission in Nairobi, Kenya, in 1942.

The Wildcats lost to Western Michigan 95-79 in the inaugural game on December 6, 1952.

Q: What famous Loyola all-American, whose uniform number #3 has been permanently retired, broke George Mikan's collegiate free-throw record at the Chicago Stadium?

A: Nick Kladis, recruited out of Tilden Tech in 1949. He sank 13 of 17 against Detroit in 1952. In 1963 Kladis served as an unpaid assistant coach for George Ireland.

1952-1953

A legendary college rivalry was suspended for over a dozen years after rowdy students from Loyola and DePaul caused a disruption at the Chicago Stadium on February 7. University officials from both schools canceled the series, which was knotted at 11 wins and 11 losses each.

Q: When did DePaul and Loyola next meet?
A: In the 1975-1976 season. The Demons resumed play, whipping Loyola 100-77.

1956

The NCAA Final Four Championship was played at Northwestern's McGaw Hall March 22-24. The final game pitted San Francisco against Iowa and drew a crowd of 10,653, a single-game attendance record for the facility. San Francisco defeated the Hawkeyes 83-71.

Q: What famous NBA center set a record by pulling down 50 rebounds in a Final Four and 27 in a championship game?
A: Bill Russell, the towering all-American out of San Francisco.

1958

Abe Saperstein brought his Globetrotters into the Chicago Stadium for an October showdown against the Philadelphia Sphas, another one of his teams. In the sellout event a crowd of 19,137 jammed the stadium to witness the professional debut of a 7'2" future NBA Hall of Famer.

Q: Who was this player, whom many believe to be the greatest player of all time?
A: Center Wilt Chamberlain. The Kansas all-American dropped out of college in order to accept $65,000 to play for the Globetrotters. Wilt scored 25 points in his professional debut at the stadium. The sportswriters of the day viewed the event, which the Globetrotters took 81 to 53, as a complete comic farce, not a game.

"The Trotters as usual, combined artistry with sheer buffoonery. And nothing so ludicrous has been seen in the Stadium

since Chuck Davey forgot to duck against Kid Gavilan. When the referee chased Meadowlark Lemon clear out of the arena, many were reminded of Davey."

CHICAGO SUN-TIMES, OCTOBER 18, 1958

1961-1962

The NBA awarded a franchise to insurance magnates David Trager and Morris Goldman, who named their expansion team the Packers because of the city's ties to the meat-packing industry. The Chicago Packers played their first season at the International Amphitheater in close proximity to the Union Stock Yards.

Six rookies and seven veterans drafted from the eight existing NBA teams vied for a starting berth. Coaching duties went to Jim Pollard, the former all-American from Stanford who had starred with George Mikan in the glory days of the Minneapolis Lakers. The Packers defeated the St. Louis Hawks 117-106 in their home opener, televised over WGN-TV with Jack Brickhouse and Lou Boudreau on October 27, 1961. With the exception of towering rookie center Walt Bellamy, the league's number one draft choice, the Packers had great difficulty putting the ball in the net and finished the season dead last in the Western Division. Walt Bellamy was the easy choice for Rookie of the Year honors, however, and was second in the league in scoring behind Wilt Chamberlain.

Q: Why was the Packers home opener delayed that year?

A: A slick Amphitheater floor made it hard for players to maintain their footing during pregame warm-ups. A maintenance crew took exactly one minute and 10 seconds to scrub and wash the floorboards before the game began.

"This Packers team would beat the Lakers I played with by 20 points!"

JIM POLLARD, OCTOBER 25, 1961

1961-1962

After being rejected twice by the NBA Board of Governors in his bid to purchase expansion teams for Chicago and Los Angeles, Harlem Globetrotter owner Abe Saperstein decided to start his own professional league. The Chicago Majors, one of the eight charter members of the American Basketball League, began playing that season and won their first home game November 11, 1961, against the Washington Tapers. A crowd of 12,073 fans had filed into the Chicago Stadium that night, but they were more interested in the second part of the bill than the cast of unknowns calling themselves the Majors.

Saperstein had shrewdly scheduled his Globetrotters for the second game in order to ensure that no one would leave the building while his Majors, coached by former Illinois whiz kid Andy Philip, went through the paces. Despite Saperstein's smarts, the ABL folded after just two seasons.

Q: What innovation, later adopted by the NBA, did Saperstein introduce to the basketball world in 1961?

A: The three-point shot. ABL players were awarded three points if they drained a shot from 25 feet away from the basket.

1962-1963

The big story this year was George Ireland's surprising Loyola Ramblers, who finished the season 29-2 and won Chicago's only NCAA Championship in Louisville's Freedom Hall on March 23. Down by 15 points with just 13:56 minutes remaining in the game, the Ramblers dug in and fought back. Vic Rouse's last-second tip-in defeated the Cincinnati Bearcats 60-58 in overtime.

Q: Ireland's high-octane run-and-gun offense got what nickname from sportswriters?

A: The coach's methods were called "organized confusion," but they worked. Loyola is still the only team to play its starting five without a break in an NCAA Championship game.

Q: Ireland was ahead of the field on another major issue that made headlines during the 1960s. What was it?

A: Ireland was also an early and strident crusader for civil rights in sports. He defied convention by starting four African-American players that season and was sharply criticized for it. His confidence was justified when his team brought home the NCAA Championship—the only time an Illinois school has won this top honor. Loyola made it to the national tourney in 1966 and 1968, but thereafter the school's basketball program lapsed into a long decline.

Q: Can you name the Loyola starting five from that championship season whose uniform numbers have all been permanently retired?

A: Guard John Egan (#11); forward Vic Rouse (#40); center Les Hunter (#41); forward Jerry Harkness (#15); and guard Ron Miller (#42).

"They used to have formulas in those days as to how many blacks you played at home, and in tournaments. You never played four at a time in tournaments."

GEORGE IRELAND, RETIRED LOYOLA RAMBLERS COACH, 1979

1962-1963

Chicago Packers owner Dave Trager sponsored a contest asking fans to come up with a new name for his team. The winning entry was Zephyrs, derived from a Greek name for the "God of the west wind."

Trager moved his renamed team into the Chicago Coliseum, hoping that a change of scenery might improve its sagging fortunes. The Zephyrs showed a modest improvement, but not enough to interest fans. Though Trager had assured the jittery Zephyr fans that the future of the team in Chicago was "secure," he later announced that Baltimore would be his new base of operations after reporting a financial loss of $500,000 in two seasons.

Q: For the second year in a row, a Chicago player won NBA Rookie of the Year honors. Who was he?

A: Terry Dischinger, an all-American forward out of Purdue who averaged 25.5 points per game that season. Dischinger is the only one of more than 50 two-time (consensus) all-Americans since 1946 not to participate in the NCAA Tournament or the NIT.

"I will show the people of Chicago they lost a good thing. Although we failed, Chicago also failed."

DAVE TRAGER, MARCH 14, 1963

1966

Though he failed in his efforts to buy the Packers from Dave Trager in 1963, Dick Klein fought to return pro basketball to Chicago. The NBA harbored grave doubts but Klein convinced the board of governors that the league could not truly call itself professional without Chicago. Amid doubt and uncertainty he prevailed.

Q: What was the new team named?

A: The new team was christened the Bulls because the owner wanted to present a hustling, scrapping ball club to the public. And what member of the animal kingdom is more fearsome than an angry bull about to go on a rampage?

"NBA owners are self-serving to the extent that each man's chief concern is the welfare of his own franchise. Every one is a self-styled emperor, despot, king or whatever you want to call it, of his own club, but you can't argue with success. The overall progress of basketball can't be denied. When the pioneers went into the forest, they shot the Indians and the turkeys and cut down the trees. So a few of them got killed. Well, a few owners got killed on the way to this league's survival."

DICK KLEIN, ON THE PREVIOUS FAILURES OF PRO BASKETBALL IN THE WINDY CITY

1966-1967

In their maiden season, the "baby Bulls" led by the former University of Illinois star Johnny "Red" Kerr and assistant coach Al Bianchi won 33 games, which still stands as a first-season record for an expansion team.

Q: What historic milestone did Jerry Sloan accomplish in the Bull's first season?
A: Defensive wizard Jerry Sloan led the team in rebounding. Michael Jordan is the only other guard in Bulls history to lead the team in that category.

The hustling expansion team made it to the play-offs that season but lost three straight games in the first round to the St. Louis Hawks.

Q: Who was Dick Klein's first choice to coach the Bulls?
A: DePaul Coach Ray Meyer nearly accepted Klein's offer, but was persuaded to remain at the university.

THE ORIGINAL BULLS DRAFT FROM THE NBA EXPANSION POOL

Player Acquired	*Former Team*	*College*
John Kerr	*Baltimore*	*Illinois*
Jerry Sloan	*Baltimore*	*Evansville*
Ron Bonham	*Boston*	*Cincinnati*
John Thompson	*Boston*	*Providence*
Nate Bowman	*Cincinnati*	*Wichita State*
Tom Thacker	*Cincinnati*	*Cincinnati*
Len Chappell	*New York*	*Wake Forest*
Barry Clemens	*New York*	*Ohio Wesley*
Al Bianchi	*Philadelphia*	*Bowling Green*
Gerry Ward	*Philadelphia*	*Boston College*
Jim King	*Los Angeles*	*Tulsa*
Bob Boozer	*Los Angeles*	*Kansas*
Jim Washington	*St. Louis*	*Villanova*

Jeff Mullins	*St. Louis*	*Duke*
Keith Erickson	*San Francisco*	*UCLA*
McCoy McLemore	*San Francisco*	*Drake*
John Barnhill	*Detroit*	*Tennessee State*
Don Kojis	*Detroit*	*Marquette*

"We won our first three games and the people were saying, 'Hey, this team's for real!' I don't know of any other expansion team that won its first three games. That was something I'll always remember."

JOHNNY "RED" KERR

1968

On November 7 the Bulls sent guard Flynn Robinson to the Milwaukee Bucks for guards Bob Love and Bob Weiss in one of the greatest trades of all time.

Q: Love set a record with the Bulls that's been beaten only by Michael Jordan and Scottie Pippen. What was it?
A: In his eight years of playing in Chicago Love scored 12,623 points, which places him third in team history behind Jordan and Pippen.

Q: Bob Love's #10 was officially retired on January 14, 1994. Who are the only other Bulls players to have their numbers retired?
A: Jerry Sloan (#4), on February 17, 1978; and Michael Jordan (#23), on November 1, 1994.

1968-1969

On May 27, 1968, Bulls owner Dick Klein hired Dick Motta as his new head coach just one month after Johnny "Red" Kerr submitted his resignation. The youthful Motta was an unknown commodity in Chicago at the time, but he had won three Big Sky Conference titles in five seasons while guiding Weber State College. The fiery, controversial Motta coached the Bulls for the next eight seasons.

Q: Dick Motta was the Bulls all-time winningest coach with 356 victories up until the 1995-1996 season. Who broke the record?

A: Phil Jackson snapped Motta's record with a victory in San Antonio on December 8, 1995.

> *"I won't be a rubber stamp coach. I'm not a good loser, and I don't intend to be a loser in the NBA. I also don't like being taken advantage of. My job is teaching and selling myself to the players."*
>
> DICK MOTTA, 1968

1969

On September 2, 1969, the Bulls traded forward Jimmy Washington to Philadelphia in exchange for forward Chet Walker and guard Shalor Halimon—the second-best trade in franchise history.

1971

The Bulls dealt for "Stormin" Norman Van Lier three days before the 1971-1972 season opened. They traded center Jim Fox and a future draft choice to Cincinnati for the hustling, play-making guard. The pivotal trade elevated the Bulls from an expansion team also-ran into a legitimate title contender. With the fiery Van Lier, Jerry Sloan, and Bob Love, the team gained a reputation around the league as a physical, no-holds-barred ball club that would kick, gouge, and punch in order to win.

> *"The word is out on the Chicago Bulls. Whenever we come to town every coach says you have to hold, grab, and slug to beat the Bulls. It's open season on us. The other players say The Bulls are dirty. You need a billy club to beat them."*
>
> BOB FEERICK, GENERAL MANAGER OF THE SAN FRANCISCO WARRIORS

1972

Amid rumors that the financially strapped Dick Klein was ready to sell the Chicago Bulls to Canadian businessman Peter

Graham, owner of the San Diego Sports Arena, the Chicago syndicate turned to Milwaukee realtor Marvin Fishman for salvation. But Fishman's bid was turned down by the NBA owners. They'd succumbed to pressure from Blackhawks owner Arthur Wirtz, who wanted a basketball team and a new tenant for the Chicago Stadium. The sale of the Bulls to Wirtz, Lester Crown, and other investors was approved by a 13-3 vote on August 10, 1972. Marvin Fishman sued Wirtz and the NBA for rejecting his sale bid. He won a $16.2 million judgment in 1984.

1974-1975

The Bulls reached the high-water mark of the Jerry Sloan-Bob Love era by winning the Midwest Division on the strength of a superb defense, but it was a last hurrah for the ball club. After this season players Chet Wacker and Nate Thurmond, along with coach Dick Motta, would be gone. With expectations for a championship riding high the Bulls coasted past the Kansas City Kings in the first round of the play-offs and were poised to knock out the Golden State Warriors.

Then disaster struck on their home floor. Before a capacity crowd of 19,594, Chicago lost 86-72 in the second half. This great defensive team just couldn't put the ball into the basket. Motta had overworked his starters all season long, and it was finally catching up with the veteran stars.

The series shifted to the West Coast for the deciding game, but again the Bulls squandered an early advantage and lost 83-79.

Q: Had the Bulls gotten to the finals that year, what team would they have played?

A: The showdown would have been with the Washington Bullets, formerly the Chicago Zephyrs.

Q: What longtime Bulls nemesis single-handedly destroyed their title chances in 1974-1975?

A: In three prior play-off series against the Bulls dating back to 1967, the burly six-foot-six forward Bill Bridges took apart Chicago with his punishing style of play. Bridges intimidated Bob Love and Chet Walker, thus freeing up

Rick Barry's deadly outside shooting in the 1974-1975 series. "I got in his jock," Bridges joked, when he was asked about his success against Bob Love.

"This has to be the biggest disappointment I ever had. I thought the good Lord was good to us for giving us another chance. I'm sure the people of Chicago are disappointed in us and me."

JERRY SLOAN

1975

George Ireland resigned as head coach of the Loyola Ramblers on January 20, 1975, citing poor health. His career record at Loyola was 321-255.

Q: Who succeeded Ireland as head coach at Loyola?

A: Jerry Lyne, who'd been Ireland's assistant for the previous 12 years and had also played under him in the early 1950s. He lasted five seasons and took the Ramblers to the NIT in 1979-1980.

1978-1979

For only the second time in the Ray Meyer era, which dated back to 1942, the Blue Demons advanced to the NCAA Final Four. The Demons had shown character and heart all season long and were confident of victory when they squared off against Larry Bird and the Indiana State Sycamores in Provo, Utah, on March 24 for a shot at the title game against Michigan State. However, Bird was devastating, and the cagers whipped DePaul 76-74 in the closing seconds of a heart-pounding contest, ending Ray Meyer's lifelong dream of a national championship.

Q: DePaul's starting lineup was called the "Iron Five." Who were they and how did they acquire that nickname?

A: Gary Garland (guard), Clyde Bradshaw (guard), Curtis Watkins (forward), Mark Aguirre (forward), and James Mitchem (center) compensated for a very weak DePaul bench by playing many more minutes than they should have. They were truly an "Iron Five" in a bittersweet season.

"I'm not depressed. I've been depressed many times but I can't be depressed now. Not when we play a basketball game. We didn't lose our lives. We didn't lose a war."

RAY MEYER, ASSESSING THE DEFEAT, MARCH 24, 1979

1978-1979

The eight-team Women's Professional Basketball League (WPBL) launched its inaugural season on December 9. Though Chicago Hustle owner John Geraty spared no expense to bring the city a winner, the concept of a women's pro league didn't catch on despite a vocal and enthusiastic core of fans calling themselves the "Hustle Muscle." Coached by Doug Bruno, the team played at DePaul's Alumni Hall. In their first season the Hustle led the league in scoring and tied for the Midwest Division title. Guard Rita Easterling won the Most Valuable Player Award.

Q: Easterling was the Hustle's biggest star, but which player won over the hearts of the fans with her personality and sex appeal?

A: Janie Fincher out of Murray State Junior College in Tishomingo, Oklahoma. When she was traded from the Hustle, many Chicago fans who supported the WPBL turned in their tickets. In desperation Doug Bruno and General Manager Chuck Shriver engineered a second trade to bring her back to Chicago.

"Some people got real upset because [Chicago sportscaster] Al Lerner slapped me on the fanny in that celebrity exhibition. Why, I never even thought about it. It was kinda funny. My dad used to do that. What an issue! A coach slapping you on the tail!"

JANIE FINCHER, CHICAGO HUSTLE, ON COPING WITH THE MEDIA AND HER IMAGE AS THE TEAM'S SEX SYMBOL

1980-1981

After 24 seasons playing exclusively at Alumni Hall, their 5,000-seat campus home from 1956 to 1980, the DePaul Blue Demons moved into the spacious Rosemont Horizon on December 1. The Demons cruised to a 74-56 victory over Gonzaga in their first game. The change of scenery reflected the popularity and success of the DePaul basketball program during this golden age of college hoops in Chicago. Despite disappointing postseason results, the 1979-1980 team was ranked number one in the regular season poll.

Q: The Demons were nearly invincible on their home court, winning the last 42 games at Alumni Hall before alternating their schedule between the Horizon and Alumni Hall. Their overall record at Alumni Hall from 1956 to 1980 was an astounding 264-68. What was the team record for home victories?

A: Between 1938 and 1956 the Blue Demons won 113 straight games at the DePaul auditorium on Sheffield Avenue. The creaky gymnasium was affectionately known as "the Barn."

1981

The Women's Professional Basketball League folded after three unprofitable seasons. Fan favorites Rita Easterling and Janie Fincher took jobs coaching basketball at Mississippi College in Clinton, Iowa.

1983-1984

McGaw Hall, the home of the Northwestern Wildcats since 1952, received a much-needed facelift. A $6.75 million renovation of the building was completed in time for the 1983-1984 basketball season. The biggest improvement was the addition of the Welsh-Ryan Arena situated at the south end of old McGaw Hall. Named in honor of the Patrick G. Ryan family of Kenilworth and Ryan's in-laws, Mr. and Mrs. Robert J. Welsh, the new facility increased seating capacity by 15 percent. Pat Ryan, the wealthy NU benefactor, is the CEO of AON Insurance and a Northwestern alumnus.

Q: When was the first game in the new arena?
A: It was formally dedicated on November 28, 1983, and Coach Rich Falk's Wildcats downed the Bradley Braves 63-42 in the inaugural game.

1984

Bulls general manager Rod Thorn selected Michael Jordan of North Carolina in the first round (third pick) of the 1984 NBA draft after the Houston Rockets drafted center Hakeem Olajuwon from Houston and the Portland Trailblazers bypassed M.J. in favor of seven-foot center Sam Bowie from Kentucky. The name of the game in those days was height, and Jordan, as great as he was at North Carolina during his abbreviated collegiate career, was considered the "lesser" of the two players by some of basketball's sharpest thinkers. Up until the moment he attained stardom in Chicago, Michael often played second fiddle, even during his prep career at Laney High School in Wilmington, N.C.

Q: Who was the North Carolina High School player of the year in 1981 when Michael graduated?
A: "Buzz" Peterson, Michael's future college roommate.

"We wish he were seven feet, but he isn't. There just wasn't a center available. What can you do?"

RON THORN, APOLOGIZING TO CHICAGO FANS FOR DRAFTING JORDAN INSTEAD OF A DOMINATING CENTER, JUNE 19, 1984

1985

Chicago White Sox owner Jerry Reinsdorf and a syndicate of investors purchased controlling interest in the Chicago Bulls from Lester Crown, William Wirtz, Phil Klutznick, Lamar Hunt, and Walter Shorenstein on March 13, 1985. Just 13 days later Reinsdorf hired former White Sox special assignment scout Jerry Krause to supervise the rebuilding of the dormant Bulls franchise as his new general manager.

Q: Who were some of the stars Krause drafted over the next few years?

A: Scottie Pippen, Horace Grant, B. J. Armstrong, Will Purdue, and Tony Kukoc. Krause brought to Chicago a cast of "situational" players who would mold a 1980s also-ran into the team of the 1990s.

Q: What other colorful baseball owner also had a piece of the Bulls prior to the arrival of Jerry Reinsdorf?
A: Yankee owner George M. Steinbrenner III.

"I saw bad chemistry. I saw players who were all skilled athletes but they were good players who could not play good together. I didn't think there was any pride in the organization. There was no pride in the uniform."
JERRY KRAUSE, ASSESSING THE 1984-1985 BULLS

1984-1985

Joey Meyer, the son of legendary DePaul mentor Ray Meyer, succeeded his father as head coach of the Blue Demons, continuing a family basketball dynasty that began in 1942. Over the next 13 seasons, Joey posted six 20-win seasons while averaging 19 victories a year. In his first season filling the big shoes the youthful Meyer guided the Demons to a 19-10 record and a trip to the NCAA Tournament, where a five-point loss to Syracuse in the opening round ended the season.

Q: Joey is one of only three Division I coaches to open his career with as many as five straight berths in the NCAA. Who were the other two?
A: Fred Schans of West Virginia (six, 1955-1960) and Pete Gillen of Xavier of Ohio (six, 1980-1991).

1985-1986

Twenty-three-year-old Michael Jordan pumped in 63 points in a double-overtime play-off loss to the Celtics in Boston on April 20, 1986. M. J. broke Elgin Baylor's single-game play-off record of 61 points, but more important, his performance in the Boston Garden that afternoon showcased "His Airness" to a nationwide TV audience who had previously looked to Larry Bird and

Magic Johnson for their hoop thrills. The "mystique of Michael" was born on the parquet floor before 14,890 howling Celtics fans. A new and exciting era of basketball that would cement the Bulls place in Chicago sports history was dawning.

Q: What is the most points Michael has scored in an NBA game to date?

A: Jordan scored 69 points in 50 minutes against the Cavaliers in Cleveland on March 28, 1990. The Bulls lost a rare one to the Cavs in overtime that day, 118-117.

1989

Citing "philosophical differences," Bulls owner Jerry Reinsdorf fired head coach Doug Collins on July 6, 1989. The dismissal of Collins caught everyone by surprise. The Bulls were on the upswing, and many observers credited the fiery young coach for building the solid foundation for the championship teams of the 1990s.

Q: What's the speculation on why Collins was let go?

A: One reason is rumored to be personal differences with Michael Jordan. The truth of the matter will probably remain a private matter between Jerry Reinsdorf and Doug Collins.

"No general manager, no matter how strong he is, can fire the head coach without the owner's approval."

JERRY KRAUSE

Q: Collins had once almost played for the Bulls. What was the deal?

A: In 1973 the Bulls offered center Clifford Ray and guard Bobby Weiss as trade bait for all-American guard Doug Collins, drafted number one in the nation by the Philadelphia 76ers. Ray's gimpy knee ruined the deal for Chicago.

1990-1991

The Raging Bulls stampeded to their first NBA championship, and Michael Jordan won the second of four NBA most valuable player awards. The 61 regular season wins were the most ever for a Bulls team up to this time.

The youthful Bulls (the average age was 25), posted the best record in the Eastern Conference and rolled past the New York Knicks and the Philadelphia 76ers in the first two rounds of the play-offs, which set up the grudge match against the "bad boys" from Detroit. In the closing minutes, when the victory was locked in, the Piston starters—Bill Laimbeer, Isaiah Thomas, Dennis Rodman, and company—proved what sore losers they could be by stalking off the court.

The NBA finals featured a classic matchup between Pat Riley's showtime Lakers, led by Magic Johnson, and the up-and-coming Bulls, appearing for the first time in the championship round. With characteristic poise and the experience of the thoroughbred champion, the Lakers squeezed by the Bulls in game one, 93-91. Thereafter it was a Chicago rout, with Michael Jordan and his 31.5-points-per-game scoring average leading the deadly triple post offense. The Bulls won the next four games, stealing the show. The championship drought was at last over.

Q: Up until then what team was the Bulls' nemesis and why?
A: The Detroit Pistons, who had knocked them out of the play-offs for three consecutive seasons entering the 1990-1991 campaign.

Q: What product of Illinois guaranteed a Pistons' victory in those games?
A: Detroit guard Isaiah Thomas, a product of St. Joe's Catholic in Westchester, Illinois. But in the end it was the younger and more agile Bulls who swept Detroit out of the post-season.

Q: Who are the only NBA players to win four (or more) MVP awards in their careers?
A: Kareem Abdul-Jabbar (6); Bill Russell (4); Wilt Chamberlain (4); Michael Jordan (4).

"This is the first team built around two guards to win a championship. It has never been done. The Lakers were built around Elgin Baylor, Philadelphia around Wilt Chamberlain, the Celtics around Bill Russell, Golden State around Rick Barry. Oscar Robertson was never on a championship team until he went to Milwaukee and played with Kareem."

JERRY KRAUSE, BULLS GENERAL MANAGER

1991-1992

The defending world champions made it look easy the second time around despite a rash of injuries in the first month of the season that sidelined center Bill Cartwright and reserve guard Craig Hodges. The Madison Street Bullies never lost more than four games in a month, en route to a team record of 67 victories. The Miami Heat were easy pickings in round one of the play-offs. However, the New York Knicks' physical style of play, so reminiscent of the Jerry Sloan-Chet Walker-Bob Love teams in the mid-1970s, forced a deciding seventh game in the second round before the Knicks bowed out 110-81.

After gliding by the Cleveland Cavaliers, who were still haunted by the woeful memory of Michael Jordan's last-second bucket that knocked them out of the 1988-1989 play-offs, the Bulls squared off against the Portland Trailblazers, coached by ex-Bull Rick Adelman, in the NBA finals. The Blazers managed victories in game two and game four, but were never really in the Bulls class. Michael Jordan stunned Portland in the first game by draining six first-half three-point field goals. With a sheepish grin on his face Jordan threw up his hands in wonderment, as if to say, "Hey, even I'm not this good."

Oh, but he was. Jordan and Scottie Pippen pounded the final nail in the Blazers' coffin on June 14, 1992, at the Chicago Stadium. The two Chicago superstars rallied the Bulls from a 17-point deficit at the end of the third quarter to pull out a 97-93 victory and salt away a second world championship in the closing seconds.

Inside the stadium the fans and the players rocked to a joyful refrain. Outside it was a different story. Rowdy fans rioted, setting fire to dozens of commercial establishments on West

Madison and breaking windows as far away as Michigan Avenue, ruining the celebration for the city of Chicago.

Q: Who is the only player to win back-to-back NBA finals awards?
A: Michael Jordan. He averaged 35.8 points per game in the 1991-1992 play-offs. His 56 points in game three of the Miami series marked the fifth time he hit the 50-mark in the postseason. No one else has ever done that.

"Last year was a honeymoon. This year has been an odyssey."
PHIL JACKSON, JUNE 14, 1992

"Let's go for the three-peat!"
SCOTTIE PIPPEN, JUNE 14, 1992

1992-1993

Phil Jackson summed up the 1992-1993 title run this way: "Truly, three the hard way." B. J. Armstrong, the sprightly 6'2" guard out of the University of Iowa, replaced John Paxson in the starting five. In order to accommodate B. J.'s deadly shooting from the outside, Phil Jackson backed away from the pressure defense that Armstrong had a problem adjusting to. But when the book was closed on this memorable season, it was the veteran Paxson who cemented the Bulls' place in history alongside the names of the great teams from the past.

Chronic knee problems sidelined Paxson for 23 games. What was shaping up to be a lost season ended happily for the veteran guard in Phoenix on June 20, 1993.

The long play-off journey with stopovers in Atlanta, Cleveland, and New York boiled down to the last 3.9 seconds of game six against the Phoenix Suns, led by the trash-talking Charles Barkley, whose verbal intimidation failed to get inside the heads of the workmanlike Bulls.

The Suns, who trailed in the series three games to two and were hoping to force a seventh game, seemed to be well on their way when Paxson delivered the fatal blow. Phoenix blew a four-point lead with only a minute to go in the game. The lead was cut to two with less than four seconds when Horace Grant dished the ball off to Paxson, who was standing wide open in three-point land. Paxson's effortless jump shot swished through the net, delivering a 99-98 victory to the visitors and the "three-peat" to Chicago. World championships were becoming quite commonplace in the Windy City.

Q: Who were the only other NBA teams to "three-peat"?
A: The Minneapolis Lakers (1951-1954) and the Boston Celtics with eight straight titles from 1958-1966.

> *"One or two plays make the difference between being a part of history and when you're a part of it . . . you cherish it."*
>
> MICHAEL JORDAN

1993

Michael Jordan's father, James Jordan, whose friendly smile warmed the hearts of the court-side patrons at Chicago Stadium, was shot and killed in North Carolina by two youthful assailants on August 13, 1993. On October 6, 1993, during a White Sox play-off game Michael Jordan announced his retirement from professional basketball. The loss of his father clouded Michael's outlook on life. He could not summon the desire to begin another grueling season of basketball. Later, when the shock of the tragedy began to wear off, Jordan signed a contract to play a season of minor league baseball with the White Sox Double-A affiliate in Birmingham, Alabama.

1994-1995

Minor league basketball premiered in Chicago with the arrival of the Chicago Rockers of the Continental Basketball Association at the UIC Pavilion. The nomadic CBA team played in a succession of cities including Toronto; Pensacola, Florida; Mississippi; and Wichita Falls, Texas, before they were purchased by the Major Broadcasting Corporation and moved to Chicago just five weeks before the kick-off of the 1994-1995 season.

The Rockers averaged just under 4,000 fans a game and advanced to the American Conference Finals in their first season, but the team lost between $700,000 and $800,000 and was virtually invisible in the Chicago media. The glut of college and professional basketball proved too much of a handicap for this team to overcome.

Attendance fell off sharply in the second season, and the team was evicted from the UIC Pavilion for failing to keep up with rent payments on a three-year lease. This forced team president Chris Devine to negotiate a transfer of the franchise to another city; the Rockers were sold to a LaCrosse, Wisconsin, group on March 12, 1996.

Q: Who coached the Rockers during their abbreviated two-year history?

A: John Treloar, who guided the Wichita Falls Texans to the 1990-1991 CBA title, was the head coach in the first season. Former Hersey High School and DePaul star Dave Corzine took over for Treloar in the second year.

1995

Somewhat of a failure at professional baseball, Michael Jordan announced his decision to return to the Bulls on March 18. He played his first game the next night against Indiana, scoring 19 points and pulling down six rebounds.

Q: What uniform number did Michael wear for the remainder of the season?

A: Number 45, the same number he wore as a member of the Birmingham Barons.

"I'm back!"

MICHAEL JORDAN TO THE MEDIA, MARCH 18, 1995

1995-1996

Four-closure! One month before the opening of the 1995-1996 campaign, Jerry Krause stunned the basketball world by trading center Will Purdue to San Antonio for Dennis Rodman. Nobody could believe it at the time. The hated Rodman, an alumnus of the Detroit bad boys, symbolized the style of play that caused Scottie Pippen migraine headaches and cost the battered Bulls a shot at the NBA finals during the early and formative years of the Phil Jackson era.

The fans were quick to forgive once Rodman donned the red and white. His off-the-court eccentricities were tolerated because his defensive heroics returned the Bulls to the top after a two-year hiatus. Dennis captured his fifth-straight rebounding title. The club won 18 games in a row to set a new team record. They did not lose at home until dropping a one-point decision to the Charlotte Hornets on April 8, and their 70th victory in Milwaukee on April 16 shattered the seemingly invincible NBA record of 69 wins in a season set by the 1971-1972 Los Angeles Lakers.

Were the Bulls this good, or was the talent thinly diluted by expansion? As the Bulls romped toward immortality the cynics and naysayers raised the specter of the great teams of the past—the Lakers, Celtics, and 76ers—and concluded that, pound for pound, this Chicago club was not as talented.

But no team, no matter what the circumstances may be, can win 72 of 82 games without drive, determination, and depth of talent. And as the Bulls sliced through Miami, New York, and Orlando in the first three play-off rounds, Phil Jackson's team offered convincing proof that they were in a class all their own.

It was an aging ball club sensing, perhaps, that there was maybe just one more year left in the current run. They made the most of their chances, taking apart a younger, friskier Seattle team in the NBA finals four games to two. The visible signs of age were apparent in the two losses sustained on the road. The Bulls appeared tired; their energy and title dreams sapped. But in the decisive game on their home floor, June 16, 1996, they routed the Sonics 87-75. There could be no further doubt. The Bulls were the team of the 1990s—perhaps for all time.

Q: Who are the only other NBA teams to win four or more NBA championships?

A: Boston (16); Los Angeles (6); Minneapolis (5); Philadelphia (4).

"A lot of people thought I'd come in and turn this organization up. I had no doubts that I could come in here and do

what I had to do. One thing that they cannot take away from me is that I am a competitor, a fighter."

DENNIS RODMAN, JUNE 16, 1996

1996

The Loyola Ramblers vacated Alumni Gym after 72 years. The final game on February 19, 1996, featured an 89-85 victory over the University of Illinois at Chicago before 4,463 screaming fans. In November the men and women's basketball teams moved into the 45,000-square-foot Joseph J. Gentile Center located on the Lake Shore campus. Given the poor performance of the Ramblers over the years, Loyola's home record at Alumni Gym stands out as one of the true fables of sport. The Ramblers finished with a 484-137 (0.773) record in there.

Q: What was the nickname given Alumni Gym?
A: The Big Brown Box That Rocks.

1996-1997

Michael Jordan scored career point number 25,000 against the San Antonio Spurs on November 30, 1996. M. J. reached this historic milestone in career game 782.

Q: Who was the only player to arrive at this milestone faster?
A: Wilt Chamberlain. He hit the mark in his 691st game.

1996-1997

An air of invincibility surrounded the Bulls as they opened the "Drive for Five" title defense. Despite a series of disabling injuries to Tony Kukoc, Bill Wennington, and Dennis Rodman, coupled with the usual off-the-court Rodman antics (getting whistled for 25 technical fouls, insulting the Mormon church, showing up at a New York book signing in a wedding dress), the rampaging Bulls breezed through the regular season with a 69-13 record, then annhilated Washington, Atlanta, Miami, and Utah in the playoffs to win their fifth world championship in seven years. It is an unparalleled accomplishment in Chicago sports history and in all likelihood will never be duplicated again.

Q: Who are the only two Bulls enshrined in the Hall of Fame?

A: George Gervin (1985-1986) and Nate Thurmond (1974-1976).

"It was a fight, a struggle, whatever you want to call it. But Phil told us a few days ago that the harder the journey the better it feels when you get to your destination."

SCOTTIE PIPPEN

BIBLIOGRAPHY

Books

The Baseball Encyclopedia. 10th ed. New York: Macmillan, 1996.

Berlage, Ingram Gai. *Women in Baseball: The Forgotten History.* Westport, Conn.: Prager, 1994.

Burrill, Bob. *Who's Who in Boxing.* New Rochelle, New York: Arlington House, 1974.

Dickson, Paul. *Baseball's Greatest Quotations.* New York: Harper Collins, 1991.

Douchant, Mike. *The Encyclopedia of College Basketball.* Detroit: Visible Ink Press, 1995.

Drager, Marvin. *The Most Glorious Crown.* New York: Winchester Press, 1975.

Evans, Charles, Jr. *Chick Evans Golf Book: The Story of the Sporting Battles by the Greatest of All Amateur Golfers.* Chicago: Reilly and Lee, 1921.

Falls, Joe. *Baseball's Great's Team: Detroit Tigers.* New York: Macmillan, 1975.

Fischler, Stan and Shirley Walton Fischler. *The Hockey Encyclopedia: The Complete Record of Professional Ice Hockey.* New York: Macmillan, 1983.

Garber, Angus G. *Boxing Legends.* New York: Gallery Books, 1988.

Gold, Eddie and Art Aherns. *The Golden Era Cubs.* Chicago: Bonus Books, 1985.

———. *The New Era Cubs.* Chicago: Bonus Books, 1985.

Gottman, Allen. *The Games Must Go On: Avery Brundage and the Olympic Movement.* New York: Columbia Univ. Press, 1984.

Grange, Harold and Ira Morton. *The Red Grange Story: An Autobiography.* Champaign: Univ. of Illinois Press, 1953.

Greenland, Paul R. *Hockey Chicago Style: The History of the*

Chicago Blackhawks. Champaign: Sagamore Publishing, 1995.

Gregory, Robert. *Diz.* New York: Viking Press, 1992.

Halas, George with Gwen Morgan and Arthur Veysey. *Halas: An Autobiography.* Chicago: Bonus Books, 1986.

Heller, Peter. *"In This Corner!..."* New York: Simon and Schuster, 1973.

Kogan, Rick. Brunswick: *The Story of an American Company from 1845 to 1985.* Chicago: Brunswick Corporation, 1985.

Leitner, Irving A. *Baseball's Diamonds in the Rough.* New York: Abelard-Schuman, 1972.

Lester, Robin. *Stagg's University: The Rise, Decline, and Fall of Big-time Football at the University of Chicago, 1890-1940.* Champaign: Univ. of Illinois Press, 1995.

Lieb, Fred. *Baseball as I Have Known It.* New York: Coward, McCann and Georg Hegan Inc., 1977.

Lindberg, Richard. *Chicago Ragtime: Another Look at Chicago, 1880-1920.* South Bend: Icarus Press, 1985.

———. *The Chicago White Sox Encyclopedia.* Philadelphia: Temple Univ. Press, 1997.

———. *Who's on 3rd? The Chicago White Sox Story.* South Bend: Icarus Press, 1983.

Logan, Bob. *The Chicago Sports Barroom Analyst.* Chicago: Contemporary Books, 1988.

Logan, Bob. *The Bulls and Chicago: A Stormy Affair.* Chicago: Contemporary Books, 1975.

Luby, Mort Jr. *The History of Bowling.* Chicago: Bowler's Journal, 1983.

Macmillan Baseball Encyclopedia. 9th Ed. New York: Macmillan, 1993.

McCallum, John D. *The Encyclopedia of World Boxing Champions.* Radnor, Penn.: Chilton Book Company, 1975.

Messick, Hank. *The Politics of Prosecution: Jim Thompson, Richard Nixon, Marje Everett & the Trial of Otto Kerner.* Ottawa, Ill.: Caroline House, 1978.

Mullan, Harry. *The Great Book of Boxing.* New York: Crescent Books, 1990.

The NFL's Official Encyclopedic History of Professional Football. New York: Macmillan and National Football League Properties, Inc., 1977.

Odd, Gilbert. *The Encyclopedia of Boxing.* Secaucus, N.J.: Chartwell Books, 1989.

Peper, George, ed. *Golf in America: The First 100 Years.* New York: Harry N. Abrams, Inc. 1987.

Peterson, Robert. *Only the Ball Was White.* Englewood Cliffs, N.J.: Prentice-Hall, 1970.

Pines, Phillip A. *The Complete Book of Harness Racing.* New York: Grosset and Dunlap, 1970.

Pridmore, Jay and Jim Hard. *The American Bicycle.* Osceola, Wis.: Motorbooks, 1995.

Roberts, Howard. *The Chicago Bears.* New York: G. P. Putnam's Sons, 1947.

Robertson, Max and Jack Kramer. *The Encyclopedia of Tennis.* New York: Viking Press, 1974.

Rogosin, Donn. *Invisible Men: Life in Baseball's Negro Leagues.* New York: Atheneum, 1983

Roth, Mark and Chuck Pezzano. *The Mark Roth Book of Bowling.* New York: Rutledge Press, 1983.

Sachare, Alex, ed. *The Official NBA Basketball Encyclopedia.* 2nd ed. New York: Villard Books, 1994.

Salvino, Carmen with Frederick C Klein. *Fast Lanes.* Chicago: Bonus Books, 1988.

Schoor, Gene. *The History of the World Series.* New York: William Morrow, 1990.

Shannon, Bill and George Kalinsky. *The Ballparks.* New York: Hawthorne Books, 1975.

Shannon, Bill. *Official Encyclopedia of Tennis.* New York: Harper and Row, 1981.

Sporting News Official NBA Guide. St. Louis: The Sporting News Publishing Company, 1997.

Sporting News Official NBA Register. St. Louis: The Sporting News Publishing Company, 1997.

Stagg, Amos Alonzo and Wesley W Stout. *Touchdown!* New York: Longman, Green & Co., 1927.

Stephans, Tim. *The Blue Demons: Great DePaul Teams and Traditions.* Chicago: Bonus Books, 1991.

Stoneridge, M. A. *Great Horses of Our Time.* New York: Doubleday, 1972.

Treat, Roger L., ed. *The Encyclopedia of Sports.* 4th ed. New York: A. S. Barnes, 1969.

Turkin, Hy and S. C Thompson. *The Official Encyclopedia of Baseball.* New York: A. S. Barnes, 1963.

Vanderberg, Bob. *Sox from Lane and Fain to Zisk and Fisk.* Chicago: Chicago Review Press, 1984.

Vass, George. *The Chicago Blackhawks Story.* Chicago: Follett Publishing, 1970.

———. *George Halas and the Chicago Bears.* Chicago: Henry Regnery, 1971.

Wendt, Lloyd and Herman Kogan. *Big Bill of Chicago.* New York: Bobbs Merrill, 1953.

Wendt, Lloyd. *The Chicago Tribune: The Rise of a Great American Newspaper.* Chicago: Rand McNally & Co., 1979

Whittingham, Richard. *The Bears: A 75-Year Celebration.* Dallas: Taylor Publishing, 1994.

———. *The Chicago Bears: From George Halas to Super Bowl XX.* New York: Simon & Schuster, 1986.

Newspapers and Periodicals (Various Years)

Bowlers Journal
Chicago American
Chicago Daily News
Chicago Defender
Chicago Herald-American
Chicago Herald & Examiner
Chicago History Magazine

Chicago Inter-Ocean
Chicago Journal
Chicago Sun
Chicago Sun-Times
Chicago Times
Chicago Tribune
Racing Forum
The Sporting News

PRESS GUIDES AND YEARBOOKS (VARIOUS YEARS)
Arlington International Racecourse
Chicago Bears
Chicago Blackhawks
Chicago Bulls
Chicago Cardinals
Chicago Cougars
Chicago Cubs
Chicago Rockets
Chicago Stags
Chicago White Sox
Chicago Wolves
DePaul Blue Demons
Hawthorne Race Course
Loyola Ramblers
Maywood Park
Northwestern Wildcats (Basketball and Football)
Sportsman's Park

ABOUT THE AUTHORS

Richard C. Lindberg is a native Chicagoan who has authored eight books dealing with various aspects of Chicago history, sports, politics, and ethnicity. Among his recent titles: *Chicago Ragtime: Another Look at Chicago, 1880-1920* (1985); *To Serve and Collect: Chicago Politics and Police Corruption* (1991); *Quotable Chicago* (1996); *Passport's Guide to Ethnic Chicago,* 2nd ed. (1997); and *The White Sox Encyclopedia* (1997). Mr. Lindberg also serves as the Chicago White Sox team historian. He is a member of the Society of Midland Authors and the Chicago Crime Commission, and was recently named to Who's Who in America for 1998.

Biart Williams earned a degree in business from Governor's State University, University Park, Illinois, upon completion of his tour of duty in the U. S. Marine Corps. Mr. Williams was a contributor to *The White Sox Encyclopedia,* and he continues to write about Chicago sports from his home in Frankfort, Illinois.

Printed in the USA
CPSIA information can be obtained
at www.ICGtesting.com
JSHW082152140824
68134JS00014B/186

9 781681 620237